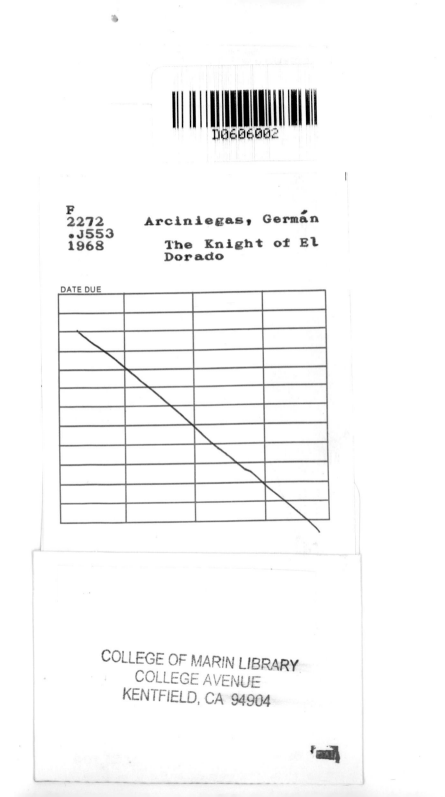

# THE KNIGHT OF EL DORADO

# ROUTE OF GONZALO JIMÉNEZ DE QUESADA
## Santa Marta, April 6, 1536 — Santa Fé, August 6, 1538
### Distance travelled, 1117 kilometres

SCALE 1 : 2,000,000

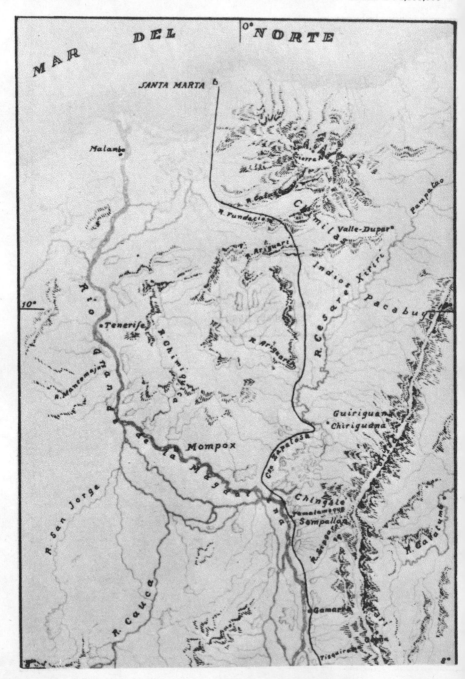

(Continued on opposite page)

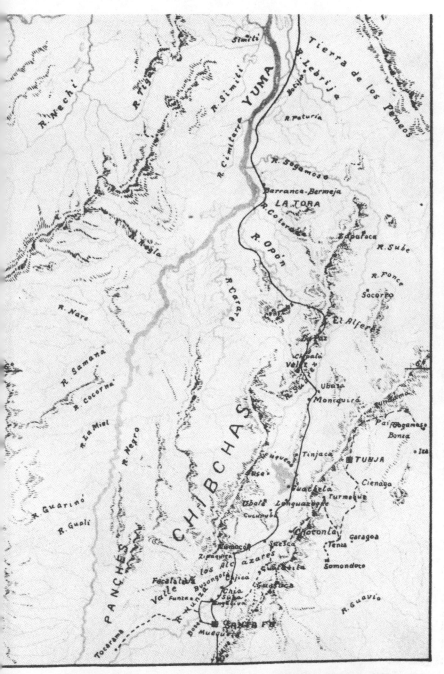

**Daniel Ortega Ricaurte**

BY GERMÁN ARCINIEGAS

# The Knight of El Dorado

### THE TALE OF
### Don Gonzalo Jiménez de Quesada
### AND HIS
### Conquest of New Granada,
### Now Called Colombia

TRANSLATED BY MILDRED ADAMS

GREENWOOD PRESS, PUBLISHERS
NEW YORK                    1968

TO

AURORA ANGUEYRA, my mother

GABRIELA VIEIRA, my wife

AURORA ARCINIEGAS, my daughter

# Contents

# I. Europe, or the Paradise of the Mad

From northern parts, and also from France and Italy, came piles of books on politics and affairs of state, aphorisms, speeches, commentaries on Cornelius, Tacitus, or on the Republics of Plato and Aristotle. This harmful merchandise was received by a venerable censor, whose candid and prudent mind was mirrored in his face; he, when such cargoes arrived, said, "O books, perilous even to the faithful, in whom truth and religion serve convenience! How many tyrannies have you introduced into the world, and how many kingdoms and republics have been lost through your counsels! . . ."

—Saavedra Fajardo

# EUROPE, OR THE PARADISE
# OF THE MAD

I n the great overturn of history which occurred at the
beginning of the sixteenth century, Spain spilled and
spread not only throughout America, but across the
whole face of Europe. On this side of the Atlantic, under the banners of those daring adventurers who sallied
forth to conquest; on the European side, in the cause of
Charles V.

Both Spain and Europe appear to have been completely
mad. The armies—those Spanish *tercios* which were to
win eternal fame—carried even in victory a certain air of
the barbarian. The culture—Humanism was struggling to
emerge, and kept breaking its head against the hard fa-
naticism of crusaders who had not so long before triumphed
over the Arabs. The men—those who left for America were
almost always the same footloose vagabonds who had been
tramping up and down Europe, now at the sack of Rome,
now going as far as Vienna to fight against Suleiman the
Magnificent. This was the very moment when Europeans
finally asserted their dominance over that ancient continent
by pushing the Turks back across the Bosporus and the
Moors down out of Spain. But there is no government, however strong, which can order and control a chaotic life that
seethes with a passion for military enterprise and meta-
physical reform.

In the caravels that set out from Cádiz for the Indies
went bandits, saints, robbers, intellectuals, capitalists—in a

word, men; men who, tried in the crucible of a contradictory struggle, would some of them take the road that is usually called saintly, while others would head for the laurel wreaths of heroism. But in the last analysis the passions which set the pattern for the movement were the same as those that give colour and motive force to all life. Chance set one man up on the pedestal of fame and buried another in the mud of infamy. Aguirre was to emerge as a tyrant, Cortés to stand forth as a god. Yet the substance out of which both were made was the same—that mortal clay common to all mankind.

"And I remember," says the historian Oviedo, "that the Catholic monarchs commanded their judges and justices throughout all Castile that men sentenced to death, or to the cutting off of hand or foot, or to other vile and bodily punishment, should be exiled to the Indies in perpetuity or for a limited period, depending on the nature of their offence, in place of the aforesaid death or punishment which would thus be commuted."

Many great men came out of this. History, old moralist and concealer that she is, thereafter sought out honourable genealogies for them, or tailored them to measure, for it is not good that heroes should emerge out of the mire of misery.

✿     ✿     ✿

In Spain the family, like the nascent state, like society that seethed and bubbled, was a cross-word puzzle. Jiménez de Quesada, the founder of Santa Fé de Bogotá and discoverer of the New Kingdom of Granada, was not called Quesada but Jiménez. This warning seems to me useful, for since I believe that whatever I write here is, from the his-

torical point of view, open to contradiction, I am tempted
to the sin of saying once and for all that in this matter of
the Americas the fictional approach is more valuable than
the historical.

Throughout the whole conquest of America one never
knows who is who. Names are always being changed about.
One never knows where men were born, who their parents
were, or what were their original names.* Sebastián de
Belalcázar, for example, was named Sebastián Moyano,
but historians waste reams of paper saying some that he
was called Belalcázar, and others, Benalcázar. As a matter
of fact he was probably not a Moyano at all but a García.
Let the reader go to Quito, Popayán, or Cali, however, and
tell residents that the founder of their city was named
García Moyano, and they will laugh in his face, if they do
not stone him to death.

Among the conquerors, Andrés López, who founded
Ibagué, is set down in history as Andrés Galarza. And Pe-
droso, that mighty conquistador who crossed the central
cordillera of the New Kingdom while fighting the Panches,
is called Francisco Núñez. As for the historians, the great
Oviedo is not Oviedo but Hernández, Gómara is López,
Ocariz is Flórez, Piedrahita is Fernández, to cite only four
among those men who wrote our first chronicles. And as
no one calls them Hernández, López, Flórez, or Fernández,
it would seem to put even the first line of their daring histories in some doubt.

Cervantes himself was to recognize this problem of transposition when, talking of the moment when the ingenious

---

* Even the locale of this story partakes of this confusion in names, for
the New Kingdom of Granada, having passed through a series of shifts
of both name and frontiers, is now Colombia.—TRANSLATOR.

gentleman was seeking a proper name for himself, he said he "determined at length to call himself Don Quixote, whence some of the authors of this most true history have concluded that his name was certainly Quixada, and not Quesada as others would have it."

Actually, of course, the great leaders of the American conquest sprang to life in America—Cortés in Cuba, Pizarro in Panama, and Don Pedro de Heredia in Santa Marta. They were born with their beards full-grown and their bodies covered with scars. Their youth has been lost amid the fantastic conjectures with which elegant biographers and indefatigable historians have tried to ennoble it. As a matter of cold fact, the real mother of Pizarro, for instance, was that straying sow which suckled him when he, a baby, was abandoned in the doorway of a Trujillo church.

Going back to Quesada, I think the transposition in his name has a very simple explanation. What happened was that through an excess of caution children in Spain were not given their father's name but their mother's, or the name of a clan or a city. Moreover, let the reader note, though he be accused of Freudian tendencies, that only the eldest son dared use his father's name, and that even in this case the public, low-minded and malicious, went on calling him by his second name, which was his mother's. An aberration similar to that found among the natives of certain American tribes which admit into their dynasties no succession except that of the king's sister, for this maternal line gives the sole certainty that the royal heirs will be of royal blood.

The amusing thing is that only Pizarro, so definitely a bastard, went down in history bearing the name of his probable father, Captain Gonzalo Pizarro, instead of the name of his mother, Francisca González of the outskirts of Huertas de las Ánimas.

In short, and to linger on this small point no longer, the truth is that in Spanish genealogies the fact of paternity, which was to grow more important as time went on, is not painted in very vivid colours. Each one chose the name that pleased him, and thus in the same family, among brothers and sisters, one became known as Jiménez, another as Pérez, while Andrea and Magdalena called themselves by the family name, Quesada, which was the name of a town.

*        *        *

But in this matter of families there is something more. When a plant puts out a great many leaves and gives very little fruit the country people say it is "going off into mere vice." Something similar seems to have happened to those genealogical trees which were transplanted to America. Some of them had their roots buried deep in the layers of the centuries and were enriched with the finest fertilizer known—the blood of Moors. This blood gives both honour and fecundity. A family that had killed many Moors would always stand in the first rank. Among the Quesadas there was a great deal of this. The very name commemorates a battle which an ancestor, mayor of the town of Quesada, waged against the Moorish quarter.

There was not a better-planted tree in the whole genealogical forest. The founders of the family were pure Goths. Then they mixed with the Moors of Toledo, though keeping their Christian prerogatives, and became Mozarabs. The noblest, and most Gothic, of the family was a princess named Palomela, who had two blue doves (*palomas*) on a silver field for her coat of arms. An author who thought this matter of trees important, like Don Juan Flórez de Ocariz, for example, would hang coats of arms on all the branches, finding Quesadas always to have been commandants, always with an illustrious lineage, and no higgling about it.

Coming down to the threshold of the conquest, we find Don Luis Jiménez and his wife Isabel de Rivera to have had seven children, Gonzalo Jiménez, Hernán Pérez, Francisco Jiménez, Jerónimo Jiménez, Melchor Quesada, Andrea and Magdalena Jiménez de Quesada. With so fertile a background one might expect a whole fistful of competing shoots. But the tree, planted with so much care, was transplanted to America, and there it "went off into mere vice," or trailed away through the invisible branches of bastardy. Taking Quesadas to America was like taking *aguacates* or *chirimoyos* to Spain. However carefully they were fertilized, however much infidel blood was shed about their roots, they did not flourish. Especially in the male line.

There is no doubt that the conquerors won, among many other kinds of riches in the New World, real treasures in the Indian women. If genealogists would only list the grafts in family trees they would find them passing on a great many fine things to history. But there were certain difficulties, due to social instability, which prevented the collection of such data, and so the trees exhausted themselves and succumbed.

❄    ❄    ❄

When Quesada came into the world at the end of the fifteenth century, the fabulous continent, the continent possessed by madness, was not America but Europe. Nor

is this the first time that an historian seeking common
sense and practical wisdom in the lives of men has had
to turn his eyes toward this side of the Atlantic. To the
fifteenth century, it was not the discovery and conquest
of America which were so impressive, but the events in
European history which were occurring at the same time.
Spain, properly enough, played a role which, in the Old
World and in those days, was of the first importance. Spanish cardinals stormed St. Peter's seat, and luxury and loose
living overflowed. Spanish soldiers invaded Rome, and
Catalans and Aragonese seemed to Rome and Naples like
missionaries of a new barbarism. There was a Spanish queen
who lost her head. There was a Spanish king who bought
the crown of Germany for eight hundred thousand florins.
And the world apparently demanded of Erasmus that he
eulogize this folly.

The infancy of Quesada, born in Moorish territory, covered the period when the monarchs were humiliating Moorish settlements and decreeing a merciless persecution of
the Jews. What the Germans were to do in the twentieth
century in the name of an Aryan fantasy the Spanish monarchs did in identical terms during the fifteenth and sixteenth centuries in the name of Catholicism. For the Spanish world the edict of 1492 against the Jews had more
importance than the so-called discovery of America which
occurred in the same year, and it even produced for it
greater riches. That edict contains such charming bits as
this:

"With the approval and advice of certain prelates and
grandees of our Kingdoms and other persons of knowledge
and understanding, and after long deliberation, we have
agreed to expel from our Kingdoms all Jews, men and

women, and they shall never return to them nor to any part of them; and to this effect we order this letter of ours to be issued, wherein we decree that all Jews, male and female, of whatever age, who live and dwell and are in our said Kingdoms and Dominions, the native-born and non-native alike, who have come by whatever manner and for whatever cause, or are in them, shall, before the end of the month of July of the present year, leave all our said Kingdoms and Dominions with their sons and daughters and servants, male and female, and attendants, old and young, of whatever age; and that they shall not dare to return to or to be in any part, either to live in or to traverse it, in any manner whatsoever: under penalty—if they fail to comply and are found in the vicinity of our Kingdoms and Dominions or come into them in any way whatsoever—of death and confiscation of all their goods for our government and exchequer; and they shall incur these penalties by this same act and decree without further process, sentence, or declaration. . . . And likewise we give leave and licence to said Jews, male and female, to take out of our Kingdoms and Dominions, by land or sea, their goods and chattels provided they do not take gold nor silver nor coined money nor other things forbidden by the laws of our Realm, but merchandise and such effects as are not contraband, or bills of exchange."

From then on, the persecution of the Jews became the most dramatic event in Spanish life, especially in the cities which had just become the objects of the Reconquest. In popular speech and in royal papers alike the Jews were called *marranos* (which means both pigs and outcasts) and it is interesting to note how the *marranos,* persecuted in

Spain, kept arriving in other countries. At convenient moments the Spanish Popes issued bulls against the outcasts. Benedetto Croce, in his penetrating study of Spain's influence on Italian life during the Renaissance, presents many very curious details; for example:

"The migration into Italy of the Jews and the *marranos*, persecuted in Spain, where they were burning them alive, increased. Sixtus IV in 1483 and Innocent VIII in 1487 published bulls against both Jews and *marranos*. In 1492 the great Spanish persecution broke out against them, and Jews arrived from Spain fainting, filthy, pallid, with sunken eyes, like walking corpses, and set up shops in our cities. At Naples, writes a chronicler in August of that year, 'ships loaded with Jews began to arrive, some coming from Italy, and others from Spain, all expelled by His Majesty the Spanish king.' In Rome, he wrote in June 1493, '*de prime parte marrani steterunt in maxime quantitate extra portam Appiam aput caput bovis, ibi tentoria tendentes, intraveruntque in urbem secreto modo.*' In Ferrara, in July, 'there was talk of certain *marranos* expelled by the king of Spain.' Among these Jews were learned men of great worth, like that Judas Abrabanel who was afterward called Leone Ebreo."

The year 1492 is famous for the discovery of the New World, but to Spain and other countries it was important for other things. Granada was recaptured in that year, the edict was issued against the Jews, and under the name of Alexander VI a Spaniard was made Pope. That same year the same Alexander VI entrusted the crosier of the bishopric of Valencia, and with it the richest archdiocese in Spain, to his bastard son Cæsar. We are, as we shall see in greater detail later, in the midst of a period when professional careers developed in Europe with extraordinary rapidity. Madness lay, we repeat, not in the new continent but in the old. Cæsar Borgia was only seventeen years old when he was crowned with the red hat of a cardinal. What a sublime and stimulating example for the ambitious Spanish adventurers who were setting forth to conquer the Indies!

But let us go on with the role Spain was playing in the European scene, for that gives an excellent picture of the kind of world it was in which the ardour of religious fanatics headed by the Catholic monarchs met and combated the licence of the Italian Renaissance. The Spanish family of the Borgias reflected the character of those days. For the second time let us quote the words of Benedetto Croce:

"Bullfights, like games played on horseback with reed swords, had not been seen in Rome since the days of Calixtus. Under Innocent VIII and using the conquest of Granada as a pretext, '*plures Prelati Hispaniæ nationis . . . tauros donarunt publice occidendos.*' Cæsar Borgia had his countrymen's own passion for bullfights. In Rome on July 24, 1500, which was St. John's Day, on foot behind the Basilica of St. Peter, with a short sword and a *muleta*, he played and killed five bulls, cutting the head off one of them. Another time, detained in Cesena, he presented the town with the death of a fighting bull as a spectacle. He and his Spanish entourage celebrated the marriage of his sister, Lucretia Borgia, to Alphonso d'Este in 1502 with a bullfight. She had various Spanish ladies at her side, including Angela Borgia, Catalina, Juana Rodríguez; on certain occasions she appeared dressed in the Spanish manner."

*     *     *

It is a curious fact that, whereas the political life of Europe was geared to the impulses of youth, the history of America was made by men of mature judgment. Charles V and Jiménez de Quesada were born within a few months of each other. But while Jiménez de Quesada was to wait thirty-six years before he began the conquest of the New Kingdom of Granada, Charles V won the crown of Germany at nineteen. And while Cæsar Borgia captured a cardinal's seat at seventeen, Columbus did not become an admiral until almost the end of his life.

When Jiménez de Quesada, like many another Andalusian, came of age the panorama spread before him could not have been more alluring. On one side of the ocean King Charles I of Spain was being crowned emperor of Germany under the name of Charles V; on the other side Hernán Cortés was completing the conquest of Mexico. But between those two events, which the youth of Spain watched with such amazement, there was a substantial difference. The conquest of Mexico fits neatly into the logic and the drama of history—it was the result of a daring war in which the military forces directed by Cortés moved in accordance with the combinations dictated by his diplomatic skill. The purchase of the German crown, on the other hand, resulted from an agreement between bankers and inexperienced youths. In Cuba, the rivalry between Governor Diego Velázquez and Cortés was a war between men full-grown. In Germany, the seven great electors were to place the crown on the brow of the lad who would pay them the most attractive sum of money.

This is the way the plot developed. When Emperor Maximilian died, the German crown was sought by three lads for whom history was reserving spacious habitations in the near future. One was Charles I, king of Spain, who was nineteen years old; another, Francis I of France, who was twenty-five; the third, Henry VIII of England, who was twenty-eight. Charles had been king of Spain since he was sixteen, Francis king of France since he was twenty-one, Henry king of England from the time he was eighteen. Initiated into governing, all of them dowered with robust personalities, all equally greedy, they fixed their eyes on a crown—and what a crown!—at the age when most lads are going to the taverns to talk to their sweethearts or to plot small local insurrections.

As I said, the victory would go to the one who most successfully wheedled the electors. It was a question of money and skill. The bankers would have the last word. The fate of Germany hung on something similar to a stock market transaction. Maximilian had already spent six hundred thousand florins buying the goodwill of the electors in favour of his grandson King Charles of Spain. But, in Wyndham Lewis's good-humoured phrase, "the sound business sense of the electors asserted itself." With Maximilian dead, the electors declared the deal ended, and again offered the crown for public sale.

The incidents of this struggle could not be more instructive. King Francis said he was prepared to spend three million florins for the crown, and he offered one of the electors—according to the biographer of Charles V, Wyndham Lewis, it was an ecclesiastical elector, the archbishop of Mainz—a hundred and twenty thousand florins and the legateship of Germany for life. The elector of Brandenburg and the archbishop of Cologne were also bribed by Francis.

For his part, Henry of England, or his chaplain, Wolsey, sent Pace so that he might have a stake in the auction. Chaplain Wolsey, the head of Henry's Cabinet, was a man of no small ambition. Twice he had presented himself as candidate for the Papacy. Leo X made him a cardinal, and he manipulated half of European politics. Nevertheless, Pace yielded before the munificence of Charles and Francis, and advised the discreet retiring of Henry's candidacy—advice which Wolsey heeded like the good Englishman he was.

Charles bought the crown for eight hundred and fifty-two thousand florins. "The archbishop of Mainz," as Lewis tells it, "expressed himself after some discussion as willing to accept Charles's offer of seventy-two thousand florins, and the other electors came into line." The bargain was made by the house of Fugger, which had lent King Charles five hundred thousand florins. From now on we shall see Charles shoulder to shoulder with those old bankers who had been gaining positions of increasing power from the time when Andreas Fugger, called by his contemporaries "the rich Fugger," was knighted in 1452. For it must not be forgotten that money creates gentlemen, or as the Spaniard will say, *"Poderoso caballero es Don Dinero."*

While these lads were thus haggling over the German crown, Hernán Cortés, already thirty-five years old, trained in the hard life of Cuba, was shutting himself up in Mexico with a few hundred men, was struggling against armies of thousands of Indians, was being crowned with victory and experiencing the hardship of defeat, until he gained for Spain a wide and wonderful land, an empire so complete and so well defined that it would be known in the chronicles by no less a name than New Spain.

These are the two examples that shone before Lawyer Jiménez de Quesada in his youth while he was litigating against his own father in the affair of some cloth dyers. It could not have entered his imagination that twenty years later he would be taking part in a scene similar to that of Charles, Francis, and Henry disputing over a new kingdom. There is a curious analogy between the case of Germany and that of the New Kingdom of Granada. Just as the three kings of Spain, England, and France met by appointment in 1519 to see who would lay hands on the German crown, so the three adventurers Jiménez de Quesada, Sebastián de Belalcázar, and Nicholas Federmann were to meet unexpectedly face to face in 1539 on the summit of the Andes to dispute the conquest of the New Kingdom of Granada.

The difference lies in the fact that those who were to contend for the Kingdom would be not three youths buying the goodwill of bishops and electors, but three soldiers, three stout captains who would stake their lives on the most daring expedition that history records. Behind each conqueror there would be no court pomp, but armies numbering fewer than two hundred survivors each, armies ravaged by hunger and fatigue, armies in which each soldier would have the individual prowess of a bandit and be capable of feats of the greatest daring. The captains themselves would be men whose titles had been won in unknown lands where neither the authority of the king nor the rule of law prevailed. Belalcázar and Quesada were mutineers who incited troops to rebel behind the governor's back and made themselves masters of their men and their destinies. Nicholas Federmann was, by one of those ironies so common to America, merely a man who worked in the name of German bankers.

But the valley of the Rhine is one thing, and the high uplands of America another. And in deciding title to the

New Kingdom, victory would go to the lawyer Quesada, while the Aryan Nicholas Federmann, backed by the German bankers, stood shivering with cold in the midst of his tattered troops.

*       *       *

The great tragic novel through which Spain, that Spain which Jiménez de Quesada had before his eyes, was moving in the sixteenth century took perfect shape in the figure of Doña Juana the Mad, who wandered back and forth across the rear of the stage like a silent and melancholy shadow. Undoubtedly it was within the very body of Europe that madness lay.

A strange and opportune fate had placed Doña Juana like the pivot of a pair of scales between her parents, the Catholic monarchs Isabel and Ferdinand, in whose reign the conquest of America began, and her son Charles V, whose reign crowned that high emprise which was so full of contradictions and absurdities.

Jiménez de Quesada would have been barely seven years old when the funeral cortege accompanying the remains of Philip the Handsome arrived in Granada. Three months earlier had this king died in Burgos. His wife, Doña Juana, had not left the sick man's bedside for a moment. The jealousies which had tormented her when Philip, well built and charming, had won the name "the Handsome" woke again as the much-loved body began to be consumed by the flames of fever. Juana, touching her husband's body with mingled longing and terror, felt the fever turn to frost. The king's hands, so soon to stiffen in death, she crossed on his manly breast. Like a sleep-walker she put an ear to the wind to listen to the music of the spheres while the king's soul

was taking leave of its mortal lodging. Not a tear misted
her eyes. No word escaped her lips.

Amid the murmuring of friars and the light of torches she
moved behind the catafalque to the monastery of Mira-
flores, where she spent ninety days in jealous vigil. Near
Christmas time Juana had the coffin placed in a splendid
coach. Four stately horses drew it. Night, and the convent
patios echoed to the clatter of horses' hoofs, the ringing of
bells, the prayers, and the murmurings. A train of servants
carried torches. The mad queen began the march to Granada. She did not want the sun to light her locks, nor to
see her face in a clear mirror. A widow, she said, who had
lost the sun of her soul ought never to show herself in the
light of day. The country children, preparing *villancicos* of
rejoicing because the Infant Jesus was born, looked out
half-opened windows at the army of shadows lit by resin
torches and moving along the road like a train of crape and
sparks against the blue enamel of the night.

When the cortege neared Torquemada, the queen called
a halt in the patio of what she thought was a monastery.
Then she saw a nun appear, and Doña Juana trembled with
horror. At once she made the cortege leave the place and
go out into the open fields. The wind shook the torches,
then put them out with a tragic sputtering that crowned
with stars the disordered head of madness. Only when the
casket was opened and she could touch Philip's corpse did
the queen grow more tranquil.

The country people carried this tale about, scarcely daring to tell it. In the cities there were moments of stupor
and amazement. The queen retired from the world. From
now on her figure, gripped by death, was never to leave
the cloisters. But all Spain is crossed with arched corridors

where simple people would see the shade of Doña Juana
pass while her son Charles, king of Spain and emperor of
Germany, also bowed his head by day and hid his eyes to
rest them amid the eternal mysteries.

✻    ✻    ✻

On March 14, 1525, the victory which the armies of
Charles V had won over the French became known to
Madrid. Francis himself had fallen into the hands of the
Spaniards. Never had the soldiers of King Charles dreamed
of a more extraordinary triumph. The messenger, strik-
ing clamour from the very paving stones with the shod
hoofs of his flying horse, took a month to carry the account
of the victory from Pavia to Madrid. His passing awoke
pæans of enthusiasm. When he reached the king's palace
he made a profound reverence. Then, his voice still ringing
with excitement, he gave Charles the news and placed certain documents in his hands. The king looked the messenger
up and down from head to foot, took him all in, and—retired to pray. In the palace the victory went muffled with
a mute, more like the echoes of a church organ than the
clarion call of a war trumpet.

✻    ✻    ✻

There was one thing in those days which might have
tormented a Spaniard if he had ever entertained any doubt
about it. That was the constant shock suffered by a nation
which still lived in the intellectual world of the Middle
Ages, and yet was battered night and morning by the ardent wave of the Renaissance which reached it from Italy,
by the biting wave of the Reformation which came to it
from Germany, by the ironic and subtle wave of Human-

ism which flowed from the Low Countries. All Europe was
in the grip of a feverish desire to change its values, to revise
its intellectual life, and only Spain with Charles V—who
retired to pray in the midst of his victories and was to
end his life in a monastery—Spain with its Catholic king,
its mad queen, remained silent and alone, tightening the
screws of the Inquisition. This was the country of Domingo
de Guzmán and Ignacio de Loyola. In the universities men
thought more about prayer than about study. For the true
Spaniard the moral struggle did not exist, nor the nightly
anguish of placing in the balances of conscience the traditional truth on one side and on the other the possibility of
denying it. The Spaniard was master of the absolute truth,
and his mission was reduced to clubbing the infidels. The
news which came to him from other countries merely fired
his desire to combat heresies, to maltreat the lukewarm, to
burn the Jews.

The same year in which the contradictory spirit of Columbus touched American soil there was born in Valencia
a man who was to adorn his life with the finest qualities of
the spirit—Luis Vives, the comrade of Erasmus, passionate
friend of the truth, philosopher of education. Like Columbus, Luis Vives felt in his bones that intelligence could
not light its peaceful lamps on Spanish soil. Once they
offered him a chair in the University of Alcalá, but Vives,
who spent his life in the Low Countries or in England
talking with the authors of *In Praise of Folly* and *Utopia*,
shunned the Spain of Domingo de Guzmán. He refused
to occupy the chair which was offered him. "To have established himself in his own country," says his biographer,
"would have rendered less service to letters, and would
have meant running the same risks as did Juan de Ver-

gara, Bernardino Tovar, Pedro de Lerma, Luis de la Ca-
dena, Alonso de Virués, and so many others of his renas-
cent countrymen who fell victim to the implacable madness
of the Inquisition."

It was in that very Alcalá that Diego López de Zúñiga,
the theologian from Extremadura, was professor. Under the
protection of Cardinal Cisneros he had had a part in creating the polyglot Bible which was to shed lustre on Spain
for so many centuries. Well, then—when Erasmus published his New Testament, praised by Leo X and the most
learned doctors in Christendom, Zúñiga called him "ignorant of the sacred Scriptures, unlearned in grammatical art,
stupid, untaught, unbalanced, a calumniator who babbles
in delirium, brutalized by his country's fats and beer."

This was the atmosphere of the universities of Spain, the
air which anyone breathed who, like Jiménez de Quesada,
was studying canonical law to qualify for his degree. The
conquerors who left for America would there have to con-
cern themselves more with human things than with divine.
Those who stayed in Spain heading the armies of the
Church would be ardent defenders of the faith. The very
year in which Jiménez de Quesada gave life and form to
the New Kingdom of Granada, Ignacio de Loyola was to
found the Company of Jesus. And while St. Francis of Borgia years later was occupying San Ignacio's post as head of
the Company, his relative Don Juan de Borja would ad-
minister the affairs of men from the Presidency of the Royal
Audiencia in Santa Fé de Bogotá.

Contrary to what is usually said, Spain was doing the real
work of propagating the faith not in America, but in Spain
itself.

And in what a fashion!

# II. Tale of Two Capitalists
## and a Lawyer

The publication on June 2, 1537, of a bull of Pope Paul III concerning the natives of America came as something of a surprise to all Christendom, to whom it was addressed. . . . From the bull, Europe learned that those strange chocolate-skinned figures with their high cheekbones and queer slanting eyes were rational beings, capable of receiving all the Sacraments and having equal rights before God with any hidalgo of Spain or lord mayor of London. . . .

—D. B. WYNDHAM LEWIS

# TALE OF TWO CAPITALISTS
## AND A LAWYER

I T seems to me clearly demonstrated that there was a certain commercial ambition in the conquest of America which shows itself in the lives of those who undertook it, or, to be more precise, in the lives of those who bought governorships in order to grow rich. Obviously the Welsers, or Federmann or Ehinger (whom the Spaniards called Alfinger), who represented the German bank in Venezuela, did not come to America as evangelists. But neither did the Spaniards.

If the spirit of the conquest takes shape in any one family, it is that of Fernández de Lugo. The Canaries were a perfect example of the way in which governors moved. It can almost be said that the whole of Spanish colonial law came into being in the course of their conquest. From the year 1400 on, long before Columbus reached America, men who lived on the slave trade had made forays into the Canaries on the pretext of converting the infidels to Christianity. Naturally, none of these man-hunters ever thought that the islanders would really turn Christian; it was as infidels that they captured and enslaved them, always handing over a fifth of the profits to the Crown in exchange for the Crown's action in legalizing the trade. This labour on the part of Spain, judged so especially healthy for the interests of the faith, was from that time on authorized by the Papacy. The king and queen, who really gained very little from the sale of ten or twenty slaves in Cádiz, who had little interest in

it, and who really did have religious scruples that sometimes drove them to the verge of madness, occasionally ob-
jected to the procedure. But whatever doubts they may
have had were not such as would keep them from renewing
the contracts for Canary conquests and accepting the bene-
fits therefrom.

The year that Columbus left on his first voyage to the
unknown world Alonso Fernández de Lugo, whom we must
consider as the founder of this particular dynasty of slave
traders, contracted with the Catholic monarchs for the conquest of the Island of La Palma, "which is in the power of
infidel Canary Islanders," and stipulated in the contract
that all the fifth part of the booty in terms of captives and
livestock which ordinarily belonged to the king should go
to Fernández de Lugo until he had reimbursed himself for
the costs of the expedition.

So the first Fernández de Lugo formed his company. It
was, as would later be said with much propriety, the house
of "Alonso de Lugo and Company, Commercial Society for
the Conquest of the Island of La Palma." What this society,
considered as a mirror of commercial enterprise, accomplished is shown very clearly in the claim which the pro-
moter's associates made before the Spanish courts for the
two-thirds that belonged to them as participating rights
in a hundred and forty captives.

The matter was this: on a certain day Fernández de Lugo
invented the charge that an uprising was being prepared
against his government, and in accord with this hypothesis
he waked the so-called conspirators at dawn and took a
hundred and forty of them captive. According to the company's rules, Don Alonso had to share this booty with his
associates; but spurred on by the hunger and thirst which

such campaigns produce, he coveted for himself not only his proper thirty or forty, but the whole hundred and forty slaves captured in the purge. Such is the natural atmosphere of conquest. And such the real business which lit the house lamps in the home of the first Fernández de Lugo.

The son and grandson of Fernández de Lugo saw this business of conquest enormously expanded by the vision of America. What had been, for the Catholic monarchs and the first Fernández de Lugo, a modest opening in which good business would be counted in terms of "some two hundred slaves" was now to develop into the most fabulous market for infidel flesh that had ever crept in under banners bearing the name of Christ.

❊　　❊　　❊

Living, as Quesada did, the common life of the time in Spain—amid brawls between friars and soldiers, inquisitors and elegant ladies, the arguments of intellectuals, the jealousy of courtiers, books of chivalry, stories of Moors, news from America, wars in Italy, and tall tales of Europe—he heard word cried through the streets of a new expedition to Santa Marta. This time the man who was promoting it and ordering its affairs was Don Pedro Fernández de Lugo, governor of the Canaries and son of that Don Alonso who had been the first governor there. He would take fifteen hundred foot-soldiers and two hundred horsemen, gunners and carabineers, cross-bowmen, shield-bearers, well-caparisoned horses and mares, supplies and ships' stores. Eighteen ships were to leave Sanlúcar first, to be followed by others which would join them in Tenerife. The lands of America would be divided among the Spaniards who accompanied him. Fernández de Lugo would do all this in splendid style, at his own expense, without the king's having to spend a single centavo. Each one was to help with whatever he could. But Fernández de Lugo was rich, and had plenty of money behind him. The ships would be his, and the greater part of the arms. He would furnish the supplies. It meant something to have a fortune in the sixteenth century.

✿    ✿    ✿

Going to the Indies—how many times must one repeat it?—was primarily considered as going to the fountainhead of riches. This was why even the bankers of Germany embarked in caravels. Don Pedro Fernández de Lugo was wealthy—his own expedition said as much—and he knew very well just how Spaniards became rich. He knew it because he was governor of the Canaries, because it was his father who had conquered those islands for the Crown, and because the Canaries had filled his money bags many times over.

The way in which the plan for this expedition, now almost ready to start for Santa Marta, was first conceived is as natural as it is instructive. One afternoon Don Pedro was thinking, as usual, that the governorship of the Canaries would end with him, and that it would be a good idea to look for other conquests in order to make more money and to install his son properly. Governorships are good, he told himself, when they carry with them the first flush of conquest gold—later they languish, and fall into mere routine administrative labours. Don Pedro was reasoning thus when one Francisco Lorenzo, a soldier who had been with Rodrigo de Bastidas in the first entry into Santa Marta, arrived in the Canaries and stumbled into his house. Just

when Don Pedro and his son were searching the horizons
for another prize, Lorenzo painted them a tempting picture
of Santa Marta, where the gold of the Taironas sparkled,
where there were pearls to be had for the fishing, and where
there were, or should be, fabulous riches to be had in the
continent which lay at the city's back, and which was still
to be explored.

Thus was born this high emprise—amid financial calculations and fantastic plans, and lit by the red glare of greed.

"Let Your Grace stay here," said Alonso Luis to his father,
"warming the governor's seat in the Canaries, while I swear
to get you the one in Santa Marta from the court by making the merits of my grandfather shine all over again. And
do you go on getting ships together as fast as possible, and
talking with people, because we will be making the acquaintance of Terra Firma in a few months, and then we'll
start piling up the gold."

And Alonso Luis went off to the capital. And he talked of
how his grandfather had conquered the islands of La Palma
and Tenerife, and of how he had beaten the Moors in the
battle of Tagaos and the African black men in the battle
of Bezebriche. And of how he had been made governor of
the Canaries for the space of two lifetimes, with his son to
succeed him.

"My grandfather," said Don Alonso, "cut a handsome
figure in the battle of Tagaos, breaking the enemies' lines
with his soldiers as a ship's prow cuts through embattled
waves in a sea of infidels. Then he rose up out of the tumult,
leaving hundreds of dead on the field. Eight hundred Arab
horsemen and four hundred foot-soldiers."

Then he painted a picture of the riches of his father, who
was preparing the expedition at his own expense. He talked

with armourers and merchants, with soldiers and men of broad ambition, inflaming all of them with the desire for conquest. And thus he set the stage for going forth to get a governorship in Terra Firma.

*　*　*

In the very name of Santa Marta lay both mystery and prestige. When Fernández de Lugo paid so large a sum for the governorship, it must have been because that governorship was worth it. A Sevillian, López de Gómara, made a picture of Santa Marta which, though some years later than when Fernández de Lugo entered it, corresponds fairly well to what the men who went out with the governor could assume the governorship would include.

"There is in Santa Marta," says López de Gómara, "much gold and copper, which they gild with a certain pressed and pounded grass; they rub the copper with it, and dry it in the fire; the more grass they use, the more colour it takes, and it is so fine that at first it deceived the Spaniards. There are amber, jasper, chalcedony, sapphire, emeralds, and pearls; the land is fertile, and irrigated; corn, yucca roots, yams, and garlic flourish there. The yucca root, which in Cuba, Haiti, and other islands is deadly when raw, is healthful here; they eat it raw, roasted, boiled, with meat or as a vegetable, and however eaten its flavour is good. They pride themselves on having their houses well furnished with dyed or painted mats of palm or rush, and cotton hangings set with gold and baroque pearls, at which our Spaniards marvelled greatly; on the corners of the bed they hang strings of sea-snail shells so that they may sound. These sea-snails are big and of many kinds, more shining and fine than mother of pearl. The men go naked, but some

of them cover their private parts with something like gourds
or pipes of gold; the women wear aprons about their waists;
the ladies wear headdresses of great plumes. . . . They
look very well in these, and taller than they are, and therefore are said to be comely and beautiful; the Indian women
are no smaller than ours, but since they do not wear clogs a
palm or a palm and a half thick, as ours do, nor even any
shoes at all, they look very small. . . ."

The chronicle also speaks of certain shameless and libidi-
nous ways of the Indian women, and vices of the Indian
men, which were a matter of common knowledge among
those Spaniards familiar with America, and which excited
the curiosity of the soldiers. Honour and the modesty
proper to this book forbid me to go further with the words
of the affable chronicler and Sevillian priest.

⸙　⸙　⸙

The son of Fernández de Lugo completed this business
of the governorship for his father at the court of Charles V
and Queen Juana. The king conceded him magnificent
privileges. His jurisdiction was to extend from the governorship of Venezuela and Cabo de la Vela, which were
under the charge of the Welsers or of agents of those German bankers, up to that of Cartagena, which was in the
hands of the noseless Pedro de Heredia. The monarchs were
interested, to be sure, in serving God. They wanted these
discoveries made without men dead, or Indians robbed, or
slaves taken. The Indians were not to be ordered to work in
the mines against their will. Each time the conqueror set
out on a new voyage of discovery he was to take with the
troops two men of the Church. The first thing to be done
when they came in sight of the Indians was to read two or

three times, in a high and intelligible voice, the catechism
prepared by Francisco de los Cobos in which they were to
be asked if they accepted the true religion of Christ, if they
believed in God and in the Holy Trinity, if they surren-
dered themselves to the Holy Ghost and to Jesus Christ His
only Son, who was born of the Virgin Mary.

Obviously all this would be agreed to by the aspirants for
a governorship. Alonso Fernández left the palace and the
capital full of plans and ambitions. To hell with this idea
of converting the Indians and going easy with them! On the
other side of the Atlantic there was only one sure thing—
booty in the form of slaves and gold. It is easy enough, he
told himself, to handle this matter of the catechism. He
laughed, imagining the faces of the poor Caribs when, in
the most pure and sweet Castilian, the snivelling friar
would ask them, "Do you believe in the Holy Ghost and in
Jesus Christ His only Son, who was born of the Virgin
Mary?" "But," repeated Don Alonso to himself, "all this
shall be done." It would be done, and if he returned some
day to Spain it would be with his pockets bursting with gold
and his saddle bags dripping pearl necklaces.

It will not be the author of this book who tells how the
soldiers for this expedition were recruited. Many people
will assume that Don Alonso went to the universities and
the monasteries to pick an intellectual here, a saint there,
and that the great families would contribute the finest of
their line so that only well-bred people directly inspired by
the fear of God should reach America. Better, in this matter,
to yield the floor to one who knows more about it because
he lived in the midst of this business of governorships, one
who knew the expedition from the inside, that wise and

sensitive chronicler, Hernández de Oviedo, governor of Cartagena. Let us hear him:

"Sent out from the court, he came to Seville with less money than he would have liked. Nevertheless, with a drummer on the one hand, and a friar or two and a few priests who later joined him under pretext of converting the Indians, they went about promising riches and turning the heads of ignorant people. The captain knew how to handle bills of exchange, and to buy old and worn-out boats which, whether they reached America, or succumbed to God's will and mercy, or to the force of doubled shot, would in no case be fit to return and to render unto Castile an account of their cargo.

"On the other hand, a youth whom he made his secretary (and who did not know what a secret was), and other smooth-tongued subordinates, whom the captain judged to be the most cunning, were charged with talking to their poor comrades and persuading them to one of two things: the one was that they should lend the captain money in return for the vain hopes he held out to them, and for a receipt which looked to him who received it like a bill of exchange; and so the poor comrade gave the little money he had, and, if the snare worked well enough, sold his cape and his smock, and remained like Quixote in his shirt-sleeves; for it seemed to him that, besides the fact that he was going to a hot country, he would arrive well clothed in the fortune that awaited him, and which they had promised. . . ."

So Don Alonso went about recruiting people for his enterprise. And among the dreamers, the despairing, the vagabonds, and the bullies who listened to him was the son of

Gonzalo Jiménez, also called Gonzalo. This Gonzalo, whom, as I have said, we must call Quesada, must have been born in Cordova, in a house which did not belong to his father's family but to his mother's, near the little chapel of Fuentesanta. He studied law, perhaps in Salamanca. And now, when he had his degree and could follow in his father's footsteps—that father to whom the legal profession had already given a certain eminence—he got into a bad piece of litigation, and found himself arguing against his father.

What had happened was that the court had started criminal proceedings against the dyers of the city for the scandalous falsifications which they had made in their dyes. Quesada undertook the defence, and lost the case. Not only did this impair his professional reputation, but it also injured his mother's family, which was in the thick of the affair with the dyers.

Quesada was living under the pressure of these misadventures. Surely in his defeat he must have sought consolation in the love of some gentle woman who would caress his jet-black beard, close his eyes with a kiss, and comfort his spirit with a song of hope. He did not let himself be downed; in public the stream of his genius, which was gay, vivid, happy, ran as freely as ever. He grew sad only when he was alone or when he opened his heart to the maid who comforted him. Behind his charming mask, however, his spirit went into deep and silent mourning. That is an essential of being a good Spaniard.

But one must not let oneself drown in vain sorrows. You, Gonzalo Jiménez, are strong and courageous. Some day you will be a leader of men. This passing reverse must not be the door that closes the future against a man of will and courage. On the other side of the sea lie the Indies. Go to

the Indies and found a kingdom, build a city like Granada
which shall be famous:

> *To the loveliest of the cities*
> *I would give the name "Granada"*
> *In remembrance of the sadness*
> *That I suffered on the journey.*
> *When on her, my gracious lady,*
> *My thoughts ever went on turning*
> *How she had, my faithful mistress*
> *Weeping, said farewell to me*
> *When I had to leave Granada*
> *For some miscreant deed of mine. . . .*

❈   ❈   ❈

And on a November day in 1535, with the air sharp and
brilliant, the ships of Fernández de Lugo cast off from the
port of Tenerife. The wind filled the grey and bellying
sails. The rigging creaked like trees that bend beneath the
shaggy hand of the hurricane. The streamers splashed the
clean blue of the sky with brilliant colour, and the women
on the beach carried in their eyes the last long memory of
those caresses which hours earlier they had been lavishing
on the virile figures of the soldiers, on their curling and
twisted beards.

The governor and the head of the expedition was, as I
have said before, Don Pedro Fernández de Lugo. As his
chief magistrate and second in command went the lawyer
Gonzalo Jiménez de Quesada.

❈   ❈   ❈

Seldom have the ships that set sail on the voyage to
America gathered between their decks so many daring men

as those that Don Pedro Fernández de Lugo commanded. The most shameless, the most greedy of them all was the son of Don Pedro, that Alonso Luis de Lugo, captain and friend of the soldiers, who had few morals, and a glittering future in Spain and America. Don Pedro himself cut but an opaque figure alongside his son. If his personality did not diminish in comparison, certainly the audacity of Alonso the impetuous loomed large.

The trip lasted two long months. Two months which everyone spent in spinning fantastic yarns about the things to be expected in Terra Firma and in elaborating plots which already included conspiring against the Indians. The sea breeze, the Caribbean sun, the physical impression of separation from Spain which the ship created when she cast off from the peninsula with her prow set toward the unknown, all wiped out as with a sponge of gold the admonitions of the Catholic king and the mad queen as to how the Indians must be treated.

When the first soldiers saw land, when everyone was straining to define the misty profile of the coast that kept surging up and then losing itself amid the tossing waves and the fiery brilliance of the horizon, all hearts swelled with excitement. A shout rose to the masthead and spread from ship to ship. The captains, in this moment of importance and command, gave their first orders and donned their finest clothes. The soldiers gathered their equipment and cast a last look at the litter of straw in which they had passed so many nights, a glance like that dogs give when they round the corner of their own house.

The ships came closer and drew into line so as to present an orderly spectacle as they entered the bay. When they passed through the natural door of this marine entrance they felt the breeze temper and thin, as if announcing that the troops would find better shelter here. The mast blossomed with flags and pennons. Friends, America is in sight! When the first group of the curious waiting on shore and the simple outlines of thatched huts came in view, the guns belched a military salute to the sound of a march. Governor Fernández de Lugo looked over his troops, his armada, the richness of his expedition, with eyes of pride and faith. Alonso Luis, his son, searched the horizon for the scene of his future enterprises. Jiménez de Quesada, he who

> *. . . had to leave Granada*
> *For some miscreant deed . . .*

stood more firm and poised, more silent, and more able.

The troops disembarked in good order, says the historian Restrepo Tirado, the soldiers in new uniforms, the officials covered with gold and silver braid, displaying precious stones and brilliant plumes, ostentatious in shining helmets and gleaming breast-plates. The few inhabitants\* of the city awaited them in cotton garments, coarsely knitted stockings, and rope sandals.

✧     ✧     ✧

Don Pedro, Don Alonso Luis, and the lawyer are now on Terra Firma. That is to say, they are in a poor settlement where the provisions are scarce, the troops sick, and the near-by Indians fierce and cannibal. The flour and grain they brought from Spain begin to deteriorate from heat and humidity. Fevers paralyse the soldiers or kill them. There

---

\* The town had been founded by Rodrigo de Bastidas ten years earlier. These inhabitants must have been all that were left of his men, and of those of García de Lerma who came after. When Fernández de Lugo's ships arrived the settlement was in the last stages of decay.—TRANSLATOR.

is an epidemic of dysentery. The governor visits the sick, directs the building of new huts, talks with the first settlers, and deals with the Indians. This, America's first greeting, does not disconcert him. He makes fantastic plans. The Indians are naked, certainly, but they have gold. With diplomatic artistry he demands tribute of them. The poor things come bringing very little, and their leader, the chief of the Bondas, does not appear at all. The governor plans his first expedition.

For the first time the settlement of Santa Marta sees an army in full array. However many have been laid low by fever, enough remain on their feet to form squads like an army in Europe. Many, seeing adventure ahead, take fresh heart and put themselves into their armour with real pleasure. The veterans, those who came first with Bastidas or with García de Lerma, watch these preparations with a slow and sceptical eye. Don Pedro does not know what America is. Only those who are now seasoned scouts would remember that gesture of García de Lerma when, possessed by terror, he cried to his servants, "Let the silver plate go! Back to Santa Marta!" Those whom experience has hardened know there are no beautiful walled cities here, no open roads, but always the mountains, the tangle of brush and briers, the sharp ascent from which the Indians hurl huge rocks—those boulders that go rolling through the chronicles of conquest for centuries—and the poisoned arrow or the pits full of thin pointed stakes into which foot-soldiers fall and remain impaled.

These newly arrived Europeans who wear fine coats of mail, who go armed like feudal knights, poised and elegant, will very soon learn that all this is of no use in America. The conquest, as an introduction to the study of the new continent, teaches that this is to be for hundreds of years a land of guerrilla warfare and ambuscade. The Indian and the mountain laugh at the European. They force him to adapt himself to the new climate and the ironic air of the inhabitant. When the new arrival sees that those who are acquainted with America dress in "cotton armour" he shouts with laughter. And there is no doubt that those horsemen who covered themselves with quilted cotton to keep the arrows from reaching their skins did look more like clowns than soldiers. At these great overstuffed figures the soldiers of Fernández de Lugo are, I repeat, overcome with laughter. But when the poison from the arrows begins to curdle their blood, they will laugh on the other side of their mouths, as those possessed of devils laugh in the long corridor that leads to the house of the dead.

The Spaniard has the arquebus, the petard, and powder, all of which fill the Indian with terror. The Indian has the poisoned arrow. He will lose thousands of his bowmen to the Spaniard, but behind them, and to replace them, stand the fecund mountains which bear hordes of them, the earth which teems with naked multitudes. The Spanish army is small, it has no rearguard, no mother to feed and nourish the paleface. The Indian trembles with terror at the sound of exploding powder. The Spaniard goes mad at the bite of the arrow.

Four centuries after the conquest Europeans will come to America to hunt for poisonous herbs from which they will extract the juice for purposes of war in Europe. War is to continue to be the greatest European industry, and barbasco (a poisonous root) will be a new twentieth-century weapon in that industry.

In the modest sixteenth century a certain chronicler,

Pedro Cieza de León, made the first investigations into poisonous plants. In his famous book on Peru he wrote a small treatise entitled "Of How the Very Venomous Herb Is Treated with Which the Indians of Santa Marta and Cartagena Have Killed So Many Spaniards." He says that the Indians dig down near those noxious trees called manchineel to get out the smallest roots. These they burn in clay pots, and make a paste. Then they hunt ants as big as beetles, very black and wicked, which with a single sting leave a man senseless, and these they grind into the root paste. They also put in huge spiders and hairy worms. These worms are so mighty that, says Cieza, "one day one bit my neck, and I had the worst night of my life, and the most painful." Bats' wings, *tamborino* tails, snakes' tails, and poisonous camomile complete the venomous formula. Far outside the village an Indian woman, wicked and condemned, stirs the mixture in a jar over hot fires until its blending is completed. Then, having taken in the fumes and the odours of so strange a brew, she swells up and violently expires.

The treatment which the Spaniards invented in order to counteract such poison was rudimentary and cruel. It consisted in opening the flesh to extract the piece of arrow which had remained in the wound. The head usually stayed in the body to the depth of four fingers, "for the Indians had thus arranged it. Then," says Fray Pedro Aguado, "they fill the open wound with as much ground corrosive sublimate as they can force into it, and then, with an iron knife and machete heated in the fire, they sear the wound and all the surrounding flesh until it is well gone over, then they come with the same glowing instruments and sear the loins from top to bottom to deaden them against convulsions, which are what the poison causes first. This done, they wrap the patient thoroughly from head to foot and put him into the darkest and most sheltered inside room so that no air shall reach or touch him, and they keep him there three whole days without eating or drinking anything; after which they give him very thin broth, eight ounces of it at most . . ." etc.

I remember reading that once in the country near Santa Marta, on the Venezuela side, the Indians rose up against *encomendero* Rodrigo de Argüello. They robbed and razed the city, and took the wife of Rodrigo, Juana de Ulloa, and her three daughters prisoners. They carried off the daughters so that the chiefs might amuse themselves, but they stripped Doña Juana and hanged her from the branches of a tree by a bridle rein. Then the whole tribe shot arrows at her with such skill and prodigality that they left her looking like a hedgehog. When the Spaniards arrived and cut the reins the body of the *encomendero's* wife fell on its feet and stood there, upheld by the art with which the arrows that adorned her had been loosed.

❖    ❖    ❖

There is no reason for dwelling longer on these wars. In the course of this book I fear that the reader will find so many necessary examples that he will grow weary of them. Let me simply say that Fernández de Lugo went forth against the Bondas like a knight and a gentleman. In accordance with the instructions of Charles V and Doña Juana, he asked the natives three times if they wished to believe in God, and in the Holy Trinity, and in His Mother the Virgin Mary, and in the whole dogma. As those wild Indians understood nothing of this, the governor charged against them, set fire to their towns, pursued them. But the end of the adventure was a fearful thing. Through rubbish and ashes and piles of corpses the Spanish soldiers, maddened by the arrows, went roaring like wild beasts. Even the veterans in their cotton-wadding armour were hardly able to defend themselves. Iron Age Europe, Catholic Europe, was left humiliated and with empty hands.

❖     ❖     ❖

But if the father had such bad luck, perhaps things would go better for the son. In any event, Santa Marta could not sustain so swollen a population as that brought by the ships of Fernández de Lugo, and expeditions had to be invented so that the army might at least find maintenance in the native towns. With this in mind, Don Alonso set out to explore the land of the Taironas. Better advised than his father, and profiting by the experience of earlier battles, he inserted himself into mountain fastnesses and around craggy corners with great care, he confronted the Indians and almost always beat them, he burned their hamlets and stole their gold. Alonso Luis was advancing through lands that were richer. After the fires the conqueror found golden nuggets in the ashes.

"Sacking a town, and taking whatever was in it," says Father Aguado, "they called 'ranching,' and the gold they got out of it they called 'ranch gold'; thus they went on painting their acts of violence and greed with exquisite and unusual words." The fact was that if many of the soldiers were suffering from hunger and dying, at least the treasure of America was gleaming in their fingers. When the gold had reached a certain amount, Alonso Luis thought about returning to Santa Marta. But his mind was already afire with the idea that he would not share the spoils of victory with anyone, not even with his father. If he went to Spain and bought a governorship for himself, he might acquire the same power and fame as had his grandfather. He felt the impetuous spirit of that conqueror of the Canaries reborn in his veins. Any compassion there may have been in his soul was burned out of it by this newly aroused ambition.

He called his captains together. He discussed with them the return to Santa Marta. A little beyond the land of the Taironas roamed a greedy German, Nicholas Federmann by name, agent for the Welsers, who had been told he could not set foot in Santa Marta. A cautious man, fearful of the forces which Fernández de Lugo must have, the German had retired and taken shelter in the lands belonging to Coro. Alonso Luis was therefore moving between his father's lands and those occupied by the German, but the day would yet come when he would have boundaries of his own. The land he had to "ranch" had already been gone over. The Indians were advancing, surrounding him, about to close him in. If they did not flee at once they would all be caught there, stuck full of arrows like the *encomendero's* wife Juana de Ulloa.

He resolved to leave at night, while the Indians were asleep. The army filed out along a narrow road between bushes and thorn trees. A hundred men went ahead, their feet shod with the sandals of care and quiet. Their eyes strained to pierce the darkness so that no tribe should spring out of the shadows to surprise them. Moving with delicate and exaggerated care, not daring to use the machetes, they broke one by one the branches that hung across their path.

But suddenly the Spaniards fell into a trap. The Indians

had barred the way with cords on which hung empty gourds and rattling bones. When the advance guard bumped into this invention an infernal din echoed through the mountains and whole armies of Indians sprang out as though on springs. But the darkness was kinder to sword-work and lances than to the flight of arrows. The army emerged from this ambuscade with very few losses, and moved on down the road to Santa Marta.

Don Alonso entered Santa Marta with a chain of Indian prisoners loaded with gold. How much gold, nobody knew. To Captain San Martín, who went along to keep account, Don Alonso declared sums that had nothing to do with the reality. True son of conquest that he was, Don Alonso looked forward to using his booty for advancing his own fortunes. The soldiers were already murmuring among themselves, the captains talked out loud, and his own father called him to account and rebuked him for trying to hide what he had brought in. The governor needed gold to pay the debts he had contracted, and the soldiers felt that gold was the only recompense for their labours. The camp was haunted by an air of new tragedy. Yet it vanished as suddenly as it had come, dispelled by Don Alonso's prudence.

When the soldiers arose on the day following the quarrel between Fernández de Lugo and his son they found that Don Alonso had fled. Loaded the gold onto a cargo boat and gone off to Spain with it. The thief left his father with nothing but disappointed hopes. The troops, who recognized that the real sufferer from this robbery was the governor, had no one on whom to vent their wrath. And as on the first day they landed in Santa Marta, the lawyer and judge, Captain Jiménez de Quesada, looked from a point apart

at this small world in ruins, and hope blazed in his dark
eyes.

*    *    *

Fernández de Lugo now became the second governor
who let the silver plate go. When he saw that the soldiers,
tired of suffering hunger and fever, arrow wounds and
misery, and, to make matters worse, robbed of all their
booty, were beginning to stir with justified murmurs of
rebellion, the poor man gave them all he had. And first his
silver service, the beautiful service which he had brought
in his role of *gran señor* and in imitation of García de
Lerma. What the devil, let the silver service go, but let
there be peace in the camp! Just the same, it seems to me
less bitter to have lost a silver service while fleeing from
Indians than to be obliged to give it up because of a thieving son.

Besieged as they all were by fever and hunger, anything
the governor could do for them served merely as a temporary distraction. When those soldiers who had been with
Don Alonso in the Tairona country came back, the epi-
demics had broken out again. The bells went on tolling all
day long, until Fernández de Lugo, desperate, forbade
their ringing. There was no time to bury the dead in separate graves, and the day came when they threw twenty
corpses into a common fosse. Those who could left the city
in any sort of boat to seek better fortune elsewhere on the
coast, or to try an adventurous trip to Cartagena. The
fevers, the flights, the faintheartedness, treachery, and
death went on widening before the governor's eyes, in
circles like those that Dante painted. Surrounded by such
agonies, he must look for a new horizon, seek out a radical

cure lest the most brilliant expedition that had ever left Spain fall to pieces in his hands.

Behind Santa Marta, in the inland country, are a series of drop curtains which fascinated the Spaniard's mind. First, of course, come the wild Indians. But beyond them, further on, there might be the fundamentals of a great country. Those enormous, muddy mouths of the Great River, the wealth of waters which betokens a huge land in the interior, beckoned discovery. Perhaps that El Dorado of which the adventurers dream lay amid the gleaming peaks of the mountains. The land of salt, where the bowels of the mountains are white, and there are rivers of sweet water and rivers of salt. It is the magic mountain of Muzo, alive with chameleon butterflies and holding veins of quartz shot with emeralds.

What a mysterious and shining spur to adventure, to follow the wanderings of a muddy river in order to reach and climb the flanks of a mountain that sleeps beneath the quiver of butterfly wings! The troops, sunk deeper in despair when they are halted in Santa Marta than when they claw their way through thickets and stand off the charge of bowmen, want to leave. They have already tasted the governor's small skill and the too great cleverness of his son.

"And when Lieutenant Jiménez de Quesada offered his services, a man who, though trained in letters and the peace of study, had a vigour and an excellence of mind and good fortune which led him to embark on this difficult and hazardous adventure, and to take into his own hands the journey to and discovery of the sources of the Great River of the Magdalena, the spirit of the governor was so moved that, expending other moneys, he set about the labour of this new enterprise."

# III. *Shipwrecks on Land and Sea*

Into the swamps through which they were wading entered crocodiles, which are, as I have said, fish that are ten, twelve, fifteen, twenty and more feet long, made like lizards, and of the ferocity of man-eating beasts or wild cannibals. Soldiers passing through certain swamps or crossing certain rivers were snatched by them with great suddenness, and plunged beneath the water, with no aid or remedy possible, and suffered very miserable and most cruel deaths.

—FRAY PEDRO AGUADO

# SHIPWRECKS ON LAND AND SEA

LET us suppose—which is not a bad guess—that there are a thousand or more Spaniards in Santa Marta. Of those, some seven hundred and fifty or eight hundred are to go with Quesada. The rest will stay with the governor. Those who set out to explore will go some by sea and some by land. Those who go by land, with Jiménez de Quesada at their head, are to cut a road through thick brush and across wet marshes until they reach the banks of the Magdalena. Those who sail, with Diego de Urbina leading them, will go coasting along the shore until they reach the mouths of the Magdalena River. Then, turning upstream, they are to meet Quesada in Chiriguaná or some other port.

The prospect of discovery put fresh heart in the soldiers. Santa Marta became one gigantic factory where everyone was working. The ships' companies spent their days twisting ropes, mending sails, building new brigantines, sawing at huge tree trunks, preparing pitch and oakum with which to caulk the boats. The Indians, full of curiosity, ventured nearer, and watched the white men with amazement. The blacksmiths blew at improvised forges. There was a constant hammering from those who worked at anvils or on the ships' planking. The horsemen went over their harness, tested the stirrup leathers, sewed the girths, put new padding on the saddles. The lances stood, cleaned, in the corners of every hut, and the captains looked to the polished brilliance of their swords.

The Indian servants, enchanted with this new life which they neither shared nor understood, went from city to hilltop, and from city to harbour carrying tree trunks, barrels, supplies. In their hearts they thought the Spaniards were getting ready to let them go free, and that the burden of servitude would pass from them to others who lived in the interior. So the tribute would be less heavy for those who remained in Santa Marta.

Quesada's captains were all men of long experience in arms. They were familiar with war in Europe, or had accompanied other discoverers across that sea of infinite routes, the Atlantic Ocean. These were no delicate youths, but hard and experienced men who had lived through hours of victory and hours of bloody adversity. Juan de Junco, chief captain under Quesada, had carried arms in Italy and Hungary, and filled out his service record by following Sebastian Cabot in his excursion to the River Plate. Junco knew how kings fought in Europe, and how it was possible that a great American discoverer, such as Cabot, could later return to Spain "destroyed, and through no fault of his, but of his men."

Another of Quesada's captains was Gonzalo Suárez Rendón, one of those who had fought under the banners of Charles V. In the battle of Pavia he saw the French king, Francis I, taken prisoner, and he was present at the siege and capture of Florence. In Vienna he watched the Turks, who had destroyed the Hungarian army, advance on Christian Europe, and then he saw the proud troops of Suleiman the Magnificent stopped before the city gates and forced to flee in disorder before the combined attack of the Spaniards and the Germans. Clearly this was a splendid school

for one who was now going to lead trail-breakers along
the banks of the Magdalena.

Nor were these cases unique. All the captains, ensigns,
and soldiers had their individual histories. Juan de Céspedes was serving in the king's forces in Spain when they
defeated the Comuneros. Antón de Olalla went as a boy to
the wars in Italy. Many of the soldiers had fought in those
regiments known as the *tercios*. They were men whom military life in Europe had encouraged to come to America in
search of new and greater excitement. And then there were
some who, like Junco, having experienced the hard row
America offered in matters of discovery, had no hesitation
in trying their fortunes there again. So they had come from
Spain in the ships of Fernández de Lugo.

*     *     *

On April 6, 1536, Don Gonzalo Jiménez de Quesada left
Santa Marta with his land army. The boats were not yet
ready, and it would take them twenty days more before
they were prepared to cast off. Don Gonzalo went ahead,
mounted on a good Andalusian charger, and behind him
some five hundred soldiers. Like men trained in the Castilian regiments they kept, in the beginning, a certain order
in their marching, and so there was about this departure a
flavour of the European, and talk of the fine army. But before long they fell into a disorder that was far more human,
for there were no roads, no formation possible, no uniforms
in an army dressed in patches. Mingled with the soldiers
went hundreds of Indian carriers who marched stark naked.
Three privileged captains had Indian women as their travelling companions. Each carried on his shoulders, in the

manner of a knapsack, a bundle such as soldiers make who do not go forth with their women for the sake of having them arrange the baggage. Eighty-five horses loaded with food and supplies looked, in this singular picture, like the work of a gipsy camp. A solitary donkey, caught in the mountains one day and kept as proof that other Spaniards had passed that way before, added a note as philosophic as it was Spanish.

It was the month of April, and this time April brought a thousand showers. Hardly had they sallied forth when torrential downpours fell, soaking the soldiers to the skin. The clouds flooded past, each dropping its load of water and leaving the earth a sea of puddles. Then came the strong tropic sun, and one could see the land steam while the air thinned and distance lengthened under a transparent sky. There was great variety in the landscapes. First the sand, the dunes, beach scenes which stretched back long fingers toward the foot of the mountains. Then the black earth which turned to mud. Then the marshes, from which the iguana, the lizard, and the snake emerged. Those soldiers who were conning the first pages of their apprenticeship in the things of America met the alligator—a monumental lizard, a lizard out of some far geologic past, with jaws which could devour a man at a single gulp, and they were stirred with enthusiasm, terror, and admiration. As if the poisoned arrow were not enough, the alligator seemed to the soldiers the first definitive sign of the New World.

They halted to make camp where the earth was less water-soaked. Some nights they passed without sleeping, in that blue electric light of thunderstorms which painted brittle, unreal landscapes and brought out the spongy green of trees. No clothing dried, there were no needles to mend the rents in it. At every crash of thunder the horses milled together, terrified. The Indians, huddled under scanty foliage, took advantage of every lightning flash to look after the terror-stricken animals. When morning dawned, if it dawned clear so the sun could warm them, their garments hung steaming from their numbed bodies, and those who had been shivering with goose flesh a moment before now took comfort in the burning tropic sun.

Sometimes they stumbled across huts which had been abandoned by their owners, and that brought great relief. If the Indians had fled hurriedly, that meant more food—yucca roots, grains of corn. Where there was farmland under cultivation the army passed like a swarm of locusts. The troops had left Santa Marta with a good supply of food—it would last all of a week. Soon it showed signs of giving out, and what mountains and rivers had to offer in the way of game, fish, or fruit was not enough to feed an army of five hundred men. The size of the expedition was in this case, as perhaps in all others, the greatest problem and the greatest hindrance. Moreover, even when it set out from Santa Marta the army was being ravaged by fever. Soon faces twisted by pain appeared, soldiers who begged a sip of water and trembled with the chills that were forerunners of death.

Only one order came from Quesada's lips—"Forward." They must reach the Magdalena. Those who could not take another step were to be put on horseback. But they were hardly more than badly covered skeletons whom life would very soon abandon. Fortunately there was no lack of priests, among them Friar Pedro Zambrano and the presbyters Antón de Lescámez and Juan de Legaspes. "My son, repent of thy sins; fear the punishment of the Inferno; I forgive thee in the name of the Father—" And then—to the grave. A grave which opened and shut with great speed—two spadefuls of earth sufficed to close it. Sometimes a hand clenched in the last agony, a hand which there was no time to cross decently on the breast, remained above ground to wave farewell to those who marched on—a ghostly troop in which those who moved in the saddles were already corpses.

Lieutenant General Quesada turned aside toward high ground in order to avoid the marshes. They had to reach the banks of the Magdalena, so they could meet the boats that would take them upstream. The sick could go on ahead then, and there would be food. Salt, cheese, wine, oil——

At times certain of the captains made forays into the country around the encampments. While the foot-soldiers were advancing so slowly, those on horseback had time to pillage. The terrain lent itself to hiding places and ambuscades. The Indians fled, hid, attacked from behind the bushes. But the Spaniards used the noses of their dogs to smell them out. And if any Indian tried to run, the dogs were loosed to tear him limb from limb. Man, horse, and dog were the conquest's great trio. After each foray the captains came back with yucca roots, corn, and new Indian carriers.

One day, while the soldiers were enjoying fresh supplies taken from the Indians, an Indian woman burst naked and weeping into camp and rushed through the midst of the group. Straight to the Indian prisoners she ran, and threw her arms around the youngest. They kissed tenderly. Jiménez de Quesada himself came to find out what all this was about—a mother who claimed a place among the captives that she might not be separated from her son. The conqueror set them both free. In this ferocious drama of conquest there was a parenthesis now and then for love.

*     *     *

As the Spaniards advanced into the highlands they entered a region populated by bowmen—the Chimilas. Poor Indians, and fierce ones, from whom the army took nothing, for there was nothing to take, but left a certain number of corpses on their hands. The rain poured down, implacable, and as the troops neared the Great River the marshes widened, so that they, like the Indians, had to take refuge on higher ground.

The veins of water swelled. The Great River overflowed, its branches overflowed. The army reached the banks of the Ariguaní. There was no fording that deep and rushing stream. The soldiers were afraid of alligators. Yet cross they must, whatever happened. They made a swinging bridge out of stout vines. Soldiers, Indians, squaws, horses, dogs, friars, mules, supplies, and weapons all were to move across the fragile, swaying makeshift. The soldiers watched the foaming, muddy water carry down dead animals, tree trunks, flowers. Under the lash of heavy rains the men worked desperately. They must reach the banks of the Great River; some safe cove where they could join forces with the brigantines which ought already to be coming upstream. Finally the troops were all across. They had lost some arms, a few supplies. But it was better now that they could move at a faster pace, and might get news of those who were coming with the ships.

They neared the shore, and in the native dialects made inquiry. There was no news, the ships had not arrived. Perhaps they had been held at the mouths of the Great River.

Perhaps they had been attacked by Indian bowmen. This was the province of the Tamalameques, so at least there were supplies, and Indians who were somewhat less hostile.

With the fleet behind time, Quesada moved ahead without such haste. The march lay through more open country now, empty plains, swamps where there was no possibility of making camp. The horsemen went out hunting game. But there were still too many men to feed. When death reduced the squads still further it would all be easier; they would go faster, there would be no difficulties of carrying the sick, and for better or worse the land would furnish food for a handful. But it takes a rich and abundant country to sustain four or five hundred soldiers and as many more Indians. Even captives began to seem a burden. As for the soldiers, they ate whatever came to hand—frogs, lizards, snakes.

After wandering for almost two months they again reached country that was inhabited. More Indians appeared every day. As there was no sign of war-making, the natives regarded the army with no suspicion. They knew what conquerors were, for the Germans under Federmann had already passed this way. But an army so worn down by weariness could safely be received under a white flag.

Soon they saw Tamalameque ahead, surrounded by fertile land and well-tilled fields. But it was not going to be easy to take Tamalameque. The city was well defended by surrounding water—it was built like an island, and could only be reached by a narrow causeway that cut across the lake. The Indians were good boatmen, and went about their business in canoes. At the rear was the Zazare River, and roundabout were many lakes and marshes. Lugo's Spaniards and those with Ehinger had come this way earlier, but

had not dared to enter the city. This time, however, hunger
and need put added courage into men. Quesada ordered
them to force an entrance along the earthen causeway.

The Indians, who had pulled up their canoes so that the
Spaniards should not make use of them, attacked with arrows. The Spaniards defended themselves with bucklers,
and attacked the nearest natives with lances. The dogs
flung themselves into the water and, biting without mercy,
terrified the Indians. Blood stains opened on the lake like
water flowers, and spread in broad red circles. The Indians
were struck in the breast, in the head. Dead bodies, naked
and copper-brown, floated past like logs from the great
American forest.

Quesada's army advanced in good order, economical of
men, without undue haste. The Indians, watching the military machine move forward step by step, recognized that
resistance was useless, and began to leave the battlefield.
Soon the army found itself in the midst of the houses, which
were full of supplies. For the first time in months the troops
could rest. The Great River was close at hand. Quesada
sent San Martín with a few soldiers to see what they could
find.

Twenty days of idleness followed, of rest, in which the
sick slept beneath a roof and watched their fevers run their
wonted course in the placid atmosphere of a hospital. Those
who had sufficient energy investigated their surroundings
and busied themselves with repairing the mountings of the
horses. The horses were the ones who most enjoyed this
rest, or perhaps that philosophic burro whose large and
mobile ears continued to surprise the Indians as much as
did the Spaniards' beards.

The Spaniards began to wonder about getting back. If

it was such a perilous adventure to come along a road so dreadful, then to go further was like defying God, who had put those perils there for a barrier so that the white European should leave the copper-coloured Indian in peace. Long as they had travelled, they were still close to the mouths of a river whose great size indicated the infinite distance which must lie between the sea and its source. After these swamps and this infernal heat there would surely come rugged mountains and cold winds that would freeze their limbs. The sick, especially, felt that their strength would fail them and that it was better to draw a last breath in the huts of Tamalameque than to push one foot ahead of the other through more marshes. In their delirium they no longer wanted the long-dreamed land of gold, but the hands of a friar who would part the air above their breasts, prepare them to die like good Catholics, and forgive them the waywardness and violence of a sinful life because of the labours they had just passed through.

Thus twenty days went by, and then a message arrived from Captain San Martín. He had reached the banks of the Great River and learned that the boats were coming late and slow. He had installed himself at the mouth of the Zazare, or Cæsar, a sizable river, and he did not want to leave for fear that the Indians might take up positions there and impede the march. Quesada accepted the message, and ordered the troops to go forward.

Those who had a little life left were again filled with enthusiasm. Adventure had become a habit, a continual thirst which allowed them no repose. Moreover, the bountiful table they had found in Tamalameque was now picked clean. Inciting them to go ahead, audacity and hunger spoke the same tongue. As though it were the first time! The soldiers arranged their gear, the Indian carriers formed in line, the horses were assigned to the sick, soldiers and captains worked with equal fervour, and the general himself tightened girths like any man in the front rank. Then the march began. Cut across lakes, throw out bridges, move machetes as if they were wide arms of an endlessly whirling windmill. And so to the banks of the Zazare. There the soldiers came together again, clasped one another's hot and dirty hands, smiled with lips that were fever-cracked.

They crossed the Zazare in canoes and entered the province of Sompallón. There they found new forests which barred their way and new channels which demanded bridges for their crossing. They counted the troops, and noted that one man out of every five had died. The army was like a clean, full set of teeth when it left Santa Marta, but now it looked broken and dirty, like the mouth of an old man. Again they halted in the fertile land of the Sompallón Indians.

Weeks passed, and still the brigantines did not come. So far, all they had had for their trouble was suffering. Other troops up from Venezuela, such as Ehinger's, and some from Santa Marta had already ranged through these same territories, so they were not even discovering new land. For many of them, however, it was the first encounter with a great American river whose stream was both wide and deep. Away on the other bank stretched a landscape blue and shimmering as alcoholic fumes. The trees looked like dwarfs. Men thrust their arms into the water and felt the steady push of the current grow stronger as the stream deepened. Even the brawny arms of machete-wielders shook in the current's grip. A Spaniard who had never been outside of Spain before had encountered streams like these only in the pages of sacred history. The Nile must have been like this, thought the priests, and the bachelors of law and letters grew homesick.

It was impossible for Captain San Martín to remain idle. Quesada decided to send him downstream until he met the brigantines. In Sampallón men went on dying. Without the brigantines the sick would never be able to set forth on new marches. Practically everything they would need for going forth to new discovery was lacking. The idea of returning never crossed Quesada's mind. He thought of Pizarro, of Cortés, of the heart of this America of his. America was already his own, and he would be a true son of America and lift up his head on top of the highest summit.

With a few soldiers and Indians behind him, Captain San Martín hurried downstream. The burro with his long felt ears, standing serene on his four feet, switching mosquitoes away with his tail, cast slow glances out of great philosophic eyes at those who went and those who stayed behind.

\*     \*     \*

Let us go back to Santa Marta. When Quesada and his men went out amid a tumult of applause and loud cries of "God and the Virgin give you luck!" from those who stayed behind, and when the last of the foot-soldiers had disappeared, nothing was left for the eye to look upon but a miserable setting of weeds and underbrush. Those who were to go by sea and up the mouths of the Great River went back to their work on the ships. Let us see what happened to them.

Here was the governor to urge them on, for the sooner they went, the sooner he would be left in peace and expectation. And here were Diego de Urbina, who was going as head of the flotilla; Diego Cardona and Diego Sandoval, who would be brothers in adventure's end as well as in name; Luis de Manjarrés, Ortún Velasco and Díaz Cardoso, Juan Chamorro and the friar Juan Zambrano. All of them flung big talk into the wind and gave loud orders to the Indians and the ships' boys. Everyone worked to speed the hour when the dirty sails of these amphibian adventurers should be unfurled above the green waters of the bay.

Moreover, there was need for leaving Santa Marta. In spite of the fact that the population was reduced, the land yielded hardly a mouthful of food. The governor himself said he would go later, behind the flotilla, to follow Quesada. It was a consolation God gave men so lost in illusion. Faced with all kinds of disaster—fevers and death and thorn trees—the mind of this type of adventurer takes refuge in thinking about a prodigious new kingdom, a kingdom where the Great River gushes out of the earth in the midst of emerald forests and sands spattered with gold.

At last came Holy Week. On Ash Wednesday they held one of those High Masses which precede long voyages. Then for some hours there was a great shouting of orders, and men stopping in the street to give one another a farewell embrace. The captains whispered of tricks to be played with the booty—phrases which fell fat and shining in the sunshine as a gold coin in the hand of a poor beggar. At last, in the afternoon, the sails were unfurled. Quesada and his men had left twenty days before. Now it was Urbina's men who were leaving in brigantines and boats with lateen rig —the fleet had seven ships, and perhaps two hundred or two hundred and fifty men to handle them—to find the country from which the great Magdalena River flows.

They passed the night in a sheltered cove. Very early in the morning of Maundy Thursday they weighed anchor, hoisted the sails, and moved out into the Caribbean Sea. Carib means a wild thing. The Caribs were cannibal Indians. "The people went Carib," wrote the ancient chroniclers when they were talking about a native uprising. The Caribbean is a wild sea, which grows suddenly rough, crisps the edges of its waves, throws up cloud banks heavy with storm like huge balls of smoke. Other times it drowses in the sun, playing with its waves and tossing up spray like flecks of cotton. It is a strange and treacherous sea.

On Good Friday it was not bad—all blue and gold, regular in its rhythm, and smiling; if it made the rigging sigh, it also made the Spaniards sing. But not so Saturday. On Saturday the daylight burned with a gusty flame and a smoky chimney. The waves began to bite at the hulls of the ships, those badly planked hulls which creaked and danced about in a horrible fashion. The greater part of the crews felt that death was pressing on their stomachs. Some rolled in the wet bottoms of the lateen-rigged lighters which danced the worst, and staggered up to seize the ropes and lend clumsy hands in the manœuvres ordered by the captains. They were men of the sea, but not of a sea so savage.

In order to avoid collision the ships drew apart, and soon were lost from one another's sight. They were now at the river mouths, but the strength of the bore threw back all that tried to enter. The rain lashed at the shadowy boats, a ghost flotilla now. The crested waves where sea and river met were more than masthead high on the lateens or the smaller brigantines. Arms, supplies, goods which the men who went by land had entrusted to Urbina's care to make their own journey easier, all went into the sea. The crews thought only of saving the hulls of the ships themselves, those hulls in which they now kept afloat like shipwrecked sailors. But the more they lightened ship, the higher and harder did the white seahorses toss them from crest to crest.

Diego de Urbina's boat crossed the bar and neared the coast on the Cartagena side. It was at once a triumph for him and a hazard for those that followed. The brigantine behind tried to do the same and struck—the force of the waves broke it into matchwood. All that could be seen in the soot-black rain was a tangle of splintered planking. The men afloat were carried to the tops of waves and flung against the scattering planks until not a single one remained alive. No one knows where corpses came up to furnish sport for sharks. Urbina's boat was carried along eight leagues beyond the river mouths. A big wave picked it up, held it clear, shook it in the air, and dashed it against a rock on the bank. The captain and the crew, caught amid rocks and sand, soaked to the skin, worn down by seasickness and fatigue, without weapons of any kind, well-nigh naked, sat and stared at one another.

The same fate befell another of the brigantines. The mainmast shivered, wavered, looked as though it was about to be torn out by the roots. Fifty men flung themselves against it, crowded in a nutshell which was visible only in the blue intervals between lightning flashes. The ship got across the bar, but more by the will of God than the skill of men. Then a single gust of wind carried it some leagues up-stream, straight as the crow flies, and wrecked it against the bank. When the men finally opened their eyes they were on dry land, but their ship was broken to bits. They were so bruised and sick that not one of them could move. The storm was over, and the sun began to dry what few clothes they had left on their bodies. The Indians descried them, motionless as something painted on the sands. With a shout, clouds of copper-coloured warriors burst from the river bank, from between the rocks, from the very sedges, and filled the air with their poisoned arrows. By afternoon those Spaniards who had tried to defy the Great River were hanging, sun-scorched and quartered like the loot of any barnyard in the hands of cannibal Indians.

Two other brigantines were borne by the wind to the other side of the Great River's mouths. By a miracle these arrived safe at Cartagena. Without their cargoes, for everything had been thrown overboard into the Caribbean, but at least the men, however terrified, were alive. They shook hands with Urbina's men, who had been brought by land in charge of friendly Indians, and stared in one another's faces like men raised from the dead, thinking with horror of the fate that had overtaken the others.

Two ships, notwithstanding, had saved themselves and were proceeding upstream. Slow sailers, they had not been able to reach that spot where the mother of all hurricanes had unleashed her forces. The first night they anchored in a sheltered spot on the coast, and the following day they entered the narrowest mouth of the river. They reached the lands of Malambo and awaited the rest of the fleet, but as days passed and no ship came, one courageous soul resolved to go to Santa Marta and tell the governor what had happened. Before he got there, and while three who had reached Cartagena safely were taking a caravel to go on to Santa Marta, the governor dispatched another ship loaded with food supplies which was also to go up the Great River

and aid Quesada's troops. This too the Caribbean devoured,
leaving fifteen survivors on the beach to bear witness to
the tragedy.

*          *          *

Don Pedro Fernández de Lugo, former governor of the
Canaries, was awaiting news of the expeditions in Santa
Marta. It was the last great dream of his governorship. He
was fondling it, savouring it, when the unhappy messengers
began to arrive. First came the three from Cartagena who
told of the wreck of the captain's ship; then the solitary
messenger from Malambo who told how the only two ships
that had passed the mouths in safety were anchored awaiting reinforcements before daring to continue the trip; at
last one of Quesada's men who told him the state of the
lawyer's troops, scourged by death and basing their hopes
entirely on what help was to come to them by river.

The men from Cartagena told how terror would not allow their companions to return. The three Diegos who had
spurred on the crew only a few days earlier by hoisting the
banners of Jiménez de Quesada took ship in Cartagena, together with Friar Juan Zambrano, and chose to go to Peru
to adventure with the Pizarros. All agreed that the storm
was a piece of hard luck and Diego de Urbina a stubborn
fool who had paid with his own failure for having dared to
pass the mouths when there were plenty to explain to him
that the risk he ran was like tempting God.

Stupidity, daring, failure. Yet the only way out still lay
in reaching the heart of those mountains that fed the Great
River. They could not abandon Quesada, nor leave the men
in Malambo awaiting reinforcements so as to ascend the
river, nor stay on in Santa Marta suffering from hunger.

On the beach were three old stranded brigantines. The governor ordered them scraped, caulked, put in order. This time the new fleet was not to be entrusted to a simple soldier; whoever commanded it would also be a licentiate of laws, for it was clear that educated Quesadas were better than mere reckless soldiers, even though the latter carried in their veins the wild inheritance of the Fernández de Lugos. So the lawyer Gallegos becomes captain of this new enterprise.

Another brigantine came back from Cartagena, and with it some of the men who had been with Urbina. With this, there would be three ships to attempt the passage of the river mouths. The men under Gallegos's command totalled two hundred. When the fleet departed, only a handful of men were left in Santa Marta. All those who were worth anything had gone off to the conquest of a new empire.

Fernández de Lugo looked not at the glassy edge of the bay but at the arquebus he held at the town's back. Not only those ships, he said, but others, and new men, and he himself would follow the quiet, well-poised head of Lawyer Jiménez de Quesada. He sent Luis de Manjarrés to Santo Domingo to buy a caravel, if possible, and three lateen-rigged boats to serve the new enterprise. The governor had some gold left—he put it into Manjarrés's hands, and borrowed right and left for this last effort at salvation.

When Manjarrés arrived in Santo Domingo, intent on nothing but conquest, the lawyers and brokers of the island, who had a great many other things to think about, laid hands on him. They reminded him he had old debts still unsettled, and a certain obligation which had to do with marriage. Absorbed in the affairs of Santa Marta, we had quite forgotten that Manjarrés was a rascal. We had forgotten how rare was the captain or the soldier who could go near a port in which justice had stationed her ministers. And so Don Luis de Manjarrés, with the small amount of gold that Governor Fernández de Lugo had left, stayed for a while buried in the prison of Santo Domingo.

Let us leave the miserable fellow in jail and go on to something else. Now I, the author of this book, am speaking in my own person.

As I have a high sense of the novel, it seems to me that I ought to take this occasion to have done with the governor of Santa Marta. This aged governor of the Canaries, son of the man who had conquered the islands with his skill, his money, and his courage, son of the man who had slain Moors and black men in the name of Christ, master of such a fortune that he was able to equip the richest expedition that had ever reached Santa Marta, found in this Terra Firma just what we have seen—Indian arrows, the treachery of his son, the hunger of the city, dysentery, Quesada's adventure, the wrecking of the fleet in the hands of Urbina, and Manjarrés in jail. I think it would be best if the governor should die. And in fact he did die. While Gallegos was going up the river, he dropped his head between the archbishop's hands, his soul whiter than his whiskers. At the same moment his son the thief was playing up and down the peninsula, snaring with gold and lies the women he met in the street.

# IV. From Court-Room to Captain of Mutineers

O dear God! That men of flesh and blood should have had only their own hands for breaking two hundred leagues across a most dense and difficult mountain, a mountain so craggy and louring that all of them together could have broken only a league or two a day had they been equipped with good iron tools.

How many sicknesses racked bodies which had been delicately reared in a most kindly region? How many pestilential fevers and other diseases put others in such a state that they could not stand upright, and with all this working with their hands, of which most died miserably?

—Lucas Fernández de Piedrahita

# FROM COURT-ROOM TO CAPTAIN
# OF MUTINEERS

THE Great River has seen on its brilliant surface only the light and slender dug-out which the Indian propels with a paddle. This canoe is as much a part of the landscape as the heron or the crocodile. The water carries it, caresses it, even exalts it, for this hollowed tree trunk has a mind of its own and refuses to be sucked in by whirlpools as it creeps along the bank making forest richness and river wealth equally available to the naked man who is fisher or hunter as need demands. In it the Indian skims safely above nests of alligators, and the alligator watches him go by, a prize he can never catch.

But the thing that is ascending the current now is a monstrosity. A wooden skeleton, plated with wood, helped out at times by sails. A floating fortress, full of men hairy as animals. The canoes hide under the low branches along the river bank so the sentries guarding these strange mechanisms shall not see them. There are four that go upstream. The Indian knows that these are enemies that come this way. If the first Spaniards to reach the coast took years to get into the heart of America, the Indians, on the other hand, sped swiftly through the intricate network of their waterways telling of men with beards, of the horses, the dogs, and even the God of the Christians.

There were tribes that grew alarmed and tried to oppose the invasion. Then the river blackened with canoes —a thousand, two thousand of them—each Indian had his own, and canoe and Indian formed a single entity—appearing out of nowhere and forcing a way through to the brigantines' ribs. The soldiers huddled behind the rigging, hid in the hold of the ship while the arrows flew overhead. After each encounter the brigantines, stuck full of arrows, looked like pincushions.

The brigantines went upstream with difficulty, almost always hauled by cables from the bank or propelled by paddles like the sampans of a later period. The soldiers were in no hurry. They were more eager to explore the shores, to find whatever luck might place in their hands, than to reach Jiménez de Quesada, of whom no one had any news. Where there was anything of a path, they followed it to see what might lie in the interior, but they always kept watch for tilled fields. Much time passed thus, until one day someone caught sight of a canoe in which shone arms like those the Spaniards carried; then they made out soldiers' figures; soon they saw Captain San Martín, who greeted them.

Gallegos the lawyer and Captain San Martín embraced. The soldiers mingled and exchanged news. The tales of shipwrecks and of discoveries in the province of Sompallón were endless. They were very near Quesada now, and they were urged to hurry in order to assist the sick. It was time to speed up the march and drop this lazy upstream pace. Gallegos put fresh heart into his men. The desire to shake the hands of those few who had emerged alive from this long adventure quickened muscles, speeded paddles, hastened manœuvres. A few days more and they all were in Sompallón.

*　　*　　*

Once united, the two expeditions rested in Sompallón for eight days. The sick were put on board the brigantines, which became floating hospitals. A cordial wave of optimism animated everybody, even in the very midst of fevers and fatigues. Quesada and his captains exchanged ideas. They must go forward. This, which the most daring endured as a bit of bad luck, Quesada carried fixed as an obsession between his eyebrows. As they went upstream the valley must narrow and there would be no more of those swamps which now made the trails impassable. The rains had come back to swell the river's arteries. Sompallón was ceasing to be the granary it had seemed when they first arrived. If they tarried longer, hunger would afflict the camp. It was decided to go on. The brigantines were to continue upstream at a much faster pace. The land forces would leave the flooded river banks and open a road through the brush. Jerónimo de Inzá was to go as head of the trail-breakers.

The friars, Antón de Lescámez, a native of Mula, and Domingo de las Casas, who had just lost his mare, took part in the discussions and cheered the men as best they could. The day of departure, when preparations were complete and horses saddled, Antón de Lescámez said Mass, which was heard with great devotion. "God and the Holy Virgin go with us, guard us, and light the way for us," repeated these miserable beings who were standing before the door to the unknown. Lescámez put a mystic unction into every movement of the Mass. Las Casas turned over a thousand ideas in his head: his Christian mission, the whole adventure, the mare which had just perished and which would be worth no less than sixty pesos. . . .

* * *

We are in the forest. It takes only a few steps, past the first tree trunks, and the Sompallón landscapes are left behind, buried in memory. Here is no light, but a diffused clarity which softens under the branches to a penumbra which is warm, humid, charged with vegetable odours. At first the soldiers found it dark, but as their eyes grew accustomed to it, the blue trunks, green trunks, red trunks, the tangle of branches, the lianas covered with mould, moss, and lichens, all took shape. One recognized the day because light awoke slow, milky, like dawn in a dream. At midday this same clarity was tinged with rose, and at twilight it faded away amid fingers of blue which foretold a night made of dark cobalt or deepest jet. Of the sun nothing was ever seen. The leafy roof was too thick for a ray to sift down diagonally or for a beam to fall straight as a golden plummet from the zenith. Depending on the hour, there was only a white clarity, or rose, or blue, which enveloped blue-green and rust-red trees, which slumbered amid the leaves, which filtered through the crowding vegetation. At night came insects with eyes that shone like candles. The soldiers kept close watch lest they be surprised by the phosphorescent pupils of a tiger.*

At times, indeed almost always, the soldiers were silent. The musical echoings of the forest frightened them. "Now we understand why the Celts used to turn sorcerers in the woods." There is a metallic hum of insects. The parakeets whir up in noisy clouds. Let him tread on a vine, and the astonished man, thinking it a snake, jumps aside as if on a spring. And the leaf that falls and the lizard that flees both

---

* This would have been a puma or a jaguar, both of which abound in the Magdalena valley and occasionally attack men.—TRANSLATOR.

leave behind them the impression of the snake. Bands of monkeys swing from the branches like festoons. An enormous blue silken butterfly, a butterfly all of mother of pearl, hangs in the air like something out of the Orient, like a reflection of the sea at midday, like a blue tile filched from the Arabs of Andalusia.

Jerónimo de Inzá's woodsmen went ahead. With mattocks, axes, machetes, they cut aside lianas and opened trails. Behind them the soldiers helped the horses, which kept slipping and falling. The strongest gave a hand to the weakest. Hunger was stalking in their midst again. They had left Sompallón almost without a grain of corn. And the forest is not exactly a granary. Hard and bitter roots grow there, juices almost impossible to extract. The thick, warm, humid air makes one dizzy, forms a palpable barrier which must be broken through. Before long the soldiers, beset by hunger, were eating everything. Lizards, snakes, frogs, leather straps cut from the harness, all went into the stew pot. When a horse died there was a banquet.

Some of the men turned stragglers. Hid behind the trees so that no one should pay any attention to them, no one oblige them to take another step, but leave them to pass quietly to the other world, which was the only new world for which they had any enthusiasm. Quesada had to redouble his vigilance in order to prevent these flights to eternity. Others were suspected of killing horses in order to get a bit of meat. The horse was the great staff of conquest, and Quesada published an edict that anyone who killed a horse would suffer the death penalty. The horrible thing about these orders is that they were carried out. Finally, in order to lessen temptation, the men were forbidden to eat horseflesh.

Of the soldiers who had left Santa Marta strong and well, one now saw himself at the gates of the other world. He went to his son and bade him farewell. "You must follow the conquest to its end, but I stay here to wait for death." The boy did not hesitate. Gathering strength out of his own weakness, he hoisted his father onto his shoulders and went on another day, and then another. Fever and convulsions shook the dying man and passed through the shoulders of his son with a continued trembling. Finally the father breathed his last. Friar Las Casas sped him on his way. Las Casas and Lescámez had divided the spiritual labours between them, and the care of the dying fell to the former. Over the old man's corpse his son sprinkled a few handfuls of earth. For those who thus remained behind, this bit of earth was the long-dreamed Terra Firma. The troops went on.

There is no reason for undue scruples. They also ate human flesh. The dead companion was transformed into bits of meat which went into the cauldron. Groups of unfortunate soldiers whispered together about these lugubrious affairs. Already they were seeing murder in the calculating glance of a companion. The night was full of terrors: fear of snakes, fear of man, fear of tigers.

Juan Serrano was sleeping in a hammock one night when a tiger approached. The first time the soldiers managed to scare him off. But the crafty animal retired on velvet paws, waited near by, and when the camp was quiet, came back and carried the Spaniard off in its mouth as easily as a cat carries off a rat. So says the chronicler.

At times they emerged from the forest. Then the soldiers had to cross swamps and marshes full of bulrushes. Game lurked among the rushes which the men on horseback soon captured easily. The swamps were infested with alligators. When they reached a river and stopped for a few days to build a bridge or seek a ford, those who were already in the grip of death were likely to hurl themselves into the water. The preying alligators followed the troops that dealt so generously with them. So great grew the danger from these beasts that when the soldiers went to get water they had to take a gourd tied to the end of a long pole. Juan Lorenzo, a good swimmer, crossed a river so as to fell a silk-cotton tree on the opposite bank and make a bridge for the army. When he started to swim back he was caught in an alligator's jaws. Feeling himself lost he cried out for help, but in an instant his body disappeared, leaving only a thread of blood floating on the surface. The puma, too, followed the army, for the army left food behind which, if not very tasty, at least was abundant.

Quesada worked unceasingly. The greater part of the way he went on foot so that his horses might be available for the sick. The rhythmic strokes of the machetes awoke in the forest a new consciousness of human life. There were still those who knew how to laugh and get fun out of the adventure. It was tragedy enough to go marching through forests and marshes without adding the useless burden of complaint. Lorenzo Martín improvised quatrains. "Forward, lads; some day we'll be out of all this punishment," said Jerónimo de Inzá, putting spirit into the trail-breakers. Quesada seemed to repeat Pizarro's words: "Thus we go to the glory and abundance of tomorrow."

Lorenzo exclaimed:

> *Your steps are sidling paces,*
> *Remiss, reluctant, slow,*

*But they'll more gallant go*
*When you have filled your faces.* . . . .

And there were those who, hungry as they were, could
still listen to Lorenzo and laugh. . . .

❖  ❖  ❖

The rains went on filling water pockets in the swamps.
Clouds of mosquitoes attacked the soldiers. There were
other insects that bored in between skin and flesh, and fat-
tened and flourished there, leaving the soldiers looking
as though worms had been doing repoussé work on their
bodies.

"The heavenly constellation," Friar Pedro Aguado was
to say later on, "was by no means favourable to our men;
for, apart from the corrupt airs and vapours which affected
the land and caused many diseases and ill health, heavy
showers fell which, owing to the peculiar influence of this
tropical sky and the exhalations from the earth itself, en-
gendered in their waters a strange kind of worm that propa-
gated in the human flesh without leaving any outward sore
or fester. Even he who was soundest of body would grow
benumbed and become host to this worm without sensing
it. Buried in the flesh, the worm would leave a very small
hole in the skin, like a pin-prick, through which to breathe,
and would grow within, nourished by the fleshy substance,
and become as large as those bred in oxen (which are
called tumours). These worms are destroyed by the appli-
cation of plasters either of diachylon or of turpentine."

The channels became torrents where the waters leaped
in fantastic forms that looked to the hungry, weary men like
sheep and horses. The winter deepened. Lawyer Gallegos,
looking out from the brigantine, saw huts. Thirty huts

which opened onto a plaza. At last there was hope of reaching country that was inhabited. The valley narrowed.
Streams tributary to the great Magdalena dropped down
the rock-faced sierras. This was La Tora of the Barrancas
Bermejas: this the site of Cuatro Brazos. Gallegos sent soldiers to inform Quesada of the find. Quesada received the
news with joy. He and his brother, with Antonio Lebrija,
Antón de Olalla, Aguirre, Velasco, and Venegas, left in
three canoes, guided by two Indians and a black man, just
as dark was falling. All night long they went up the black
waters of the river. The crisp air was vibrant with the music
of cicadas. The seven conquerors were seven sentries that
never closed their eyes but constantly searched the banks
without seeing anything. When dawn broke they caught
sight of one canoe. The Indians fled, terrified. There in a
bend of the river was La Tora. When the Spaniards landed,
there was not an Indian left in town.

      ❈    ❈    ❈

Soon all the Spaniards were in La Tora. The town was
surrounded by tilled fields. A series of paths pointed to the
possibility of scaling the cordillera's flanks. Moreover, the
rivers that joined the Magdalena here were so big that
brigantines could safely enter them. To follow the course
of the Great River would mean to prolong the adventure
endlessly. It was time to seek a change in direction.

While the greater part of the army was resting and waiting for the rains to cease, Quesada ordered small bodies of
men to go exploring. The brigantines started up the first
river in sight. As the wind gave no assistance, the boat had
to be propelled with paddles, or pulled with cables, while
the sails hung limp and flapping from the masts. The brigan-

tines went on for thirteen days and found nothing. Then
the explorers returned wth empty hands, and disappoint-
ment weighed heavy on all hearts. But Quesada was in-
sistent. He sent other men to hunt new routes in other directions, and many soldiers to explore paths and side
streams.

There were fields of corn in La Tora, but Quesada issued
an order that whoever touched an ear of it would be punished with death. After their past starvation the grain had
to be doled out bit by bit in order to accustom stomachs
to receiving food again. Any soldier at the point of death
was thrown into the water. Whispers of rebellion began
to circulate. Six months of marching and they had found
nothing. Better Santa Marta with its Carib Indians, where
at least the ships kept coming from Santo Domingo, Cuba,
Cartagena. This place, with its swollen rivers and a soil that
offered little sustenance for human beings, was a charnel
house. Finally someone raised his voice to the general and
said, as Piedrahita tells it:

"Who, Señor Licenciado, could see the army, so fine
when it left the coast, so impaired now before it has pene-
trated more than a hundred and fifty leagues, without asking himself what the danger is that threatens its final ex-
tinction? These stout hearts bred in Spanish provinces are
not intimidated by hostile Indians, but by hunger and epi-
demics, against which courage avails little. Never did so
brave a leader suffer direr hardships than he who guides us,
and it is therefore the more lamentable that he should perish where he would leave no trace and where no record of
his invincible valour would remain. Thus far the suffering
of so many miseries could be endured, and for as long as
hope lasted, but on leaving here, and with hope gone, forti-

tude becomes mere desperation. To see only barren mountains devoid of civilized beings, offering no sustenance, overrun by ferocious beasts, threatening inevitable hazards, is no diversion to be pursued unto death; and the more so when there are no tidings, however false, to spur men on to an imagined rest. Fame is not to be won by a stubborn obstinacy that spurs its possessor forward when enterprises that would justify it are lacking, but at moments and in places where the sword may open the way to a glorious end. And so if we go back to our governor, he will read in the record of our many dead the hardships through which those of us who return alive have passed, and even the most ambitious will recognize that the determination of an unconquered heart could go no further."

This is the kind of speech that is always addressed to men of the conquest as a prelude to their *noches tristes*. Certainly many hardships lay ahead, but for the ambitious to go back was as sad as to meet death in the forest. If they went forward, they might reach the same end as those who had already fed the crocodiles. But—would Santa Marta give them any better burial?

Quesada's mind was busy turning over a series of ambitious ideas. He knew that if he found rich territory, if he discovered and conquered a kingdom, he would rise to command, could turn his back on the governor, would himself become a governor, or perhaps even a viceroy, and would have more wealth than that miserable Fernández de Lugo. But, crafty man that he was, Quesada did not make direct reply to those who urged him to return. He let the rest do the talking. In this crowd of the despairing he searched, not for those who might give tongue to terror, but for those who might serve as the mouthpiece for ambition. He manœuvred so that the most adventurous should seem to impart fresh courage to him. Gently at first, and then with resolute decision, he urged the troop forward again into the green hell of this adventure. Urged it, yes, but his resolution was tinged with melancholy.

Here they are surrounding him, pressing in on him, listening to him, their eyes brilliant with fever; the soldiers with curly beards and dishevelled locks looking in their ragged clothes like a crowd of unlucky beggars; men who have lost all hope and men of great faith who first had staked that faith on El Dorado and who now, defeated and melancholy, place that faith in God and the Holy Virgin.

The friar Las Casas, in whose veins runs the same blood as that of Bishop Bartolomé, defender of the Indies, is the same man whose mare died in Sompallón. He has more daring and ambition than many in the threadbare troop. He exalts the soldiers' honour, the apostolic mission of the conquest, the duty of following the general, the prospect of the riches which they all are going to find when the adventure ends.

Antón de Lescámez and the donkey look at Quesada from an angle apart. The soldiers, doubtful, wipe away the sweat with ragged sleeves. The horses slap mosquitoes with their tails. Captain Fernández de Valenzuela, who thinks he has surprised a shade of sadness on the general's face, makes him a speech which Fray Antón, the son of Mula, will later put into a ballad:

> *Fernández de Valenzuela*
> *In this way spoke to Jiménez:*
> *Do not grieve thyself, Gonzalo,*
> *Make show of thy gallantry.*

*One time we must needs all perish*
*But not several times a day.*
*Rendón goes as thy companion,*
*Flower of all chivalry,*
*And the steadfast Lázaro Fonte*
*Makes thee valiant company.*
*Do not grieve thyself, Gonzalo,*
*For with thee García travels*
*And has with him many soldiers*
*Both of horse and infantry.*
*So, as well becomes a Christian,*
*Yield not to a coward's fears;*
*Thou art thorough Granadino,*
*Cunning, and with gallantry.*
*Show a face that's never frowning*
*And a spirit full of joy,*
*Launch thee bravely in the trial*
*'Gainst a hostile wilderness*
*As it were against the squadrons*
*Of the heretics and Moors.*

This hour held for Quesada something of the same problem that furrowed Cortés's brow. He had reached the same point Columbus reached in the last days of September 1492, when, on the verge of sighting the American horizon, he found himself besieged by a crew in which doubt had almost become despair; when "all day and all night those who were awake never ceased complaining; those who could joined others to whisper and plan how they might turn back again." Quesada was at the same point Pizarro reached on Cock Island (Isla de Gallo) when he drew the line and said, "That way to Panama, to eat bitter bread, to live vanquished and insulted. This way to the hunger and misery of today, but also to the abundance, the riches and fame of tomorrow." But Quesada, at this point, had his own quarter of an hour of melancholy:

*And the circumspect young lawyer*
*In this fashion made him answer:*
*Fernández, it is not I that*
*Ever'd wish to shun the fight.*
*Than retreat I first would rather*
*Give the last drop of my blood.*
*Thou art, Valenzuela, loyal,*
*Good, and to a high degree;*
*So with thee for my companion*
*I would greatly heartened be,*
*And o'er all this kingdom triumph*
*And these high peaks soon surmount—*
*Hold four worlds in dominion*
*And have spirit left for more.*
*And to king, and Spain, and me, then*
*I would bring a great renown*
*By the prowess of my weapons,*
*Finest in all chivalry,*
*And then later in my fashion*
*My heroic deed recount,*
*For I am a man of letters,*
*Quill pen like a sword I wield.*
*But my homeland, the Alhambra,*
*Always makes me very troubled,*
*Seeing how my people, stripped there,*
*Making no resistance, died. . . .*

*       *       *

Salt and woven cotton! These were what Albarracín and Antonio Díaz Cardoso, who had followed a trail to "ranch," brought back. This salt was fine white salt in cakes, which bears no resemblance to that which men take from the sea. This salt could come only from a country that was white at heart. And it was salt which the troops coveted. They had gone on for days without this indispensable condiment. In the neighbourhood of Sompallón, the Indians made it "from human urine and palm dust." This salt, the salt which Albarracín and Cardoso struck, was strong and came in cakes that were "like lumps of sugar." And with this salt in his hands, symbolizing the country which at heart was white, Quesada answered all those speeches.

Captain San Martín soon went out with twenty or twenty-five men in canoes to identify the route they must travel to reach the land of salt. As the canoes advanced he felt hope reborn. At the first stream they met he left the canoes hidden in the bushes and took the land route. First he found two or three huts, then six, and as he advanced toward the spurs of the sierra he went on finding habitations where there were always lumps of salt and cloths of red cotton. Also there was corn. He caught sight of the well-worn trail which must lead them to the Chibcha empire. When they reached the actual foot of the range, he recognized that it was time to turn back. With only twenty-five men the captain could not venture into a nation of Indians who surely must be numerous.

When San Martín entered La Tora draped in a cotton manta, with salt in his hands and his arms held high, he was already a victòr. Quesada was the first to rejoice and to communicate his enthusiasm to the others. Though La Tora was a hospital, hope always gave the sick new heart. Before they left, Quesada wanted to see with his own eyes the road San Martín had found, and among those who were most healthy and most determined he enlisted sixty men. If the road looked to be safe, they would set out from La Tora to conquer the New Kingdom. This time they would go with horses and well provided with arms.

But the water rose against them. As the exploring party advanced with Quesada in the lead, the river swelled, dragged all sorts of things down with it, covered its waters with spray, seeped beneath the forest which edged its banks. The freshet lasted ten days. Against the handicap set by this new enemy, the men advanced through water to their waists. At night they climbed into the forks of trees in order to sleep. The horses plodded through water up to their girths. Food began to give out. The general set a maximum ration of forty grains of toasted corn. For two days the company had to wait on a flooded island until the crest of the current dropped. Then they went on through the mud. What tremendous effort it took to build a fire to dry their clothes! But they went forward.

"There was no mangy dog they did not devour, no bit of refuse they declined to eat." Here is what Aguado says:

"The greatest prize they took in these fourteen leagues of land and water marches was a stray dog which had followed them from La Tora. The feast this provided for the leaders seemed to them as splendid as those which certain Roman emperors used to give, and upon which they squandered a large part of the revenues of their realm. And it may well be believed—as some of those who were present affirmed—that the dog's feet, paws, head, entrails, and hide were as completely devoured as though it had been the tenderest mutton, and even more so, for it is seldom that the skin of a sheep is made use of, unless for the confection of some insignificant article, whereas that of the dog was used as food."

And the march went on. The waters had dropped. The army started up the trails. They advanced with difficulty, for there was no path for the horses. Soon they arrived at San Martín's huts. They appeased their hunger with cakes of corn which the soldiers themselves ground. Another time they threw yucca roots into the cauldrons and had salt with which to flavour them. These soldiers grew fat and thin like accordions, had flesh on their bones one day and only skin the next. In the same way the direct glance from their eyes sometimes hid behind clouds of scepticism and at other times, as by a miracle, burned with the flame of hope.

As it became harder and harder to advance with the horses, Quesada resolved to halt at huts that had good fields about them. Lázaro Fonte, Antón de Olalla, and Céspedes went ahead with a few soldiers. These were the leaders who must do the exploring. They were given ten days in which to return. They accepted, but planned secretly to make it twenty. No one could do anything in less time. If they were not back by the twentieth day, let them be considered dead. Those who stayed behind hardly left the camp even to pillage, so busy were they washing clothes, grinding corn, making cakes "very full of straw." In those Spanish camps they made everything, even turning them at times into sandal factories. Out of rags, out of rawhide, of whatever God put into their hands, they made foot covering for those who had covered most of these marches on bare feet.

From now on prospects improved for the expedition.

Those who went ahead as scouts found a good village which the Indians had abandoned on first sight of the Spaniards. There were ten or twelve houses, and good fields: potatoes, yams, yucca roots, kidney beans. News of this soon reached Quesada. Everything pointed to their being on a sure path. But to drive the horses up these steep ranges was a difficult undertaking, possible only with the whole army. Quesada resolved to stay behind with eight soldiers to take care of the horses, and to send all the rest ahead on discovery.

Soon the exploring party ran across Indians who spoke a different tongue. Then they spied small villages. Paths and tilled fields began to multiply; they sensed the nearness of a great nation. They stumbled on a group of aborigines, and an Indian woman took a liking to the Spaniards and came over to their side. Apparently she was in bad standing with her husband, the chief. The first interpreter of these conquests, the Indian Pericón, marched with the soldiers. Some of the greediest went "ranching" and found gold and emeralds. Cotton cloth, salt, gold, and emeralds —these were the keys to the new empire. With these in hand the soldiers went back to Quesada. He was ill, but firm in his hopes. With these things in hand, no more vacillation. He left the entire company in camp, and with Céspedes, San Martín, Valenzuela, Cardoso, and three soldiers returned to La Tora. Now the adventure was really beginning.

*    *    *

When Quesada and his companions arrived, La Tora took it as a miracle. The freshet had not swallowed them, nor had they met the fifty canoes full of Indian bowmen who had beset the Spaniards in camp only the night before. La Tora was no more than the shadow of what it had been in previous days. Death had gone on thinning out the army, and there was a pervasive hospital odour that made it hard to draw a breath. With rain and sun had come clouds of insects which descended on the troops and poisoned them. The four keys to empire which Quesada brought attracted only half-hearted attention. To men in that condition their value was at best dubious, and represented poor compensation for the amount of further suffering their pursuit would entail. For the second time his men tried to dissuade the general from continuing with his project. They told him that to venture into the ranges of the Opón with a miserable company like this was to be foolhardy. To go on would be to despise one's own life and the lives of the soldiers. It would be tempting God. But Quesada, who in the common life of the encampment laughed and talked with all the charm of the true Andalusian, now looked illumined by fever, his throat dry, and his eyes afire with forest wizardry, as though he had stepped out from the pages of a book of chivalry; and he reasoned just as Don Quixote was to do later on. Faced with the avalanche of good arguments with which they surrounded him, pressed him, and tried vainly to dissuade him, he was fixed in his idea, simple and invincible.

"None of these things," the chronicler would say, "sufficed to change the general's mind. Fortified by a brave spirit, he desired to achieve a memorable deed which would do service to God and his king; and so he replied to those who counselled him otherwise that, although their intention might be good, the course which they wished him to follow was against his honour, as it could justly be said of him that he had, by his inconstancy, turned his back upon the gates of a most promising land; and that, although he should die on the way, he considered death in that enterprise more glorious than life with such infamy as would be his if he turned back; and he begged them that, if they wanted to preserve his life and his friendship, they should refrain from such advice; that nothing could so quickly consume and destroy both these as to persuade him to return."

Do not these pages foreshadow the whole drama of Cervantes? Note that the gentleman who speaks thus is a lean man, with beard uncombed and clothes ragged, his garments full of holes, muddy to the neck, his breeches tattered, worn and ridden by hunger, fever, and ambition. It is all laughable, and none of it is laughable. Certainly the miserable creatures who were under the lawyer's spell could not laugh. His mind was set on a fabulous castle: Castilla de Oro—Golden Castle—Castilla Aurea, as the maps say. He sees a new kingdom within his grasp. To make his madness the more complete, he thinks, as Fray Antón de Lescámez says, of a lady:

> To the loveliest of the cities
> I would give the name "Granada"
> In remembrance of the sadness
> That I suffered on the journey.
> When on her, my gracious lady,
> My thoughts ever went revolving
> How she had, my faithful mistress
> Weeping, said farewell to me
> When I had to leave Granada
> For some miscreant deed of mine. . . .

But no—what might be and has been fiction in Europe is true for us, the very stuff of life. After these talks will come the adventurous achievement. Let those who wish to go forth to conquer march beneath the banners of Lawyer Jiménez de Quesada.

He lay prostrate on his bed and from his bed prepared the expedition. He talked with another lawyer, with Gallegos, and told him, "Let Your Grace wait here with the brigantines, and if six months pass and we do not return, better go back to Santa Marta and blot us from your memory, for we shall all be dead."

Then he ordered the sick to go to the boats and the well to form in marching order to leave at once. The well? There was none. All of them went forth staff in hand, a haversack over one shoulder, like a beggar's bag holding a few grains of corn. They were as tattered as the poor pilgrims who journeyed to Santiago de Compostela. These conquerors—conquerors!—were bitten by mosquitoes, discoloured by fever. And their hair! Long locks without order or combing, stuck together by sweat; that hair of beard and moustache which gives each face the impress of virility. It was the same Spanish hair, the same fuzz, the same beards as might be seen crowding around the convent doors of Toledo begging a plate of soup. The same locks, the same beards behind which Castilians look out at the public from any canvas, whether in palace or sacristy. Thus the Æsop of Velázquez will look, thus Ribera's beggars and his apostles. . . .

Quesada was first of all a good Christian. Before leaving he ordered a Mass to be said. There was no church here, no belfry, no altar, no altarpiece. Only the one white solitary Host which was lifted high in the hands of a priest hardly able to uphold it. In the silence which bowed the heads of these talkative Andalusians, these loud-mouthed soldiers, came the warm breath of the tropics. A mosquito hummed. From the near-by trees sounded the chatter of monkeys. The air stirred the beards of these world wanderers, and a mystic emotion oppressed the heart. Besides, there was the sermon of Fray Domingo de las Casas. . . .

Finally those who were to stay with the brigantines embraced those who were to start out in search of El Dorado. The general, drunk on the drugs he had taken to banish his fever, gave any kind of order to the troops. Ambition could hardly serve as inspiration for this march. There was something magnificent, something both mad and audacious which beat amid the rags. With the beggar's haversack went the friar and the burro naturally enough. It was the whole romance of Spain. A novel in human form which set out from hospital doors to cross the channels that run to the Magdalena, to bury themselves in the mire of the trails, to thrust thin, greedy, hard, dirty claws into the flanks of the cordillera, into the ranges of the Opón.

Five hundred, eight hundred, a thousand had left Santa Marta to crown this enterprise with victory. Some in brigantines, some through the mud and thickets of Terra Firma. Of all these there are hardly two hundred left. Nor will two hundred reach the top of the Andes. Two hundred lame men, whose clinging hands catch like live tendrils at the ragged fringe of Quesada's garments. Two hundred lame men beneath a fabulous standard which carries blanch, vert, and gules—salt, emeralds, and gold. . . .

At this point the general's mind, moving in the contradictory fashion essential to such romances, was already busy with the idea of turning himself into a captain of mutineers. Lawyer Gallegos, who was to stay there with the brigantines waiting until those who were leaving should return or not, would be left planted there for the rest of his life. In vain would he one day bring suit in an attempt to have his right to a share of the booty recognized. He will get nothing. All he had suffered and endured going upstream at the same pace as those on shore will, when he litigates against Quesada, dissolve like sugar on touching water. For Quesada first of all studied law, and studied it so well that at times he imposed his own law, and would always have done so had not a certain scepticism and melancholy, a certain marginal irony which, as I have said, borders the edges of history, sent his spirit along unusual and capricious paths.

❖    ❖    ❖

The march began again. The river route was abandoned for ever. Soon the whole troop would be reunited. They knew the path that led to the land of salt, and this time they must take the horses up it. As they mounted the flank of the cordillera the air grew temperate, so that when they reached the country of the Chibchas their muscles revived. With mattock and machete, with axes that slashed noisily at the mountain's heart, they widened way for the horses. But there were moments when the rock was so sharp that the horses could not climb. Out of vines they had to make slings to hoist them up. Finally after a great deal of hard work they reached the valley of La Grita. A broad panorama rolled away before the eyes of the company. Small grey mounds that were huts showed thin columns of smoke that announced the presence of man in every direction. Many roads snaked their way amid brush and between fields.

The emotion stirred by this new kingdom showed clear on all faces. The survivors numbered some hundred and seventy. They were all that were left of the fine army that had bidden farewell to Fernández de Lugo and his despairing overlordship in Santa Marta.

The Spaniards stayed in La Grita eight days to rest and mend their gear. The Indians watched them from a distance, held back by the beards and the presence of the horses. The horses are said to have created such a panic among the Indians one night that they fled, possessed by terror. It was like a stratagem Cortés used in Veracruz when he loosed one of the horses that it might go, amid the terror of the Indians, to seek the company of a mare. This time, however, the horses worked on their own. In open camp their strength returned, and one night they began frolicking with the mares. Overexcited, the mares broke into flight. The horses followed. In a tumultuous band they invaded the Indian camp. Then came chaos. The Indians thought the Spaniards had sent the animals to destroy them. They left their huts in a rush. When dawn awoke the soldiers, they found the Indian camp deserted and the horses straying among the huts.

Quesada got the troops in shape. All threw their canes away and with their fingers began to comb their hair and set their beards in order. It was as though they had come back to life and were preparing to appear at court. A breath of cool air had given them back their youth.

The general made no war against these Indians. He sought parleys. He instructed the interpreters to say that they came in peace. In the beginning the Indians did not understand, but when they saw that the Spaniards did not want to eat human flesh, when they sent an old man and the Spaniards failed to set tooth in him, when they threw children down some of the hills and the Spaniards refrained from roasting them, and when instead of showing such Carib tendencies, the Spaniards sent them glass beads and trinkets, they dared to come closer. How strange that along these same routes where fighting Indians had come at other times these who came now should not be cannibals. No, these were hairy types; some who had the disposition of men were provided with sharp sticks that shone like the rays of the sun, and others were animals that walked on four feet. So the Indians came nearer, cautious at first, then more confident until they ended by offering the Spaniards banquets—game, corn, potatoes.

Quesada felt himself transported from the world of arms to that of politics in which a supreme court is conceived and formed. The moment had arrived for defining the essential point of their adventure—how much of the work accomplished should fill the pockets of Fernández de Lugo and how much those of Quesada and his soldiers? Should this continue to be a perquisite of the governor of Santa Marta, or was it to be a new kingdom created by their own force and valour? The question must be defined now with complete clarity. Gold and emeralds would soon fall into their hands—soon there would be booty to divide. There they are, for the solving of the problem—Quesada, who is skilled in the law, and the friars, who know plenty about morals. But, above all, there are the soldiers themselves, whose efforts must also be consulted as to the natural reward for these marches.

It is exactly the same situation Cortés was in when, from

the beaches of Mexico, he said to Diego Velásquez, "Farewell, my dear Governor. From now on we shall require nothing more of Your Grace."

We have reached the exact moment in which Jiménez de Quesada, who had left Spain as chief magistrate, is to be acclaimed captain of mutineers. He takes stock of men and horses, reviews the troops, and . . .

This is how Bishop Piedrahita, in whose hands luck placed Quesada's papers, is to tell this stupendous part of the story:

"And so, having made the list and conditioned the horses, it is the accepted opinion throughout the realm that Gonzalo Jiménez de Quesada, considering the great conquests that he had in hand, and that these must be undertaken amid such manifest perils as war carries with it, wherein failures would be judged against him personally by his impassioned rivals, and wherein successes would redound to the glory of the governor, Don Pedro Fernández de Lugo, for whom as lieutenant he governed the camp; and trusting hopefully in the affection and good standing he enjoyed among his soldiers, he (having assembled them for this purpose) artfully renounced the office which he held by appointment from the governor, saying that he did not feel himself capable of commanding them in an enterprise that must result so gloriously for them all. He asked that, by election of the camp, a captain general be chosen whom all must obey, since they had reached the turning point which admitted of their doing so without failing in their duty as faithful vassals of His Majesty. He would be the first to abide by the choice they made, and would obey the chosen one as his chief and follow him on the march unto death itself. And as there are words which, efficaciously employed, can persuade to the very opposite of that which they propose, his were heard by his followers at just the time when there was no one to fill the place of so well-loved a chief whom they were accustomed to obey. They discussed it among themselves, and in consequence Quesada was newly elected and was acclaimed by the whole camp as captain general without dependence upon the governor of Santa Marta—an acclamation which he accepted with pleasure, thanking them for the goodwill thus shown to him. . . ."

# V. Mud, Chiggers, and the Indian Woman

The chiggers are a universal plague. There is no defence against them, they enter through stockings and shoes, penetrate into the living flesh with pain and a burning itch; then they form a web, and within it, in twenty-four hours, they have tiny eggs laid for the creation of a whole swarm of chiggers. They are like tiny fleas, which dust engenders.

It is indispensable and urgent that a servant, with pin or needle in hand, go carefully over the feet every day. It is customary to find four or six chiggers to take out daily, another will have fifteen, and another many more, according to each one's fleshly humours.

—FATHER GUMILLA

The Indian woman went off with another.

—OLD SONG

# MUD, CHIGGERS, AND THE
# INDIAN WOMAN

I<small>N</small> Tinjacá, in Gachancipá, in Cogua, in Ráquira, man
talks with the earth. These are the pottery towns of
Cundinámarca. The Indian sits down, spreads a piece
of hide across his knees, pats a pancake of clay, handles it,
shapes it. A current of warm air plays across his face. From
time to time he wets his hands, for the clay dries in small
patches parched by the breeze, and then he goes on with
his potter's art. The sky is clear, and the tiny clouds, mere
puffs of harmless fleece, chase one another gaily across the
hills. The heavy clouds, the threatening, dirty rain clouds
have all passed by. They dumped their load of water on
the hut and soaked it through as though it were made of a
single thin branch. Now one can see open country again.
The rise and fall of the hills gives the horizon a feeling of
slow movement. The water runs through their folds, clear
and singing.

The Indian hollows the clay with his fingers; now gives
it the form of a cup, now deepens it to make it round and
smooth, now turns its rim. What his father, what his mother
did before him, he goes on doing, while his straying
thoughts lose themselves in vague ideas like those which
pass across the minds of sailors as they gaze through the
smoke from their pipes. Now the fresh, smooth, round jar
stands on the damp hide. This is a ewer. He thrusts his hand
into its mouth and goes over the inside with his fingers so
that it shall be clean and smooth as the rounded surface

109

which shines damp and glossy in the sun. One or two children, dirty as the earth on which they were cradled, take a handful of clay to make pellets. Or bring brush to stoke the fire.

The cordillera, which is defended by such steep escarpments as it descends into the depths of the Great River of the Magdalena, here breaks into gentle hills. The landscape flattens into little valleys with no depth to them, into musical undulations, into meadows where the water no longer runs but stands poised in lakes. The higher the land rises, the more the light tempers and softens. Here the daylight hours are not glowing with golden rays but simply infused with clarity. The trees are not corpulent trunks wound around with vines and creepers like those that dulled the machetes of Jerónimo de Inzá, but scrub which crinkles the flank of the hills with creeping bushes and tries to hide the skein of gleaming threads that are minute rivers. Along paths worn by the feet of Indian runners move the women pottery-makers, their baskets of jars on their shoulders.

Now the jar is big-bellied, hollow, handsome, ready for the sun to dry it or the flames of the oven to caress it. Like a wise and contemplative god, the Indian fastens two handles on its neck. And by a logical continuity of ideas, with a certain languor that smiles in his eyes and on his lips, he makes two small rolls of clay and fastens them from belly to neck of the jar with all the art of a master decorator. They are his symbols, and so placed on the surface of the jar that a frog moves, or a snake crawls, or the nose, eyes, and ears of a warrior are visible on them. The Indian, seeing his work finished, gives a sudden laugh, and the youngster with him laughs too.

Many paths go off from the hut. Toward the cornfield which is coming into bearing. Toward the far-off salt mines, toward the distant fairs of Muequetá, toward the harsh lands of the Muzos. The empire of the Chibchas is crossed by a narrow network of paths. Seen from the air, the Indian runners look like quick-moving ants, coming together in black clots at the salt pits and the fairs. This Indian pottery-maker who has finished his jar makes a fire by rubbing dry sticks together. Flat on the ground, he blows until a blue flame starts. At last red tongues lick round the belly of the vase. Soon the small column of smoke announces the success of his blowing. Inside the hut his woman grinds the corn or spins with a spindle turned by a whorl of baked clay.

❀   ❀   ❀

Tac, tac, tac . . . the Indian taps gently at the baked jar, and the jar answers with a voice at once sonorous and confidential. It has been well made, there is no crack in it. Perhaps this means that the Indian is going to have many happy moons, that he will not go to war again, for the Zipa is content and neither the Sopoes nor the Guatavitas, the Muequetaes nor the Chías will come to attack him.

In his malicious eye, poorly shielded by short, straight lashes, shines the memory of that day when the Indians from the city of Junza (now Tunja) defeated those of the Bogotá plains! The men of Bogotá were more accustomed to war. Fighting every day against the Panches who came from the hot country, they had learned to handle the arrow with skill, they were treacherous. In the fairs and the drunken feasts those who came from the Bogotá side and those who came from the Junza side usually insulted each

other—because the one came too near the other's wife, or
because the other gave the one some jars that were faulty,
or because one deceived the other in the matter of woven
goods or tubers. But the final result was clear—the Junza
men put those of Bogotá to flight. The Zipa himself had
to flee, carried by his servants in his litter. A few days later
he died, while his adversaries were celebrating their victory with intoxicating *chicha* in the midst of a terrific
racket. The Indian still remembers the embraces he gave
his wife that night, the bites and the squeezes, both of them
exhilarated by victory and *chicha,* while the happy squaw
laughed and twisted, showing teeth as white as the yucca
and gums like the red anatta.

But now we are at peace. In the whole vast territory
which goes from the sides of Vélez to those of Jacatativá
and Jusagasugá, there is not a hearth where the fire is out.
One must travel many leagues, many days' marches, many
moons, in order to go from one end to another of this immense nation. The country of the Aztecs or the Incas is
hardly larger. All the tablelands, all the fields which here
form an end to the Andes, are peopled and cultivated,
tended, provided with roads by these Indian pottery-
makers, farmers, weavers, miners, who pass their days
holding dialogues with clay, struggling to raise potatoes,
hunting rabbits, making their cornfields bloom with gay-
tasselled ears. And all this work that they may frolic at night
on their beds of woven strips or of matting, with no other
witness than the eye of the guttering candle which trembles
on the hearth.

We are at peace—so at least think those Indians who
gather water at the salt beds in Nemocón, set it to boil in
great clay pots, and never cease to feed the fire until the

snowy lump of white salt stands forth, white as the teeth
of the Indians. We are at peace—so think the fishermen
shut into the labyrinth of canals and lakes which the river
forms in the broad savannas of the Bogotá men, ingenuous
fishermen who laugh when they catch a fish slippery as a
serpent or when they feel the bite of a crab. There are
Indians who hack firewood from the hills with their stone
hatchets. Others on crude looms in rude workshops weave
the black-dyed, red-dyed threads into fine and gaudy blankets. There are some who beat skilfully on a sheet of gold
to bring forth a ferocious image which they have previously engraved on a bit of stone. Not a few of them go to
the fair at Muequetá with small bars of gold, cakes of salt,
loads of corn, small green stones from Somondoco, cotton
mantas, in order to barter and exchange. But all of them
feel that a cordial air of friendliness protects them, that
they are wrapped in an atmosphere of peace.

Two great lords, great chieftains rule this immense nation: on the Bogotá side, the Zipa; on the Junza side, the
Zaque. The Junza lives to the north; his lands extend to
the temperate extremities of Vélez, where a wind blows
warm and fragrant; they reach as far as Somondoco, where
the small green stones come from, crystals which look like
little avocados, emeralds born amid white nests of quartz.
On his side is the lord of Suamoz, the Sugamuxi, who reads
man's future in the passage of the stars and knows the fate
of the harvests. The Zipa of Bogotá lives to the south. Puffed
up by the victories he won over the Panches, he took arms
against the Indians of the east, at Ebaqué. Then he went
north and conquered Ebaté. And when he tried to penetrate the Junza dominions, the two armies met in Chocontá.
In the potter's imagination that seemed like an encounter

between a hundred thousand Indians, and thus the chroniclers will describe it later.

*     *     *

After all, this land with such gentle levels, such quiet
plains, such broad horizons, which serves as terminus to
the Andes, is like a miracle inviting to labour and to peace.
The Indian who has planted the poles of his hut in the
earth, who sits down in the afternoon to knead clay, who
spends his spare time hunting rabbits in the brush, feels no
desire for battle. He sees that the paths which lead away
from his hut toward all the pointings of the weathervane
are innumerable, and sometimes he follows them to go to
a fair or to barter with his neighbours. The son of the
house who ventures farther will perhaps go down to the
valley of the Magdalena some day, and perhaps he will
never come back. The Caribs who clamber up the hard
flanks from the river and fall upon the mountain plains
soon grow bent and lazy, cover themselves with blankets,
no longer eat fish, feed on potatoes and other tubers, and
after not very many moons become peaceful labourers.

The lands of Bogotá are so high that the cold strikes to
the bones. Sometimes in the early morning the water turns
to ice. A crown of hills surrounds the plain. Standing at
the summit of these hills, or on certain peaks and outcrop-
pings where the tableland seems to hang suspended over
the abyss, one can look down to the depths of the Magdalena. There are five thousand, six thousand feet between
the two levels. Many times the living spurs of cordillera
rock stand stripped and naked as if to show on what kind
of concrete the land of the Chibchas is founded.

The Zipa lives in an immense circular hut surrounded

by a palisade into which are woven painted woods of vivid colours; the walls are covered with the finest cloths. The litters in which he goes forth to visit his dominions are plated with gold. His subjects hunt game in the brush and roast it a golden brown in their ovens. In the afternoon the landscape of the savannas is a tapestry. There are forests of myrtle with its twisted trunks, its branches decorated with a moss that hangs in long grey beards; canal-crossed swamps where the rushes grow; smooth waterways for the rafts that the Indian fishermen propel with a paddle; the river, muddy and troubled in its flowing, traces a bed meandering and capricious; maize fields here and there, dry leaves stirring sonorous under the hand of the wind; ears of corn wrapped like children in their swaddling clothes and showing a red head already blackened and crisped by the sun; from time to time a hut, grey and gilded like a sheaf of wheat; on all sides lakes which turn vermilion under the afternoon sun.

The afternoon is one long hour of quietude, the first call to rest, which dissolves amid cloud flecks of gold. The wild game stop, cautious, raise their heads with round startled eyes as black as jet, and hold the twilight suspended like a golden banner on their branching horns. Into the west, swift and proud, falls the sun of the cold country: the clear sun of the wild.

The Zaque of Junza lives in an enclosure with sheets of gold at the entrance over which the breeze wanders as though it were playing amid the cymbals. The priests, after powdering their skins with gold dust, wash themselves in certain lakes. The Indians make frogs and lizards out of gold and offer them to the Mojanes to obtain their good-will. In Sugamuxi a temple dedicated to the sun is covered with gold. In some places there are goldsmiths who work for the Zaque and for the Indians in good standing. It is the gold, the cursed gold of America, which determines so many undertakings, both good and bad.

＊　　＊　　＊

The Indians move about like ants. Like ants they travel along winding paths to the hot country and exchange salt cakes for golden statuettes. The tale of the Indians who have salt, who weave cotton cloths, who worship the god of the lakes travels into far-distant lands.

But now there is something strange in the atmosphere which heralds catastrophe. The virgin flanks of the cordillera tremble. Whispers of terror run through the towns. On clear nights the Indian looks at the goddess Chía in the moon and questions her. From the rocks that serve as balconies by the lakes the Indians watch the goddess Sia in the water, she who guards the sacred frog under her crystal skirts. In the sacred mirrors they try to divine the truth about the future. A warrior shout comes up from the bottom of the valleys. The monster horse whinnies in their ears. On the wind runs the voice of bearded men who carry poles brilliant as the sun's rays. The pottery-maker strikes the rounded surface of the ewer which he has just taken from the fire, and the jar responds with a cracked and hollow voice. The Indian looks at it, terrified. . . .

From the north, from the south, from the east come rumours of the invaders, like the sound of rising waters tearing out a tree centuries old and playing with it as though it were a straw. From the north come the troops that set out so recklessly from Santa Marta. In the south sound the arquebuses of Belalcázar, who makes the thrust for the

conquistadors of Peru. On the east climb the troops of
Federmann, the soulless Germans who have become hardened in the crucible of treacherous crimes; they are diabolic forces which ascend like fire that bores upward to
crown the mountains with a flaming crest. It seems the
fulfilment of some absurd prophecy that three unknown
captains with their troops of vagabonds should arrive at
the same time as if keeping tryst with the devil. And all of
them carry the cross of Christ in front. But we are getting
ahead of our story.

❖　　❖　　❖

Quesada was the first to arrive, the most punctual. The
sight of these pleasant and cultivated regions put new heart
into his soldiers. When in the distance they saw huts that
dotted the landscape until they were lost against the horizon, the enthusiastic conquerors exclaimed, "This is the
valley of our dreams!" After such arduous marches, with
the rude flank of the rugged cordillera well behind them,
there was not one who did not seek rest here, a chance to
pitch his tent, to found a lasting home. Father Castellanos
was to capture this feeling with rare perfection in his verse:

> *Tierra buena! Tierra buena!*
> *Land that puts an end to sorrow!*
> *Land of gold and land of plenty,*
> *Land to make for ever homeland,*
> *Land with good food in abundance,*
> *Land of large towns, level land,*
> *Land where one sees people clothed,*
> *Where in season cooked foods taste good;*
> *Land of blessings, bright and clear,*
> *Land that puts an end to sorrow!*

The land is not exactly a land of gold, as the priest says. It is a land of labourers, of farmers, where a conquistador who comes in search of fabulous riches will find only an elusive, fleeting splendour that slips between his fingers. Yet the Spaniards entered as though they were going into Aladdin's cave, with their eyes wide open and their poverty plain to be seen in their most miserable appearance. This was their New Kingdom. Malaria, hunger, and fevers had left their mark. At the first feasts, with an abundance of game, potatoes, corn, rabbits, the colour came back to their faces; their bodies grew stronger. Out of the beautiful cloths woven by the Indians they made themselves new garments. The horses frisked gaily. Clean, new air filled the lungs. Past hungers were forgotten, and they looked only for riches. And when those riches failed to materialize, when the would-be "ranchers" found only emptiness, "in their sadness they clearly showed the motives with which they began so arduous a conquest," as the melancholy Bishop Piedrahita says.

From this time forward the Indians displayed their whole game, which was to make sly fun of the Spaniards. Quesada, with his air of a wise statesman, borne on the litter of authority, began to dictate his first laws, in which he condensed a fine Machiavellian principle into these words —"to ensure the chase with art and to subdue these nations with cunning." Clearly Quesada had not had Belalcázar's experience in founding cities, as that former donkey-boy was to throw in his face later on.

While those who had rebelled against Pizarro were marching to Cundinamarca by the beautiful valley of Popayán, by the broad vale of Cali, Quesada was scaling the cordillera with his body suspended in vine slings and the

horses going up in baskets. He might not know how to found
a city, but he did have an illusive concept of what justice
was. He was stubborn, fantastic, extravagant, magnani-
mous, full of illusions, as befits this type of caballero. Here
is the speech he addressed to his soldiers, boldly confront-
ing his conquest, in full view of that land which was to be
the subject of his governing:

"Brave Spaniards and my comrades, the time has arrived when the chain of hardships with which you have
been fettered in these imprisoning mountains has been
broken, and you see before you, in the broad spaces of this
surrounding country, the well-merited reward of your efforts; the multitude of natives, the neatness and order of
their persons, offer clear evidence of the benign influences
they enjoy; the land, less cautious than its inhabitants, gives
open sign of rich treasures in the shape of copious lodes
upon which our hopes feed. I have well tested your valour
in the quick obedience with which you have carried out
my orders, overcoming enormous difficulties; and on the
occasion which now confronts us, I would not want to im-
pose delay, for speed in action increases fear in our opponents, whom we must subjugate more through terror than
by force of arms; and this will be the greater in their minds
in proportion as they feel more haste on our part. When
Marcus Cato was asked how he had conquered a certain
city in Spain, he answered that it was by covering in two
days' time what would ordinarily take four days, for if fore-
sight has the force of thunder, execution should have the
speed of lightning. What good will we have reaped from
calamity if we do not attain the glory which fortune holds
out to us? What good to have saved our lives while so
many close friends perished, if we do not risk those lives

so that our names may be eternal or an honourable death vindicate us? Compared with that fortitude which heaven freed from such enslaving misery, our enemies, numerous as they are, are not powerful. If the purpose of exalting the name of Christ is served by the display of a bold valour, even more is it served by bearing it victorious through greater dangers. Good soldiers never seem few, nor do enemies seem many when they fight in disorder. The hazards that await us carry no greater risk than those which you have already overcome in so many encounters; and those who knew how to emerge so gaily from the first can hardly anticipate failure in the second. Those who have no confidence in themselves become the posts on which the victories of our opponents will be engraved; and those who are not afraid when the die is cast become the darlings of fortune whom she courts with the same favours she showered upon Julius Cæsar. All this is understood when the way must be opened by force of arms; but otherwise it is an error, which prudence condemns, to provoke a combat when the end can be achieved by gentler methods. Some of the greatest successes have been won through the mediation of peace and friendliness, both of these being advantages which even the most barbarous desire. And since it is so important to reconcile these Indians to our presence, it will be sound judgment to try winning them by flattery, and forbear breaking with them until occasion demands it. If they believe us men of honour, they will not shun contact with us, and if by our deeds we belie all reason, they will defend their rights with their lives, and will, first of all, and to our great loss, secrete all their possessions. So the most judicious course will always be to ensure the chase with art and to subdue these nations with cunning, since fortune renders him who fears her incapable of winning her by force; and if pacific means are likewise simple we shall gain superiority by keeping our pact and not breaking our word; but if they fail to respond to our friendly advances, I shall not hesitate to take stronger measures until they do respect them."

Quesada was energetic in enforcing the laws which stemmed from this discourse. Having reached open country, he allowed no flouting of his military ordinances, and he wanted everything to move as by the magic of a single spring. A shifty little Indian approached the soldiers' camp one day with a load of blankets, and on the way ran into Juan Gordo (Fat Jack), who was one of Quesada's good men. Gordo had stolen off from the camp in secret to strip the flesh from a horse that had died near by. Seeing him, the Indian dropped his load on the ground and took to his heels. Gordo understood this to be an offering and took the blankets for himself. Recovered from his fright, and seeing that the Spaniard had walked off with the pile, the Indian turned his steps toward the camp and laid his complaint before the general. Quesada investigated, found that Gordo was the guilty one, and executed him. As Castellanos says:

> *It did not save him to be nicknamed "Fatty,"*
> *For, following the usage of these peoples,*
> *His neck, where he was thinnest, broke the rôpe.*

In matters of law the lawyer's ideas were in accord with that feudal attitude which inspired the laws of Spain, and of which the *fueros* of the cities and the *partidas* of the wise King Alfonso X were a faithful expression. They were cruel laws, mystic and ingenuous. "The day of the Assump-

tion of Our Lady," says the chronicler, "there was no reason for marching. What was done meanwhile was that the
general and other chief personages confessed and received
the Sacrament in order that they might go with more devotion and attendant contrition to rob the chief of Tunja,
thus putting themselves right with God so that the robbery
should not be on their conscience."

What the army really needed was order, to obey one
person; and that admirable captain of mutineers, Quesada,
well understood that the natural thing was that the order
should be of his establishing and that the troops should
think through his head. "Troop," thinks the lawyer, "comes
from *troppus,* flock. I am the shepherd. Rob—yes. But
when I order it. And let no one murmur or contradict."
There goes Lázaro Fonte saying that when they reach the
coast he is going to denounce the general for hiding emeralds in order not to pay the king's fifth. Who ever heard
of such a thing! From that moment forward the general
thought only of hanging Lázaro Fonte. Let the soldiers see
him dangling in the air like any Juan Gordo. Quesada
invented a subterfuge to give his sentence some foundation. He contrived to have a soldier denounce Lázaro Fonte
as an emerald thief. The general had said, "No one is to
steal emeralds except on my order." There were "ranching" days in which everything was allowed, and days of
no "ranching" in which everything was forbidden. And
Lázaro Fonte made an error in this simplest of calendars.

To receive the accusation against Lázaro Fonte and to
condemn him were one and the same thing. No question
of proofs, no opportunity for the accused to defend himself. Anger was working within Quesada's mind. "So I was

stealing the king's fifth, and you were going to denounce me, you great rogue!"

But this time, my dear general, this is no Juan Gordo. This is no less than Lázaro Fonte, flower of the captains. This is Lázaro Fonte who went ahead with San Martín to the discoveries of the Opón. He is the best of the horsemen, the one who outran the swiftest of the Chibchas in races which left the Indians astounded at the efficacy and the wonder of the horses.

Lázaro Fonte demanded an appeal to the king, but Quesada refused to concede it. There was a movement of horror in the army. Captain Suárez advanced, and in the name of all of them asked that the sentence be commuted to exile. "The sentence which Your Grace has pronounced," he insinuated, "might be taken as the fruit of rancour." The blow struck home. Quesada retreated. He changed the sentence and Lázaro Fonte was disarmed, and ordered forth to exile in the lands of the chief of Pasca. For Quesada this was equivalent to a death sentence. To fall disarmed into the territory of wild Indians, already known for their treachery, was to head straight for death. A good escort went with Lázaro Fonte to the native town. They were twenty-five Spanish horsemen, a body that, to the Pascas, meant the town's destruction. The Indians, seeing them come, fled to the hills. Then the soldiers abandoned Lázaro Fonte in a hut, and left him tied.

But Lázaro Fonte was one of those captains who make themselves beloved. There was an Indian woman who had become attached to him and who followed him. She passed the whole night at his side while Lázaro was commending his soul to God. The copper-coloured maiden had no intention of letting the Pascas sacrifice her captain, her man, the handsome Spaniard with the curly beard which her fingers caressed, while the captain was running his hairy hand over her abundant tresses. As soon as dawn broke, the Indian woman went out to the entrance of the town. The Pascas were already coming back. She advanced to meet the chief and told him that Lázaro Fonte had been bound and tied for having opposed his companions' plan to burn the town. And thus was Captain Lázaro Fonte saved.

❖    ❖    ❖

The new land defended itself from its conquerors only through irony and dissimulation. The Spaniards advanced full of confidence, for they were going to conquer more by diplomacy than with arms. From now on this would be a war in which there was no fighting. The swords that were covered with blood in Hungary and Italy, the lances that in Santa Marta had carried thin vermilion points after battle, as though crowned with red carnations—those same swords and lances were blunted by the mists of the high plains, and turned the colour of lilies. Everything moved on a level of malice, cunning, sagacity. And thus it would be for centuries in this new world of guerrilla warfare, ambuscades, and delay.

When the army entered Sorocatá, they found abundant supplies. Here was the laden table of which they had dreamed in those far-away days in Spain when the eloquence of the governors had turned these vagabond heads. The potato fields were just ripe. And of the potatoes Castellanos says:

> *To the roots of this aforesaid herb,*
> *Which in height may grow perhaps three spans,*

*Underneath the earth these are attached.*
*They are more or less of an egg's size,*
*Some bulbous-shaped, but others growing long.*
*In colour they are yellow, white, or purple,*
*Mealy roots and pleasant to the taste.*

The army, then, decided to rest. After two or three days of idleness, they all felt as though their feet were laughing or at least smiling. Their toes itched with a delicious tickling. When they sat on their piles of straw, or on their beds, it was delightful to rub one foot against the other. But on the third and the fourth day the pleasure turned into something quite different. Their feet burned, itched, hung like red beets, and were unable to move. The army had caught a foot infection. It was the chigger, the white chigger of America, which had worked its way into the flesh.

*Minutest fleas that inward drilling*
*Bury themselves 'twixt skin and flesh*
*Where feeding on the fat they grow*
*And wax, should they be overlooked,*
*Until they are as large as peas;*
*And that fatness is all full*
*Of issue similar to the mother*
*That go spreading through the soles*
*And multiplying their generations.*

But soon it became evident that the Indians, or at least the Indian women, did not wish the Spaniards to disappear. These bearded men had a grace all their own. The passion which dominated them gave them a certain prestige. And the Indian women resolved to give them back the use of their lower limbs. The Spaniards, shoeless, rested against the walls, or sat on the beds, and stretched out a foot to the Indian women, who, squatting before them, amused themselves by picking out the chiggers with straw needles, with long thorns, working in the weeping flesh with a care and a gentleness that were a delight. . . .

\*     \*     \*

The conquest of New Granada has many entertaining things about it. Just as the land laughs in mockery, so did the Indians, and above all the Indian women. There is a certain coquetry in virgin land. It was the same amusement which moved the Indian potter to laughter as he drew the ferocious image of the god of war on the jar's neck. It was the laughter of the child when he thrust his hands deep into the clay of Ráquira and smeared himself to the eyebrows. It was the same gaiety that made the Portuguese soldier's squaw split her sides with laughing.

Father Castellanos was to make the tale of the Indian woman and the Portuguese soldier immortal in a certain passage of his *Elegías*. The Indian woman was well formed, well made, well disposed. The Portuguese who saw her said, "This one is mine." This Indian was one of those women who stand out wherever they are. She had personality, she had charm. The Portuguese had no wish to drag her off by force; he sincerely wanted to make her his according to the proper legal and religious formulæ. And he dressed her in a good slip, he had her baptized, he prepared feasts and a real wedding for her.

The Spaniards and the Indians watched all this with pleasure. Some laughed at seeing the Indian woman in so foreign a costume and the Portuguese in so deep an ecstasy. When night fell, a dark night, the Portuguese took the Indian woman to his hut. Up to this point she had said nothing, as if her will had no tongue. She was shy, frightened, silent. The Portuguese took her to his hammock and pressed her lovingly against his breast. She trembled like a little bird, and did not close her eyes. Suddenly, with much cunning, she indicated that she must rise a moment "to go to do some necessary business." The Portuguese released her gently from his arms, and watched the Indian woman, in the white slip he had given her, move across his room and go out through the door's black hole. The white silhouette stopped under the branches of a tree at the entrance to the hut. Some time passed. The Portuguese looked and looked again at the white form which moved gently in the same place against the shadows. The Portuguese called his sweetheart, demanded her, but she made no answer and she did not come back.

> *My own Tereya, come to me,*
> *To thy lover's arms who yearns for thee.*

But the Indian woman made no answer, came forward not one step. Nor could she come, for what the Portuguese saw was only the white slip which the Indian woman had left hanging on the branches of the tree, while her swift feet carried her far away from the hut. The Portuguese grew impatient.

> *Seeing no response, 'twas his desire*
> *To rise, and this he did with ardent fire,*
> *Saying, "Guard thou that I should not see?*

*Why, thy clothes betray thy place to me."*
*He put a hand to her, and found the skin*
*Now empty of the lovely flesh within.*
*So he returned with nothing but the shirt*
*And nearer tears than laughter at the hurt.*

# VI. The Indian Kings

Mine is not a bed of roses. . . .
                              —CUAUHTEMOTZIN

# THE INDIAN KINGS

ALL these histories are alike. The heads of all the kings in America were detached in the same manner, and a grey wave of defeat ran from Mexico to Chile in which Aztecs and Chibchas, Incas and Araucanians, all met the same fate. There was a moment when the Spaniards, moved by the simple dignity of the native monarchs, bowed before them, but greed gnawed at their vitals. Their appetites were whetted by the first small samples they took on the coast, and the pupils of their eyes dilated as if gold had been belladonna. The tale of El Dorado implied inexhaustible treasures. And as there is no limit to the desire for riches, the Spaniards were firmly convinced that the Indians hid some part of their wealth. It was not possible that there should be no more than one small mound of gold in the neighbourhood of the Zipa or the Zaque. How could it be that Atahuallpa was hardly able to fill one single room with jewels? Who doubted that Cuauhtemotzin had thrown millions into the lakes in Mexico? Then came the torture—systematic cruelty organized to tear the Indians' secrets from them. And perfidy, and treason, which should not be considered as moral vices, but as natural consequences of the thirst for gold which was stimulated by the very atmosphere of America.

Let us, for a moment, turn aside from Quesada and the Chibchas in order to look at what was happening under the conquerors. In so doing, we will evoke the figures of these native kings who all seemed moved by the same noble spirit until they were pulled down by an identical greedy hand.

*     *     *

One day Cortés and his soldiers went to Montezuma's palace with the secret intention of seizing him. Montezuma was the king, and Cortés an intruder. Cortés had asked an audience. His first words were veiled in politeness, but then, brusquely changing his tone, he said:

"I am very much surprised that you, so valorous a prince, and our avowed friend, should have ordered your captains on the coast near Tucupán to take arms against my Spaniards, and to dare rob the towns which are under the protection of our Lord and King, and to demand of them Indian men and women for sacrifice, and to kill a Spaniard who is my brother, and a horse."

The king had done none of these things. Surprised and terrified, he listened to the demand and "taking from his arm and wrist the sign and seal of Vichilobos" he ordered an immediate investigation. But Cortés had scattered his soldiers about the king's apartments, and the king was alone and unarmed. It was hard to attack a man who was loyal and honourable. Cortés set forth certain arguments, but his soldiers cut short his discreet words and broke out in a manner which left no room for discussion. "What is Your Grace doing with so many words? Either we take him prisoner, or leave him stuck full of sword thrusts. Therefore tell him that if he shouts or makes outcry we will kill him, for this time it is more important that we make sure of our lives than that we lose them."

So they took Montezuma prisoner, and held him in jail under heavy guard while he was swearing to remain Spain's vassal and trying to calm down the Mexicans. Montezuma's nephews went about stirring up the Indians in order to free him. There were Mexican uprisings. The king went to the jail roof to quiet the crowd, but everything he did in an attempt to pacify his people was useless. The Indians in the streets were growling with anger. With stones, sticks, and arrows they let fly at the Spaniards. Some of the stones reached Montezuma. He met the injury with tears in his eyes, and fell into melancholy silence. He saw life slipping away from him, and refused to try to hold onto it. He would not eat, he would not drink. The Spaniards, to whom their own defence was more important than that of a prisoner, abandoned him. "While we were otherwise engaged they came to say that he was dead."

With Montezuma dead, there still remained Cuauhtemotzin. He fought in the defence of his people like a lion. When the Spaniards finally defeated him the city of Mexico was covered with the bodies of Indians who had died rather than surrender. In the streets, in the plazas, in the very houses there were piles of human heads. Never was invader resisted with such intrepid courage. Díaz del Castillo says, "I have read of the destruction of Jerusalem, but I am not at all sure that the mortality was greater there than it was here." Says Torquemada, "Torrents of blood ran through the streets as water runs when the rain is hard." Cuauhtemotzin had asked the priests if he ought to continue fighting, and as their reply was in the affirmative, he said, "Then as you wish it that way, guard well the corn we have, and the supplies, and let us all die fighting; and from now on let no one demand peace lest I slay him for it." And the Indians promised to fight "night and day, and to die in the defence of the city." And thus they did.

Death put an end to the combat. Cuauhtemotzin, surprised by a small group of soldiers, fell into Cortés's hands. Seeing himself lost, he asked only freedom for the women, and peace for the vanquished. The Spaniards were already thinking of the gold to be had. What they had found in Montezuma's chamber was not enough. The Indians had had to hide the jewels, and their leader must know where.

To drag out a confession, they put him to the torture. The knotted cords worked on his flesh. The king had nothing to say. Whether much or little, he indicates that they will find something in the bottom of the lake. Wrath mounts in the soldiers. "Where is the gold?" they demand furiously. Their eyes seem about to start from their heads. Their lips are dry, their faces marked with blood and anger. "Let's burn his feet," some demand, "until this villain talks." They put oil to heat in a cauldron. They pour it over his feet until they become a mass of raw flesh. A slight odour of frying assails the nostrils of the hungry Spaniards. But nothing else comes. Not a word.

Another leader was put to the torture at Cuauhtemotzin's side. This was Tlacopán. When he felt himself burning, and when the boiling oil began to bite to the quick, he cried aloud, and twisted about. Cuauhtemotzin, who had been enduring this martyrdom with the utmost imperturbability, turned his head toward his companion and reproached him gently, "Am I in some pleasure nest, or bath?"

✿　　✿　　✿

The capture and death of Atahuallpa at the hands of Pizarro was identical. He was invited to an interview with Pizarro. Atahuallpa agreed, and came one day so slow and majestic that it took him four hours to cover a league. "He came in a golden litter, lined and decorated with many-coloured parrot feathers, which men carried on their shoulders, and seated on a rich golden cushion garnished with many stones and placed above a block, or throne, of gold. He wore a coloured *borla* or fringe of finest wool which covered his eyebrows and his temples, and which was the royal insigne of the kings of Cuzco. He brought three hundred or more liveried servants to bear the litter and to clear away sticks and stones from the path, and they danced and sang before him, and many great lords were borne on litters and hammocks in token of the majesty of his court."

While the king was advancing, Pizarro and his men stationed themselves behind the doors of the hut where the interview was to take place, in order to fire at Atahuallpa and assassinate him if it came to that. Among them was Sebastián de Belalcázar, who as a boy had herded donkeys in Spain and who now figured as one of Pizarro's grandees. So the king came on in slow majesty. A Dominican friar, Vicente de Valverde, who reminds one a bit of Tomás Ortiz of Santa Marta, advanced to receive him. The friar said to the king:

"Does Your Excellency believe in God, and in the Holy Trinity, and in the Holy Ghost, and in Jesus Christ His only Son, who was born of the Virgin Mary?"

In short, that same speech of Don Francisco de los Cobos which all the friars had learned, and which left Atahuallpa as perplexed and amused as it had the Indians at Santa Marta. Fray Vicente, who wasted no time getting to the point, thus ended the creed:

"Who was resurrected on the third day, ascended within

forty days into heaven, leaving as his vicar on earth St. Peter and his successors who are called popes; they have granted unto the most powerful King of Spain the conquest and conversion of these lands; and thus Francisco de Pizarro has now come to beg you to be the friends and tributaries of the King of Spain, Emperor of the Romans, Monarch of the world, and to obey the Pope and receive the faith of Christ, if you believe in it and that it is most holy, and that the faith you now hold is most false. And know that if you do the contrary, we will make war on you, and tear your idols from you, so that you may quit this false religion, and your many and false gods."

It seems to me that Atahuallpa was no fool, for he answered thus:

"Let Your Grace be assured that, as I am free, I have no reason to pay tribute to anyone, nor can I listen to any statement that there may be a greater lord than Atahuallpa. Nevertheless, I am willing to be a friend to your emperor, and to recognize that he must be a great prince, inasmuch as he has sent so many armies throughout the world, as Your Grace says. But I will not obey that Pope of whom you speak, for he is far away and I will not yield to one who has never seen my father's kingdom. As for religion, mine is a very good one, and I am content with it, and I do not wish even to argue about a thing so old and tried. That Christ of which Your Grace speaks died. The sun and the moon never die. How does Your Grace know that it was your God who created the world?"

Friar Vicente was in no mood for theological disputes with a savage such as Atahuallpa. Up to this moment he had been speaking with crucifix in hand. Now he took his breviary and advanced toward the king. "Let Your Majesty read these pages," he said, "and you will see whether what I am saying is the truth or not." The king took the book, looked at it, leafed through it with a certain curiosity, gave a loud laugh, and dropped it on the floor. The priest at once lifted his hands toward heaven and cried vengeance.

"The Scriptures on the floor! Vengeance, Christians! Have at them, at those who wish neither our friendship nor our laws!"

That was what they were waiting for. The soldiers threw themselves forward with daggers, swords, lances, and bludgeons, and began hacking at the litter-bearers. For every Indian that fell, another Indian of the retinue took his place. The king rocked amid a sea of heads, screaming tongues, swords which waved in the air, white at first, then red. Pizarro threw himself forward, put hand to Atahuallpa's mantle, and pulled him down. Confronted with this horrible sacrilege, the Indians were aghast, their hands fell to their sides, their eyes opened wide with horror. And panic took them, and they rushed away leaving clouds of dust behind them. The soldiers led Atahuallpa to Pizarro's room.

The Spaniards wanted gold. "I will give you gold until it chokes you, if in exchange you will give me liberty," said the king. The Spaniards stretched their ears, they listened. "More, more, more," was the word that rang in their heads. They were in a room twenty-two feet long by sixteen feet wide. "I will fill this room with vessels of gold and silver until they reach the height of my hand on the wall." The king raised his hand, and the Spaniards marked a line along the wall. They could hardly believe that the king's treasure was so great.

All the roads of Tahuantinsuyo filled with Indian carriers going to Caxamalca with the ransom gold. From the remotest confines of the empire all roads, paths, broad Inca trails become veins, roots flooded with gold to feed a tree of greed and to make sure that when the golden apples ripen, the king shall get back his liberty. Already they are pouring out their loads on the floor, covering the earth with jars, disks, breast-plates of gold. It is a musical cataract which gives the Spaniards a feeling of amazement and admiration. This is Peru, the "Piru" of the Peruvians. It is Spain's Golden Age. In the shadows the men of the conquest unsheathe their daggers so as to make themselves felt when the moment comes for dividing the loot.

Now the treasure is heaped before them. Now they must laugh at all compromise and hang the king. Pizarro is as delicate in this as any advocate, and he opens criminal proceedings. Felipillo is the accuser, an interpreter who is "in love with and a friend of" one of the wives of Atahuallpa. This Felipillo is the Indian traitor who always figures in every criminal proceeding of the entire conquest. Pizarro and Almagro agree on the king's death. A friar helps them —Valverde.

"When the sentence was communicated to him," says Benjamín Carrión, "Atahuallpa rebuked Pizarro for his falseness. He reminded him that he had fulfilled the ransom agreement; and he told him that while he and his people had had only a kind and friendly feeling for the Spaniards, they had been repaid with death. Seeing his reproaches useless, he again returned to his attitude of apparent serenity and, in accordance with his rites, recommended to the mercy of the conqueror the fate of his wives and his children. He then conversed with the priests and sages who surrounded him. They reminded him that the

soul of the Inca cannot return to the sun if his body has
been consumed by the flames of earthly fire, and they
counselled him to allow himself to be baptized so that
eternal punishment would be commuted. This was the
moment of Valverde's dark revenge. There in the plaza,
under the gallows and surrounding the piled faggots ready
to be lighted, was the group formed by the Inca and his
butchers. The sun had hidden its face. A few wavering
torches lighted the fateful scene. Valverde was muttering
psalms, and after the Inca had declared—through the dog
Latin of an acolyte—that he abjured his infamous idolatry
and embraced the Christian religion, the priest poured the
baptismal waters over the head of the great king and with
the aid of oil and salt imposed on him the grotesque name
of Juan Francisco. . . .

"The death sentence. The friars recite their office of the
dead. The soldiers kneel. In the corners of the plaza the
Indians, like men drugged and drunken, listen to the death
agonies of the Son of the Sun."

"*Chaupi punchapi tutayaca*": darkness fell in the middle
of the day!

◆          ◆          ◆

Among warrior peoples the Indian kings fell fighting;
thus Cuauhtemotzin in Mexico and Caupolicán in Chile.
Among agricultural peoples the kings fell into the snares of
the conquerors; Atahuallpa in Peru, Sacresaxigua in the
kingdom of the Chibchas. In the last analysis it was all the
same. The same legend of treasure thrown into the lake,
the same tale of the king plotting uprisings, the same friar
who stirs the bonfire and assists in proper dying, the same
captains who hide behind the doors, the same pressure of

the soldiers to get on with the torture and continue the victorious emprises of Spain. As there are always some among the troops who have read the letters of Cortés on the taking of Mexico, or have fought with the Pizarros, a tradition grows up. On the death of the Zaque of Tunja Castellanos writes:

> *Fernán Pérez de Quesada caused it*
> *. . . and this with no great prudence*
> *And the encouragement of bad advisers*
> *Who came there from Peru. . . .*

The death of Caupolicán must be placed as a proper climax to these first enterprises which began with the heroic martyrdom of Cuauhtemotzin. Caupolicán represented fighting valour. He fought in the land of the Araucanians. He was chosen captain because he had proved himself the strongest in the military trials. He got his troops in order, and for his first battle chose a new scene—the sea. When the Spaniards in two or three ships arrived at Peuco he hurled himself into the sea to hold them off. The men from Spain shot off their cannons. Caupolicán threw himself on the cannons, tore them from their bases, flung them into the sea. Then came a second battle, Lagunillas, this time on land. Here the Spanish forces created havoc, and Caupolicán paused to consider. Ordinary shields were of no avail against powder, so in the next attack at Cañete he presented his army protected with planks for shields. He had arrows thrust into the piles of hay which the Indians paying tribute to the Spaniards brought into town, and thus provided that the attack should come from within as well as from without.

But the Spanish weapons were always more effective.

Caupolicán fell prisoner. He was impaled, thrust through
with arrows until his body looked like a St. Sebastian. His
wife, who had come running like a madwoman across the
near-by hills, arrived in time to throw the body of his son
at the feet of the dying Caupolicán. The Spaniards pursued
the conquered Indians, offered them new battles. After
the battle of Quiapo six hundred native prisoners were
hanged. From then on the history of Chile developed in
an atmosphere of cruelty. They cut two toes off the feet
of the Indians who worked in the mines so that they could
not flee.

* * *

Against such a background of contemporary activity,
let us return to the tale of Quesada and the Chibchas.

Sacresaxigua, king of Cundelumarca or Cundinamarca,
in whose lands Quesada found himself, was to die under
conditions very like those of Cuauhtemotzin and Atahuallpa, but as these uplands are wrapped in a cold which
makes even the dead grin, the tragedies of his suffering
and death were to be mixed with humour. Sacresaxigua
knew right well that death was snapping at his heels, but
he still had spirit enough left to make fun of the Spaniards
as did that Indian girl who left her nightgown hanging
at the door of the Portuguese's hut.

The Spaniards entered the kingdom of the Chibchas
resolved to get their fill of gold. "The spies," as Father
Aguado says, "kept their eyes turned in all directions." The
army seemed to be set in the centre of a roulette wheel.
They did not know which way to move for the lucky number. The green uplands were like a gaming table. King
Bogotá, in order to rid himself of Quesada, pointed out

that the emerald mines lay to the north, and the soldiers Pedro Fernández commanded went prowling around Somondoco until they stumbled on the nest of precious stones.

Then an Indian woman told about a city, which was Tunja, where the hut doors were hung with "great pieces of gold which strike against one another, chiming and making a noise," so the general moved down Tunja way, imprisoned the chief, and laid hands on his treasures.

In Tunja they said there was another city, Sogamoso, where the temple of the sun was lined with sheets of gold and the floor covered with mats made of golden thread so that it shone brilliantly within. The Spaniard put spurs to his horse, the troops marched through the midst of warrior nations, but nothing kept these sons of greed from going where they meant to go. They reached Sogamoso and at nightfall entered the gigantic sanctuary of Remichinchagagua with blazing torches; sheets of gold gave back the light in a thousand reflections. Torch in hand, the soldiers drew near to touch that unbelievable treasure, and suddenly the tongues of flame licked the wooden columns, soared to the ceiling, sang amid the dry thatching, and turned the whole thing into a gigantic bonfire that burned for a solid year. More singed than enriched, the Spaniards returned to Tunja by the light of this fire, and it was then announced that the greatest riches were not toward the east, in Sogamoso, but to the south in the possession of Bogotá, king of Cundinamarca, to whom all towns were tributary. And Quesada left like a soul borne by the devil, followed by the thieving rabble, to clap irons on Bogotá. But Bogotá had taken advantage of Quesada's absence to hide himself.

*    *    *

It was not going to be easy to lay hands on Bogotá. Cunningly hidden, the Indian moved through certain hills which only his friends could reach. From his retreat he watched Quesada through the thousand hidden eyes of his spies. The savanna was a deceptive plain covered with marshes. The Indians, moving on rafts, slipping along paths known only to them and to the lizards, fired or shouted from behind the rushes, and no one could find them. They had no greater order nor accord, for their captains were far away. One day Lázaro Fonte and Maldonado caught sight of two Indians hidden behind the weeds. They confessed to being spies. To make him speak the older one was put to the torture. The Indian let fall nothing of value. The Spaniards increased the torture. The Indian was silent. They multiplied the pressure of the infernal machine. The Indian was silent. Finally the body was empty of blood, the flesh of the tortured man darkened, his limbs fell apart: the Indian was silent and dead.

The same torment was prepared for the younger Indian. He, having seen what awaited him, chose to tell where the king hid. With this informer as guide, Quesada and his men began the hunt. The king lived in a sort of monumental cave formed by two fissures of the cordillera: it was the Mouth of the Mountains. Neither he nor his soldiers offered open resistance, they scattered and played a delaying guerrilla game. By pure chance someone killed Bogotá. Once more the treasures slipped through the Spaniards' hands. They searched, hunted, smelled about, but found nothing. Neither army, nor palace, nor treasure.

❋ ❋ ❋

Now they would surely get their hands on Sacresaxigua.

Many days had passed since the grey soul of Bogotá vanished into the impenetrable world of shadows, and the conquerors ranged from Muequetá to Chía, from Chía to Tunja, from Tunja to Bosa, hunting rich gold, hunting emeralds. Over the vast stretches of the plateau they ranged like hounds on a scent. Only one question concerned them: what had happened to Bogotá's treasure? The rumour spread that he had thrown it into the lakes. It was that same Mexican fable, now applied to every chief who disappeared without leaving trace of his riches. But no; it was known that Bogotá had left a successor. This was Sacresaxigua, who lived in that same Mouth of the Mountains. Quesada and his followers recognized then that it was better to hunt him with cunning than to risk him in the hazardous game of a military undertaking. Once more it was proven that what availed there was politics, diplomacy. It went beyond that: Quesada remembered again that he was an advocate. That he had won his place in the world of law. That Sacresaxigua must be taken, but without omitting legal formula. And Quesada himself—"who peradventure sought his counsel"—had Hernán Pérez present him with a written demand for the capture of Sacresaxigua for having failed to swear fealty to the king of Spain and for having concealed the treasure of Bogotá.

The first part of the hunt was a game of hide and seek. The Indians, practising their art of concealment, first learned to conceal their bodies. Sacresaxigua, who well knew how Bogotá had fallen, never slept two nights in the same place, but wandered from nook to cranny amusing himself by watching, with a smile and a shiver, the general's efforts to find him. These tricky Indians were always like that. When the chiefs were required to visit the general they never said "No," but dressed their servants as chiefs and stayed in the back of their huts, convulsed with laughter at the thought of the gifts and the genuflections which the general would lavish on those who were, in reality, nothing but poor serving-men. Sacresaxigua amused himself with the general for many days, until the general managed to find out exactly where he was. Then Quesada, with soft, melodious, and skilful phrases, began to persuade him to pay a visit. Messages went hidden in glass beads, tongues told him that everything would be done to the tune of peace.

Until one day, like Montezuma, he was captured by twelve cross-bowmen, his fetters were double-locked by twelve cross-bowmen, and twelve cross-bowmen mounted guard. Then, as with Atahuallpa, there was the king's catechism, that catechism we first began to hear in Santa Marta, and which already had been modified most artfully in Peru.

"Know, my dear Señor Sacresaxigua," Quesada said to the chieftain, "that I shall surely treat you with all courtesy, like the great lord that you are, if, relieving me of having to take more strenuous measures, you turn over to me all the gold of Thysquesuzha, the king of Bogotá, for, since his property is that of a rebellious vassal, it belongs by right to the king of Spain. For you must know that the Pope, that sovereign monarch who through God's might has supreme authority over all the men and kingdoms of the earth, saw fit to give the king of Spain this new world that his heirs might succeed to it, in order that the barbaric peoples who inhabit it and live so blindly in their idolatries might be instructed and indoctrinated in our holy Catholic faith, recognizing only one God, Author of everything created," etc. . . .

Sacresaxigua listened to all these reasonings, and they seemed to him so diverting that he could only smile. He had not the slightest doubt that he would suffer the same fate as Atahuallpa, and he therefore resolved that the last chapters of his life should constitute a fine and ironic farce. With his fetters double-locked, he could no longer slip out and evade the conqueror by hiding in the pathless hills, but he had all the resources and cunning of the spirit left to him, and perhaps the hope that, by using them to make fun of Quesada, he might some day escape like the wind through a crack in the door. So the king laughed, and answered Quesada with a promptness which saved further speech-making:

"If what Your Grace desires is Thysquesuzha's gold, I will order it gathered for you this very moment. And within forty days Your Grace will have this room filled with gold to half its height. And then, is it not true that Your Grace will let me out of this imprisonment and return me a free man to the hills, that, at liberty, I may see my town and be happy?"

The Spaniards looked with greedy eyes at the circumference of the hut, and saw it as a solid cylinder of gold, to be divided among them like a wonderful cheese that would make them all richer than King Crœsus. They nudged one another, looked at one another, and rejoiced. The pact was made. Sacresaxigua gave orders to his Indians. They were to go to every nook, through the king's hiding place in the mountains, along the lake edges, hunting the gold of Thysquesuzha, and bring it in heavy sacks to empty it in a room next to the king's, so that Spaniards would not always be looking at it and the lantern of their greed be lit.

Each afternoon the Indians came with their loads. He

who carried the gold sweated and bent almost double under the weight of the metal. Thirty-six peons followed him, well wrapped in cotton blankets, provided with cudgels, and their faces covered to the nose, as if they were engaged in a ritual. The Spaniards watched the procession avidly. The Indians emptied the sack in the place reserved for the ransom treasure, and the Spaniards heard a cataract of golden vessels, jewels, and idols that tormented the imagination. "I'll give you not only gold," Sacresaxigua had said, "but three gourds full of emeralds."

The Indians came out in front of their king, reverent and silent. With two or three words Sacresaxigua dismissed them. The Spaniards, knowing how Atahuallpa had kept his promises, never doubted but that they would be made as rich as the Peruvians. And thus the forty days passed. Sacresaxigua never ceased looking for a way of escape every night. But the cross-bowmen, unsleeping, zealous, implacable, guarded him. On the fortieth day Quesada entered to look at the mound of gold. His bearded countenance wore an air of victory. If the pile were not big enough, he would press the king until he kept his promise. He would not reduce it even one inch. The king said two or three things he did not understand. When Quesada entered the room, the king smiled behind his back. The room—holy heavens!—was empty, swept clean: Nothing on the floor but the plain black naked earth. The general swore angrily. The soldiers bellowed with rage. The king's head trembled beneath the circle made by the captain's fists.

"Great villain, deceitful dog, filthy liar!" the general shouted at him. "Where is the gold the Indians brought? Is not your life forfeit for this promise?"

The king shrank back, his spirit wound within him like
a ball of yarn, and through a certain trembling that passed
along his skin like an electric current he began to thread
a cautious speech, full of fawning and subtlety, to which
the Spaniards listened without losing a word:

"What could I, fettered here, know of what the Indian
carriers did? What I have seen, your cross-bowmen have
seen: that the Indians entered bowed down beneath the
weight of gold, then left with the bags empty. But I know
what has happened. It is those ingrates Quixinimpaba
and Quixinimegua, my enemies, who have contrived this
trick to see me die. It is a scheme of those miserable men!"
Here the king showed an energy that emphasized his indignation. "Have those chiefs arrested, and Your Grace
will see the pile grow as if by magic art."

The Spaniards held onto this hope. No one could doubt
the sincerity of a king as gentle as Sacresaxigua. Everyone
saw the Indians' trick clearly now: the leader had emptied
the sack, and each one of the peons had picked up one
piece, hid it in his sack, and carried it out again under the
cotton cloak with as much skill as dignity.

The Spaniards rushed for the two accused leaders like
hunting dogs. Twenty-four hours after Sacresaxigua had
spoken, they were in Quesada's hands. Sacresaxigua, who
saw them on the road to the torture, smiled. He was going
to repay two Indians who had never been faithful to him.
Quesada reflected: one must be politic, one must proceed
according to law. With due measure he made the demand
in the name of the king, and then applied torture at the
same pace as the questions. As a matter of fact, the two
chieftains knew nothing of the treasure and had nothing
to answer. That was so clear that there was no point in

going on with the questioning. But the dilemma was final: either they should speak or they would be hanged. A shiver of fear ran through the souls of the other Indians when they saw the two chiefs swinging on the scaffolds.

Quesada came back, his voice muted by anger, and with measured firmness announced to Sacresaxigua that, if he would not confess where the gold was, he should hang on the scaffold like his two enemies. Once more the lawyer in the general acted to express things in order and clearly:

". . . The captains and soldiers accused Sagipa [Sacresaxigua] to their general, saying that he had absconded with the gold and emeralds of Bogotá which for the above-mentioned reasons belonged to the royal exchequer and to them; and, the necessary testimony having been given by the Indians of the country themselves, who said all they wished to and all they knew, the poor prisoner was condemned to questioning with torture, that he might declare where the gold and emeralds of Bogotá were, having been first of all provided with a healer, and the process having been most judiciously substantiated that there might be no errors of procedure, in an affair of such importance. . . ."

The king still sought a way out. He still kept a certain wheedling smile that he thought might save him. "If you will remove these shackles, allow me to go with a good detachment of troops to search for the treasure myself—for I suspect where it might be—I shall bring it to you." Such was the greed of the Spaniards that it was converted into trust. The gyves were struck from the king, and with a rope about his neck he began travelling toward the Mouth of the Mountains, to look for the treasure. The king thought: "If I could at least fling myself off a cliff and die of my own will, in order not to give this old man the pleasure of hanging me . . ." And by rough gullies and hard ridges and difficult hills he led the soldiers to a place where the rock fell off steeply. "*Xisysa, xisysa*"—"This way, this way"—he said hoarsely and wheedlingly. And when he was on the edge—to the abyss! He launched himself in one leap, but failed. The soldiers, who had come to suspect him, pulled back the rope in time, and this time the Indian returned, defeated, to be mounted on the rack.

Five months was the king of the Bogotá men in prison. He no longer misled the general with smiles. The contest had been very long, and the king was beaten. Melancholy enveloped him. He was carried to the rack, but said nothing. It was a hard silence, cutting and aggressive, the fruit of long bitterness. In vain was the lash plied, in vain did the blood run. They worked over him for two months. They did not want the king to die, because, with him dead, all hope was gone. The king stood it in silence, like Cuauhtemotzin. All the captains were present at these ceremonies, with the anxiety of relatives about a dying man's bed, waiting for the king to speak his last word. But the king was tired and said nothing. Two horseshoes were heated red hot, and with them the soles of the king were slowly burned. Suddenly, his eyes fixed like two eyes made of glass and the sweat on his brow froze. Four centuries were to pass, and herdsmen would still be hunting for the treasure of Sacresaxigua.

# VII. *Meeting of the German, the Andalusian, and the Donkey-Boy*

To ensure the chase with art and to subdue these nations with cunning.

—QUESADA

Arriving at the provinces of the said New Kingdom, Belalcázar found in it Licentiate Ximénez de Quesada with certain soldiers who were as men leaderless and lost and who did not understand what it was they had to do in the settlement of the said land, on account of which the said Adelantado Belalcázar, as an old and skilled conqueror, gave them order and policy in settling, and moreover furnished them with many horses and arms and other very necessary things.

—PROOF OF THE MERITS AND SERVICES
OF SEBASTIÁN DE BELALCÁZAR

I, Nicholas Federmann the younger, of Ulm, embarked in Sanlúcar de Barrameda, a port of the province of Andalusia, in Spain. I went appointed by Messer Ulrich Ehinger, in the name of Messers Bartholomew Welser and Company, as captain of a hundred and twenty-three Spanish soldiers and of twenty-four German miners whom I must lead across the great Ocean Sea to the country of Venezuela, whose government and dominion His Imperial Majesty has ceded to the said Welsers, my masters.

—FEDERMANN

# MEETING OF THE GERMAN,
# THE ANDALUSIAN, AND
# THE DONKEY-BOY

THE time had come to seek a little rest. Up to now they had taken all the gold which the ingenuity of the Indians had failed to hide. The general, the priests, the captains, and the soldiers had their pockets well stuffed. They would have liked more, but what they had taken and counted was plenty. From now on the metal was to elude their fingers as the shade of Sacresaxigua had escaped them. As a matter of fact this land was poor in minerals. There was not a single mine within its boundaries. What the men of Spain had found was what had been accumulated for centuries by the venders of salt and of cloths in their barterings with the Natagaimas or the Coyaimas in the hot valleys where the rivers wash down golden nuggets. But the Spaniards had not yet set foot in any Potosí.

In the five months they had been roaming through the kingdom, the conquistadors had had no thought of founding a city. It was time to do so. They looked about them, but the savannas were an uncertain terrain and subject to flooding. Only to the east was there solid ground leading to the foot of two hills: it was the place where King Bogotá used to rest in the rainy seasons. "What made them determine to establish a town on that site," Fray Simón was to say, "was the advantages to be found there—such as a city judiciously founded should have—for the ground is high enough for superfluous water to run off without leav-

ing the streets muddy; there are two streams of sweet and
potable water which flow gently down from the summit of
the sierra without flooding the streets and plazas, one of
them so abundant that even in dry years it turns the mill-
wheels of the city; there is plenty of stone for building,
sufficient firewood, good air . . . the sky is usually clear,
the outlook of the city to north and west is long and extended, with no barrier; but what was not a little noted in
choosing this site was the protection given on the east by
the hill and the whole range, for on that side the nation
could not be molested by its enemies. . . ." Alcedo was to
say in his dictionary, "The winds which regularly prevail
are the south wind, which is called Ubaque and is at the
summit of the mountain from which it comes; it is subtle
and cold, and so beneficial that the natives say it should
be received with open mouth; and the one from the north,
from which they protect themselves, for it is humid, tempestuous, and intemperate. . . ."

Quesada drew up his army in the midst of a great con-
course of Indians. A scribe took notes on what was happening. The Indians looked on without understanding any of
it. At the edge of the crowd the burro flapped his ears in-
differently. Father Las Casas prepared the altar cloth for
the Mass. Quesada advanced very solemnly to the centre
of the field and pulled up some blades of grass. This meant,
and he proclaimed it roundly, that he took possession of
the country in the name of his lord and master, King
Charles V. Who would dare to contradict him? A very
good horseman, he mounted his horse, drew his sword, and
asked the assembled multitude if there was anyone who
dared to dispute this conquest. These actions and these
words are like a chapter from the *Siete Partidas* of Al-

fonso X, made flesh and blood. No one contradicted. The
scribe made his record.

The priest Las Casas was ready now. All faces were
turned toward the altar. Quesada got down from his horse,
which a peon took by the bridle. The knight, so proud an
instant before, was now to bend the knee. The soldiers,
those adventurers who clutched at their pockets in order
to feel the material possession of gold, the same who had
heated white-hot irons to torture Sacresaxigua, closed their
eyes and bowed their heads. Before a Christ painted on a
cloth, the friar elevated a chalice made of lead. A droning
of Latin hummed through the limpid air of August, that
clear month of August which seems to pour a golden glow
over the savanna. . . .

Then the voices of the leaders were heard again. A new
undertaking, a new going to and fro. The general had said,
here would be the church, here the houses of the captains.
The Indians opened trenches in the black earth, set up
corner posts, brought bundles of wild cane on their backs,
drew water from the Vicachá—which is the river of very
sweet water—made clay, trod it out with broad and dili-
gent feet, prepared straw for the roof-tops. Very soon there
would be twelve houses which those from Spain, or some
of them, would occupy. The others would be more at their
ease in a camp a little way off. The chroniclers would say
that the twelve houses were founded in memory of the
twelve apostles. The city which was thus founded is called
the New City of Granada.

> . . . I would give the name "Granada"
> In remembrance of the sadness
> That I suffered on the journey. . . .

❧     ❧     ❧

But strange winds began to blow. The flanks of the cordillera were trembling again. Toward the summit of the Andes which backed these twelve huts of straw, clay, and wild cane were moving other adventurers. First came those from the north. The humid, tempestuous, and intemperate wind announced it. They were Federmann's foot-soldiers who had started out from Coro. They were broken soldiers under the command of the gentleman from Germany. Lázaro Fonte, who stayed a prisoner in Pasca, sent word of it to Quesada by a runner, writing it on a bit of deerskin. The history of these gentlemen of Germany merits a word by itself.

*     *     *

I have already told how the Fuggers gave the necessary money to elect Charles emperor of Germany. There is more. As the shameless electors who auctioned off the crown, and in whose hands the fate of Germany lay, had no reason for trusting the word of the melancholy lad who was king of Spain, and as the election was partly on credit, with the price of the votes to be paid later, the Fuggers deposited a bond of one hundred and thirty thousand florins in order to guarantee the obligations of the future Emperor Charles V.

Among the portraits which the elder Hans Holbein painted is one of Jacob Fugger. He is a man with a hard eye and thin lips, wearing his velvet beret perched over one ear. He is the image of adventure plus shrewd calculation. Once they asked Jacob why he never rested, why, when he had plenty of money with which to do as he pleased, to play, to amuse himself, he never left the bank for a single day. And Jacob answered, "As long as I can make money, I will not stop making it, nor will you ever see me idle." Jacob was not only the emperor's banker, he was also the Pope's banker. His power went so far that he even founded a city, the Fuggerei, with a hundred and six houses which he built with his own money along six streets or avenues. A thick wall defended the Fuggerei, ornamented and protected by three monumental gates, on which were the banker's coat of arms.

Competing for power with the Fuggers was another banking house—the Welsers. Fugger and Welser were born in the same Bavarian city, Augsburg. Their power grew like two parallel trees stemming from the same root. In those first decades of the sixteenth century we must consider these two houses as having power and splendour similar to that which the Medicis of Florence displayed earlier. The Fuggers and the Welsers acquired noble titles, patronized the arts and sciences, and were building in Antwerp such rich palaces as those northern cities had never known, cities where the guilds covered the coats of arms on their houses with gold. They were called "Fúcares" and "Belzares" in Spain, and the Spaniards looked with amazement upon these people who moved behind the empire and the Papacy, managing the king or adorning the Pope with threads of a gold more brilliant and more skilfully managed than that of Atahuallpa, whether in the hands of the Pizarros, the kings of Spain, or the priests of Toledo.

While the Fuggers were monopolizing the political enterprises of Europe, the Welsers were turning their eyes toward America. And therefore Charles V gave them the captaincy of Venezuela. While Jacob Fugger was receiving noble titles, the Welsers, who were no less able, were doing something more substantial. Filipine Welser, daughter of Bartholomew, was secretly marrying a nephew of Charles V—King Ferdinand of Bohemia. So the business prospered. The contract regarding the captaincy of Venezuela could not have been more advantageous. The German colonists were to go to Venezuela with fifty Austrian miners, many Negro slaves, Spanish foot-soldiers, eighty horses. The leaders would be Heinrich Ehinger and Hieronymus Sayler, or, failing these, Ambrosius and Georg Ehinger. They would take with them the right to enslave, to erect strongholds, take out gold, import horses, discover, conquer, and populate. They would not pay salt taxes. They would not return to the king a fifth, but a tenth, of the gold they mined in ten years. And whoever carried out the agreement would be governor and captain general for all the days of his life, with an annual salary of three hundred thousand maravedis.

While the terms of the agreement were being perfected and completed, the Welsers did not sleep: Ambrosius Ehinger was already moving about Hispaniola as the bankers' agent, pointing with pride to the power of his house— "our house." When the papers arrived, everything was ready. Soon vessels were crossing the Caribbean en route to Coro. In the bow the ferocious face of Messer Ambrosius, and in the hold of the ships "the worst fellows who ever left Spain for America, and he who is worse than the worst of his men." Germans, Portuguese, Spaniards, Negroes from Guinea, all would soon leave Venezuela marked with the iron of their ambition.

*    *    *

I do not really believe that in matters of cruelty the Germans were any worse than the Spaniards. The natural thing, of course, is that the Spanish chroniclers should fling all the dirty water of the conquest at these blond meddlers. The conquistador had no homeland; he was a conqueror and nothing more. And the conquest, as I have said many times, was hard. Ehinger marched, investigated, hunted along the banks of the Maracaibo, through Guajira, through Tamalameque. "He took with him lines of Indians carrying food and baggage, and they all went tied around the neck with the same cord; as the rope made a ring or loop around each head, it was not possible to release one of them without beginning with the first in line; for this reason, when an Indian grew tired, they cut off his head, if he did not cut it himself, without undoing the chain or calling a halt."

Ehinger got some gold, but not enough even to pay the soldiers. On the other hand, he got reports of the fabulous country of the Chibchas. It was said that there were Indians in a certain town whose task it was to smelt in special forges. "And they have their forges and anvils and hammers, which are made of tough stones. The hammers are the size of eggs, or smaller, and the anvils as big as a Mallorcan cheese, made of other tough stones; the bellows are as thick as two fingers or more, and as long as two palms. They have delicate scales with which to weigh, and these are made of a white bone which looks like marble, also there are some of a black wood, like ebony."

Nevertheless, Ehinger did not complete the undertaking. His cruelty was punished by the Indians or by the Spaniards themselves. Suddenly, with no one knowing where it came from, a poisoned arrow pierced his throat. There were four days of a furious struggle between life and death, in which the red-head spat blood and unintelligible revilings, while the poison spread through his veins and his body swelled. On seeing him suffering the agonies of a man condemned to death, even the Spaniards, who hated him, felt their hearts oppressed. That he might have a broad tomb and a legend to recall his name, the valley in which he drew his last breath was baptized the Valley of Messer Ambrosius . . .

With Ehinger dead, Johann Sinserhoffer became governor. He was a quiet, phlegmatic banker, made for the life of a cashier in Europe, weighing gold and specie, rather than for the business of killing wild Indians and dying with an arrow in the throat. So Sinserhoffer installed himself in a chair, while his lieutenants hunted Indians in the near-by regions. But the Welsers wanted something more positive and the soldiers something more tangible. So the governorship soon passed from Sinserhoffer's hands to those of Georg Hohermuth. He brought Messer Nicholas Federmann as his second in command.

There is something exotic about finding these names with a harsh German flavour—Welser, Ehinger, Sinserhoffer, Hohermuth, Federmann—running through the history of the conquest of America. The tropical paradise is to swallow them all. Or the green hell; as you wish. . . .

❧    ❧    ❧

When Georg Hohermuth and Nicholas Federmann saw themselves masters of the captaincy in Coro, they found this poor, thin stage as sterile as was Santa Marta to Fernández de Lugo and Jiménez de Quesada. In the back country were the plains, fiery savannas in summer and in

winter covered by the waters of rivers that had overflowed
their banks until they looked like mirrors traced by the
flight of scarlet flamingos. Behind the plains, and mounting
the flank of the cordillera, it ought to be possible to reach
the town where the Indians smelted gold. This gold of
America must clink in the bank of the Welsers in Amster-
dam. Not the gold that the avid claws of the Spaniards
snatched from the Indians, but that which was to be discovered by the red-blond Germans, who were about to
prove their nerve and their courage in the captaincy and
the adventure of Venezuela.

Messer Georg Hohermuth and Messer Nicholas Feder-
mann looked toward the interior and ordered the march.
Messer Georg must follow in Ehinger's footsteps; Messer
Nicholas must await him in Coro. But when the tread of
Messer Georg's troops ceased to echo in Coro, Messer Nich-
olas could not resist, and he himself went out to explore.
Georg had ordered Nicholas to go to Hispaniola to bring
back from that island more men, more slaves, more horses.
But Nicholas was not so simple-minded, and he forgot those
orders.

I need not now recount all that Georg Hohermuth suffered in his long peregrination through those lands. I will
only say that he wore his fingers to the quick in trying to
climb the flanks of the cordillera without ever succeeding
in doing it. Higher, ever higher was the land of salt and
emeralds, the land of the Chibcha nation, where men were
eating beautiful baked potatoes and the flesh of game, and
drinking good corn wine, while the German, not knowing
it but sensing it, groaned with hunger on the vertical slopes
of those same mountains. The elusive El Dorado spurred

Messer Georg on, but always escaped his grasp. It is the constant jest and coquetry of our America, so unyielding, so deceptive, and so beautiful.

One day Chief Guaygueri said to Messer Georg, "March two moons more, and you will reach a town where the Indians eat from vessels of gold and silver, where the land is flat and smooth and the wind urges flocks of fat sheep across peaceful cultivated fields." Messer Georg advanced, and found nothing. Another time the Spaniards lost a great raft which they had built to cross the Opía. Indian enemies managed to seize it, and then amused themselves by passing up and down on it in front of the Spaniards, performing their dances of war and lust on this floating stage, to the sound of diabolic music.

These Indians of the plains and the steep slopes were fiercer than those of the cold country. When they advanced against Messer Georg, they did it with a very martial air. They beat hard drums and blew on rosy snail-shells. They marched in squads. First came the lancers, then the bowmen, then the women with ropes, jars, and food. In America women have always followed the armies, when they have not preceded them. One day the soldiers will call them the Juanas [Janes], and the Juanas will be the most typical note in our wars.

These Indians loved the sun and the moon. It is told of Salammbo, the most beautiful star of the hot Carthage nights, who communed with the moon on the temple's flat roof, taking off her clothes in order to adorn herself with the impalpable light that flowed silently over shoulders, breasts, and knees, that one night when there was an eclipse she flung herself to death. The Indians whom Georg Hohermuth saw also went mad when the moon disappeared and, during an eclipse, hurled "brands, sticks, stones, clay, and whatever they might have in hand," begging it desperately not to flee away through the hazardous corridors of eternal night.

*        *        *

Nicholas Federmann was more daring, or more lucky, than Hohermuth. While the latter was losing three years and destroying his army on an unsuccessful expedition, Messer Nicholas, his second in command, a man not very tall but stout, with blue eyes and curly red whiskers, agile and stubborn, reached the summit of the Andes and the kingdom of the Chibchas. When Hohermuth got back to Coro, he found neither his second in command nor any trace of him. One day he would be writing to King Charles, "I marched more than five hundred leagues, as far as the Choques, and, being no more than twenty-five leagues from what I sought, I found myself so weakened in men, horses, and arms that I had to go back to recuperate in order to renew the march."

Not so Federmann. He went thrusting himself into the mountain like a wedge. Two things made him climb: the desire to reach El Dorado and the fear of meeting Hohermuth. As is obvious, his soldiers died, he suffered hunger, and there were weeks when the troops fed on the flesh of horses, which were stricken by some strange ailment. But he climbed, climbed until he reached the high uplands, until the soldiers felt as though blades of ice were penetrating their flesh—those selfsame soldiers who had come from plains where it was the blades of an implacable sun that had pierced them. When the troops reached the land of the Chibchas, they were poorer and more miserable than Gonzalo Jiménez de Quesada's men. Three years and a half did Federmann spend roaming through an unknown world. His soldiers had not a stitch of clothing left on their bodies, but went dressed in the skins of wild animals.

Lázaro Fonte, who remained in exile in Pasca, sent, as I have said, a runner to Jiménez de Quesada, announcing the German's coming. Quesada, as if not sure whether to believe the message, sent out spies. Federmann's scouts and Quesada's met face to face. The two armies confronted each other. There was a miracle; the soldiers of Quesada numbered a hundred and sixty-three, and a hundred and sixty-three were those of Federmann. But Quesada's men were refreshed by food and rest; they wore cotton garments and Chibcha blankets, and there were twenty thousand Indians whom Quesada had ranged in the manner of an army belonging to him as lord and master of these lands.

The red beard looked at the jet-black beard with jealousy and amazement. The two strong hands first faltered, then clasped. The soldiers embraced. For an instant, the Spaniard suspected that these miserable foot-soldiers had come to rob him of his conquests; soon he was convinced that there was none of this. What was needed was to give them a few grains of corn so they could resume their old habit of eating. The amusing chronicler of El Carnero summed up the results of the interview between the two generals, "They received each other very well at first, and soon were exchanging various jests which the gold converted into laughter; they remained very good friends, and agreed that the soldiers of the two generals should be fed in the conquered territory thirty at a time. . . ." Later, when Rodríguez Fresle made up the roll of Federmann's soldiers, he began it in these terms, "Soldiers of Nicholas Federmann who were fed in this kingdom . . ."

It was a never-ending source of amusement that a few poor fugitives from Santa Marta who had been living on snakes and lizards, and who in Spain were never more than adventurers swaggering around church porticoes, should have fed the agent of the Welsers, bankers as great and as rich as those that had bought the crown of the German emperor for the king of Spain.

❉ ❉ ❉

It is hard to say whether the Indians or the Spaniards themselves were regarding this meeting of the troops with the more surprise, when a no less unexpected bit of news arrived to amaze Quesada and to leave the Indians and the soldiers stupefied. It was brought by the south wind, the wind called Ubaque, that cold and subtle wind which the natives say should be received with open mouth. . . . The news concerned certain soldiers under the command of Don Sebastián de Belalcázar who, having left Peru years before with destination unknown, were now riding their horses along the other flank of the cordillera. It was as though the hidden reason for the illegal venture on which all three captains had embarked was leading them irresistibly toward these desert uplands. The three generals were all mutineers. Just as Quesada had mutinied with the troops which Fernández de Lugo had confided to him, so Federmann had mutinied with those Hohermuth had confided to him, and Belalcázar with those Pizarro had put in his charge.

This city of mine which was shortly to receive its he-

raldic bearings from the mystic King Charles and the mad
Queen Juana could not have had a more honourable origin.
This is the way all noble cities are born; the best dynasties
and the finest family trees are rooted in the same soil.

But let us be a bit more definite about the coming of this
Belalcázar, who was, as everyone knows, a mere donkey-
boy in his own land. Whenever, years before, could that
poor lad's head, nodding up and down between the burro's plushy ears, have dreamed of the stupendous future
which America had in store for him!

> *Sebastián very often was accustomed,*
> *By reason of his elder brother's order*
> *Or his own will, to go into the forest*
> *To carry cord-wood out upon his donkey.*
> *Once, leading it full-loaded by a trail*
> *On which a lashing rainstorm barred the way,*
> *The skinny pack-beast fell with all its burden*
> *Into a slippery pit, and stuck in mud.*
> *He stripped it of its halter, cords, and panniers,*
> *Then urged it, shouted, begged it to get out,*
> *And, sweating, tried to lift it by the tail;*
> *The skinny donkey did not budge an inch.*
> *Then he, seized by a fit of childish anger,*
> *Took up a sturdy cudgel in both hands,*
> *Saying, "Know, beast, that if I'm angered,*
> *By force I'll make thee lift thyself and trot."*
> *At last, without intending such great damage,*
> *He aimed one of his blows behind the neck*
> *And with such fury did the beast belabour*
> *That the unhappy donkey, he fell dead.*

*An ill-advised one will not linger longer,*
*But flees when once his madness stands out clear.*
*So leaving wood and rope and panniers mired*
*And throwing off a poor and narrow life,*
*He went to win a new and better fortune*
*Imagination painted far from there.*
*It seemed a finer thing to be a warrior*
*Than stay and till the fields he knew at home.*

So Belalcázar fled from home because of the death of a burro. Somehow he enrolled in one of those expeditions which were going to the Indies. He reached the Antilles, explored in Hispaniola, went to the mainland, explored in Darién, "ranched" for gold, traded, bought, sold. The lad became a man; the donkey-boy a captain. He stored up money, and when the harsh voices of Pizarro and Almagro and the persuasive speeches of a certain friar who was financing expeditions in Panama said, "On to Peru!" Belalcázar's eyes sparkled and burned.

One day, when Pizarro was raging like a wild beast in Peruvian territory, Sebastián de Belalcázar arrived on the coast of Ecuador, or what we were later to call Ecuador, to reinforce and serve him. He had come from Nicaragua in a big ship and he brought twelve horses and thirty men. Belalcázar was now a man grown, sparing of words and effective in action, who kept his thoughts to himself and made his calculations before he acted. He was one of those with naked swords who had helped Atahuallpa into prison, and he was ready to drive that sword in up to the hilt if it was necessary. Ninety-nine hundred gold pesos and four hundred and seven silver marks came to him when the booty was divided. Pizarro, though fearing him, gave him command over the city of San Miguel. Belalcázar went as captain, and nine horsemen accompanied him.

As Belalcázar got farther away from Pizarro, he had only one fixed idea—to become a governor. He had seen that Atahuallpa came from the north, from the kingdom of Quito, and he thought that in Quito the gold would stand about in piles. San Miguel did not hold him long.

Shortly after establishing himself in the city, he had set sail again. From ships that came from Panama and Nicaragua with new troops for Pizarro, he took two hundred men and sixty horses. "Let us go," he said to the soldiers, "to the land of the king who filled a room with gold in Cundinamarca. To the land of Atahuallpa, where his sons are now." And without Pizarro's knowing anything about it, he left that poor city of San Miguel and set out for Quito. In order to place himself in the right, he arranged a petition. In a declaration made by Bartolomé García, ship's captain, the trick is told thus, "The citizens presented him with a request that he go to Quito, and he said he could not do it; then the citizens entered the council and told him that if he did not want to go, they would put another captain in his place; and as he saw that they intended to do it, he said, 'Then, as someone must go, I will' . . . and he began to gather a force. . . ."

*     *     *

"And he began to gather a force" and set out for the north. To get away from the Pizarros and the Almagros, Belalcázar said that he was going to punish the Indian Ruminaguí, who was Atahuallpa's successor in position and wealth. Ruminaguí opened battle against Don Sebastián.

He dug wide ditches for the horses to fall into, but the horses avoided them. The Indian battalions opened like fans and let fly their arrows. The Spaniards shot off their arquebuses, and won the round. Ruminaguí re-formed his army and offered new resistance. He hung dead horses' heads on the road and decorated them with flowers to give pleasure to the Indians and warning to the Spaniards. But again powder conquered the arrow. And to add to the Indians' terror, the earth trembled and Cotopaxi wore a crown of fire. Then the Indians abandoned Quito. Ruminaguí, wounded and sarcastic, went back to the women, "to his great seraglio of wives and concubines," and said to them, "Rejoice, for the Christians with whom you can amuse yourselves are coming." Some of them laughed, says the chronicler, as women will, perhaps not thinking any evil at all. Ruminaguí throttled those who laughed loudest.

Belalcázar went on. On the site of the city which the Indian king had burned and abandoned, he founded San Francisco de Quito. One night, guided by certain bright stars, he climbed the two cliffs, Oromina (gold mine) and Copagua. He did not find the treasures they all were hoping for. The soldiers grew impatient. Belalcázar went on to Guayaquil, founded a city there, and returned to Quito. In Guayaquil he had left a small force. As soon as he was out of sight the Indians rose against the Spaniards, because "they began to understand their importunities and the speed with which they demanded gold and silver and beautiful women."

But this meant nothing. There was news that El Dorado lay to the north. In the lands of Cundinamarca was an Indian king who anointed his body with turpentine and, covered with gold dust, went to bathe in the lakes, while the priests offered their gods golden idols and emeralds by the handful. Belalcázar had a letter from the Spanish empress congratulating him on his discoveries and his conquests. In the service of so great a lady, he had to go forward. While they were doubting him and building up resistance against him in the council, Belalcázar got his army ready. In the hands of the former donkey-boy that mysterious letter from the empress became a talisman. Until he left Quito one day with everything that had any value for the army. Five thousand Indians marched in his train; he carried a silver service with him, and a hundred hogs. The city was left with no garrison and no horses. The town council, alarmed, told Pizarro so without giving Belalcázar a copy of the letter "for lack of paper."

Belalcázar left behind him Peru, the land on which a fatal destiny was weighing. In those years, the history of Peru, from which the prudent and ambitious Don Sebastián thought it well to disassociate himself, can be summed up in a few words. Listen to them: Francisco Pizarro, its founder, assassinated his companion Diego de Almagro. Diego's son assassinated Francisco Pizarro. Vaca de Castro strangled that second Almagro. The viceroy Núñez de Vela put Vaca de Castro in jail. Gonzalo Pizarro killed the viceroy Núñez de Vela. The lawyer La Gasca strangled Gonzalo Pizarro. And the Contreras tried to assassinate La Gasca. If he had not returned to Spain, I think they would have devoured him alive. That is all. Incidentally it might be noted that Friar Valverde, who helped Atahuallpa to die so nicely, ended with a cudgelling well and skilfully administered by the inhabitants of Puna.

Consequently it was not a bad idea for Belalcázar, already skilled in the matter of conquests, to go on further

to the north. To traverse the harsh wasteland of the Guái-
tara, to cross the simmering plains of the Patía, to reach the
broad and beautiful valley of the Cauca, to found cities
there, and to set up there the imaginary centre of his future
governorship: Popayán, which had a pleasant climate and
a fertile soil. "Having reached Popayán, and finding himself
in a beautiful valley which stretched for a space of fourteen leagues from there to the headwaters of the Great
River, a valley no less abundant in streams and rivers stemming from the Andes than in charming fields and plains
where the multitude of farms and gardens showed the fer-
tility of the country, Belalcázar decided to settle there,
electing as site a high tableland whose temperature was
moderate, avoiding the extremes of Quito as to cold and
of Cartagena as to heat; and whose benign though rainy
sky, and fields adapted to the best grain, have made Popayán famous as containing the best sky, land, and bread in
the Indies."

This did not mean that Belalcázar, conqueror that he
was, ceased to march in the midst of blood and fire. On
leaving Quito, he divided his army into three sections, and
put one in charge of Juan de Ampudia. "You must follow the
footpaths of the cordillera," the chief told him, "and not
engage in any dangerous action. We will follow you." It
was not difficult for Belalcázar to follow in the leader's footsteps; for, as Ampudia burned all the towns he ran across
and strangled all the Indians, Don Sebastián could be
guided by the ashes and the blood.

It would be long and tedious to repeat the tale of a
march which in no wise differed from that of the other
conquistadors. Belalcázar spent four years in discovering,
conquering, founding, and populating, until the natural

force of his destiny led him toward the kingdom of Cundinamarca, toward the site where Quesada and Federmann were. And by a strange coincidence he arrived, as I have said, at the same time Federmann came up through Pasca. Belalcázar came across the valley of the Magdalena, and touched the spurs of the mountain on whose summit was Quesada. While the lawyer was receiving the,news of the German from Lázaro Fonte, Indians brought him the news of the man from Peru who was coming up the opposite side. Quesada treated somewhat hastily with the German while his brother was advancing to talk with Belalcázar. And in less time than it took for them all to recover from the surprise Belalcázar, who refused to let himself be distracted by conversations, came forward with his troop, which consisted of exactly the same number of men as Quesada had on the one hand and Federmann on the other. In the geometry of military forces, this is called an equilateral triangle. The only thing in which they differed was their clothing. That of the men who came with Belalcázar was better; it was the clothing of men from Peru, the rich and the fortunate. He who in his childhood had walked only with burros came now "eager to find the gilded man," dressed in silks and fine stuffs, with good coats of mail and many Indian servants. He brought a silver service and a herd of pigs. Belalcázar's present eminence and his former profession were balanced between the plate and the pigs.

# VIII. Play and Gaming in Europe

As he carried a great deal of gold, General Jiménez de Quesada wished first to see Granada, his homeland, and to amuse himself among his friends and relatives. After some time there, he went to court in pursuance of his affairs, arriving during the period when the court was in mourning for the death of the Empress. They said here that the Adelantado entered in the scarlet clothes adorned with much gold braid which were worn in those days, and that he was seen crossing the plaza by Secretary Cobos, who called out from one of the palace windows, "What madman is that? Throw that lunatic out of the plaza," and at that he left. If it was true and he did it, as was said in this city, there is no reason why I should not write it. The Adelantado was absent-minded; I knew him very well, for he was godfather to a sister of mine, and a close friend of my parents, and I valued him in spite of all he cost us in the second voyage he made to Castile, when he returned ruined from hunting El Dorado, for on this voyage my father went with him, with a deal of good money which never came back, though both of them returned.

—Juan Rodríguez Fresle

I N THAT great plain at the top of the Andes, enamelled by
the trembling blue of the lakes and shaded by emerald
clumps of underbrush, lies, I think, the very heart of
America. Three men started from three different points—
the green bay of Santa Marta, the ruddy coast of Venezuela,
and Quito, seat of the Incas—to hunt for the centre of Terra
Firma, and as though they had been climbing the three
sides of a pyramid simultaneously they came face to face
when they reached the summit, their hands still bloody
from having torn themselves to tatters on the rough rock
flanks. One came by the Great River of the Magdalena,
another followed the waters of the Meta, the third came
up the Cauca; when they began unfolding the tales of
their prowess the whole narrative was braided through with
the mysteries of those three rivers into whose broad streams
fall the gurgling cascades of the Andes and are silenced.

The petals of all the winds come together here as in the
rosy heart of a flower. The cold and subtle wind from the
south and the tempestuous wind from the north caress
the backs of the swift and tremulous deer, or thin out
above the waters of the Funza and fold their wings to follow
the slow pace of Indian fishing craft which glide through
the sleeping shallows. The hours of anguish which the
troops of the conquest passed when they were crossing the
eastern flatlands or overcoming Carib resistance, or breaking the pride of the last of the Inca kings, ended here in the

light from the zenith. Those troops were mingled to form a
single, restless, noisy army which included men from Spain,
Portugal, Greece, Italy, and Germany, soldiers whom fate
had decided to bring together on a single day in this poor
land of the Indians, crowds that darkened and hummed
like a swarm of hornets.

Of the three captains, I may say that the Andalusian,
armed only with his own eloquence, imposed his will on
the others. He was again the good politician, who disarmed
Federmann's pretensions, if he had any, and Belalcázar's,
which were many and plain to be seen. Federmann was
not exactly a fool. On his first trip through Venezuela he
wrote, or had the scribe write, a fantastic account which his
brother-in-law was to publish under this title, *Charming
and Agreeable Account of the First Trip of Nicholas Federmann the Younger, of Ulm, to the Indies in the Ocean Sea,
and of All That Happened in That Country until His Return to Spain, Written Briefly and Diverting to Read.* In
this account the Welsers' agent decided to cede nothing
to the most prevaricating of the chroniclers and told in
prolix detail of his trip to the land of the dwarf, where the
largest living being was only four palms tall. In the prologue, which Kiefhaber wrote as a dedication to Messer
Johann Wilhelm von Loubenberg, of Loubenbergerstein,
he said as follows, "Dear and Gracious Lord, I have known
you not only as a lover and a connoisseur of ancient things,
but also of the oversea expeditions carried out in our era,
which have, by the grace of God, produced the discovery
of new islands called the New World, where a quantity of
gold, precious stones, spices, and fine woods is found, prov-
ing God's great goodness to humankind; many things still
remain hidden, which we shall discover before Judgment

Day, as your great wisdom doubtless has taught you earlier than I."

But notwithstanding Federmann's excellent aptitude for serving his masters the Welsers and for making good use of his eloquence, he was now, at the head of troops which the Venezuelan plains had thinned and ravaged, a beaten man. "Federmann" means "Featherman." But in this instance the man who handled the quill was the man of law, Quesada. And the plumage of the German who arrived dressed in uncured skins might better seem to refer to the kind that the poor American Indians wear on their heads.

Belalcázar's case looked a bit more serious. That gentleman, who arrived with a great show of swine and servants, had been founding cities everywhere. He was the first technician in the art of creating towns. He kept explaining to Quesada how colonization should be carried out. His schooling, which consisted of conquering Indians in America, had been better than that of the Andalusian, who had burned the midnight oil in Salamanca reading Cæsar's *Commentaries on the Gallic Wars*. Nevertheless, Belalcázar could consider his ambition satisfied with Popayán, the land of the best bread. It would be absurd to pretend to gather under a single governorship all the broad territory his legs had measured, and perhaps for that reason he was not so demanding.

All in all, as it was a matter of three lieutenants who with their troops had mutinied against their governors, but who might find the merit of those enterprises serving for something before the court, they agreed that the Spanish monarchs themselves should decide the fate of this New Kingdom; at once they took the necessary steps for going to the peninsula. Belalcázar pressed the empress's letter to his heart, Quesada clutched the booty emeralds in his fist, and Federmann caressed the plumage of his name. . . .

*          *          *

Let us be brief. There go the generals down the road to the Magdalena, which is to say, the road to Spain. Each has gathered all the gold he could, and his imagination is busy with old friends in Spain whom he now hopes to meet. The tales of their conquests, their riches, the contact with the grandees of the court, will open a circle of praise and admiration for them when they begin to talk in the taverns, when they approach girls of good family, when they hold forth in church porticoes to the throngs of idlers who gather to listen to them. Those who have conquered a New Kingdom can put an arm about the waist of the prettiest girl in town, and just as they had previously felt a warm wave of the tropics, so now, as they bring an ear close to the breasts of European women, they will hear the heart-beats jump. Into their dreams of returning to the peninsula these captains put all the swagger, the Don Juan audacity, the boastfulness of Spaniards in the best theatrical tradition.

And so the three captains went down the gentle slopes on this side of the cordillera, which the Indians had webbed with paths. The governing of the new lands had been left in the hands of Hernán Pérez, brother of the lawyer. Almost all Quesada's soldiers and those of Federmann stayed with him. Of Belalcázar's, only forty were left there "whom he agreed to feed," and the rest were sent to settle other regions. They were too enterprising to be kept in the new colony. Belalcázar pondered on how he had let Quesada gain a great deal of territory, and he even played with the idea of rising against the chief on the pretence that a group of soldiers was insisting on it. Quesada managed to read these ideas in the donkey-boy's mind, and hastened to defend himself before the other could do anything about it. Quesada won that new move, and the game was over, for the wish to go to Europe with gold was stronger than the temptation to do battle in the Peruvian manner, which is to say, in the style of the Almagros and Pizarros.

The three captains reached the Magdalena. They embarked with certain of their entourage in ships built by Captain Albarracín, and soon the current was bearing them down waters which for the first time were reflecting Spanish faces that were placid and smiling. For a moment each one remembered what he had left in the New City of Granada, which they had at the last moment decided to christen with a new name at once Christian and indigenous. They would call it Santa Fé de Bogotá. And Belalcázar thought wistfully of his swine, Federmann of his hens, Don Gonzalo of the burro. Those were the humblest details of this conquest, and the only ones which were to become a part of Indian life as democratic acquisitions. Let three or four centuries pass, and of those days that were so stupendous the Indians would see only Quesada's burro, Belalcázar's pigs, and Federmann's hens, which would be ranging through the gardens and fields of their ranches.

* * *

Among the captains and the soldiers heading thus gaily for Cartagena, and soon to be crossing the Ocean Sea toward the port of Sanlúcar de Barrameda in Spain, went a certain Dominican friar already familiar to us—Father Domingo de las Casas. He also busied his imagination with restless dreams. Taking part in the gay amusements which

those who came home from the Indies were wont to pro-
mote might not be entirely outside his programme. The
soldiers saw no saint in him. They even said that during the
conquest he usually threw the major weight of spiritual
labours on Lescámez, and kept the easiest and simplest part
for himself. Of his apostolic zeal the chroniclers preserved
no very good memory. Fray Pedro Simón, speaking of the
founding of the New City of Granada, says, "Quesada
named neither judge nor regiment, nor did he establish gallows or guillotine, nor any of the other things so important
in the governing of a city, nor a priest for the church." On
this last point, the major responsibility rested clearly on
Las Casas. But Las Casas had other worries.

Among those other worries was money. The fact is that
when Quesada divided the booty taken from the Indians—
those twenty million ducats in gold and emeralds—he made
the distribution

> *Giving each his share, but favouring*
> *The two priests they had brought with them. . . .*

And as though this were not enough, Fray Domingo had
himself paid for the mare that died on the road. And not
yet content, he addressed himself in a moving speech to
the soldiers, instructing them as to the use which they
should make of their gold:

> *Before they carried it into their huts*
> *They must not lose all at playing dice and cards.*

The idea that the friar then put into action was very simple. Those soldiers who had, by a miracle, reached the be-
nignant lands where they now found themselves owed
their lives to the Virgin. The Holy Virgin had saved them

from the plague, from hunger, from Indians and wild beasts. There was not sufficient gratitude in the heart of any one of them to repay her for such good fortune, nor could any tongue ever reach in her praises a height of eloquence which could properly express what was due her. So what they ought to do was to raise an enduring monument of thanks to María Santísima. Build a chapel near those Seville wharves which saw the soldiers depart amid a shout of "God carry you safely, and the Virgin go with you!" from the women on shore. Yes, that was the spot where the conquerors of the Chibchas must lay the foundation stone of their Christian faith and their love for the Mother of God. "Out of the gold which is his, let each one set aside a portion and place it in my hands," said the friar, "for I am going to Spain, and by my faith I will have the chapel built. And on a day I will return to this Christian land and give account of my labour—which is to be the labour of all of you—to the captains and the soldiers."

The friar had never, perhaps, talked so long and with such high eloquence as on this occasion. He softened all their hearts. For one thing, they were more enthusiastic about spending money when their pockets, which had always been empty, were newly stuffed with it; for another, it was truly a miracle that they had reached this port of safety. And so, while the bark was dropping downstream, the friar, instead of counting the beads of his rosary, added up his bits of gold.

❖　❖　❖

For his part, Quesada took out gold and emeralds in an amount which is not known with exactness to anyone. In addition to what had gone to him as his share of the booty, it was said that he took money from the royal strongboxes by force, on the ground that he was going to hand it to His Majesty in person. This would be told to Seville officials in a letter which was never to reach them. Later, another letter from Hernán Venegas, Pedro de Colmenares, and Juan Tafur said, "At the time when the lawyer Gonzalo Jiménez, captain and lieutenant governor, left this New Kingdom to make his report on the discovery of this kingdom and on its natives, we wrote Your Honours what you should know in order to be forewarned concerning what had happened to the gold and stores which belonged to His Majesty as his royal fifths, and also to the thirteen thousand castellanos of sixteen- to eighteen-carat gold which Hernán Pérez de Quesada, the lawyer's brother, who remained in his stead, took out of His Majesty's box by force and against our will, in order to give them, as he gave them, to the lawyer, who said that he would take them to His Majesty; not being certain about this, we are advising Your Honours that these may be collected."

As a matter of fact, there would never be any way of knowing how much the Indian loot amounted to. Gold and emeralds were hidden in prudent, or imprudent, quantities so that the royal fifths should not be increased. Denunciations came from time to time, out of jealousy of the conquerors. But as we have seen, the letters were lost, sometimes in the long trip across mountain and ocean, sometimes through trickery on the part of the captains, sometimes because the pile of letters and reports that reached Spain climbed higher and higher, without eyes enough to read and pass on them.

What Venegas, Colmenares, and Tafur said of those thirteen thousand castellanos that Don Gonzalo took would agree with the denunciation they themselves made, first in another letter which was lost, and later in one that said, "We wrote Your Honours by Captain Juan de Junco to tell how Captain Hernán Pérez de Quesada had taken another six thousand castellanos of good gold out of His Majesty's box by force and against our will, saying that he was taking them for the discovery of the Sierra Nevadas because he had had great news of them, which six thousand castellanos he gave to Jerónimo Lebrón in payment for certain clothing and a horse bought of him for the journey; and because force was used against us in this matter we have decided to advise Your Honours of it."

It ought not to surprise us that these adventurers and conquerors, having never handled anything of more value than copper coins in Spain, felt dizzy as they awoke to the sudden sense of wealth. Thrust thus into Aladdin's cave, they filled their pockets with gold and grabbed fistfuls of emeralds in such an orgy as had never been known before. Even Don Gonzalo himself lost his head and his sense of discretion as he neared the shores of his native land. The poor lawyer who had left in disgrace after losing the dyers' lawsuit was coming back in triumph to dress in fine clothes, with an inexhaustible stream of gold gushing from his pockets.

*     *     *

The ship that bore the three conquerors dropped anchor at Málaga. The peninsula that they had left poverty-stricken years before was now, under the feverish impulse of discovery and with the aid of conquest gold, bursting forth into a froth of stone. What had happened to the lucky conquistador was now happening to Spain. Simple churches

grew into presumptuous piles, with twisted baroque columns hanging against their façades like stone corkscrews.
In Toledo, Granada, Salamanca sounded the noise of the
stone-cutters. Charles V built a gigantic palace within the
Alhambra and destroyed certain Moorish monuments in
the process. The empire felt the need of affirming itself
above infidel ruins and humiliations. In Toledo the Alcázar
grew to monumental proportions.

The first loads of gold taken from the Peruvian kings
went ringing into the royal coffers, and Hernando Pizarro
amazed the court with his fantastic description of the
treasures of Atahuallpa. They say that when he unloaded
his ship "the customs office was filled with solid bars, vases
of diverse forms in imitation of animals, flowers, fountains,
and other objects, executed with more or less skill and all
of pure gold, to the great astonishment of spectators, who
came in great numbers from near-by towns to look upon
the marvellous products of Indian art." In the face of the
physical reality of Peru, the stories Cortés told began to lose
their importance. The first time he came back he had daz-
zled the country and almost eclipsed the imperial majesty
of Charles V himself, but now, back a second time, he was
to seem only the younger brother of the Pizarros, those
Pizarros who had risen from Trujillo swineherds to be the
court's bright stars.

Quesada, coming out of the unknown, was besieged by
people eager to hear about this other kingdom which had
risen from his hands as if by magic. He brought the latest
news. When he passed through Granada he declared that
he carried a hundred and fifty thousand gold pesos in his
pocket. Pale envy snapped at his heels. Cobos, knight com-
mander of León, wrote the fiscal agent of the Indies dilat-

ing upon this fortune, and pointing out that the conqueror, in place of landing at the customs office in Seville, had stopped in Málaga so as to escape inspection. But Quesada was now the most important figure in Málaga, Granada, Cordova, and Seville, and for some days they left him in peace.

Naturally, Quesada was burning with the ambition to have the governorship of the New Kingdom placed in his hands. Fernández de Lugo had died some time before, and his thieving son wandered about the court claiming the right to succeed him and carrying his pretensions even to the lands discovered by Quesada. In Seville, Quesada obtained permission to go to court, and left to seek out the king and queen. He thought that if Peru had been given to Pizarro, New Granada should be given to him. But Alonso de Lugo had a head start, and Quesada decided that the best thing would be to buy the governorship. Alonso, married to a lady of high degree, was acting very much the gentleman. He was everybody's friend, and he was adept at using the gold he had stolen from his father in giving parties and placing bribes. Quesada proposed purchase, Don Alonso was disposed to sell. The lawyer advanced certain moneys. But the court did not accept the transfer, and there now began an interminable suit in which the lawyer tried to get back the money he had advanced to Don Alonso.

*     *     *

Quesada certainly began under an evil star. This golden age of Spain was full of intrigue, denunciations, and what Ignacio de Loyola and the friars of the Inquisition called "Christian spirit." Charles V had reached the peak of his

greatness, and his greatness coincided with the formation
of the first militias of the Company of Jesus. In the same
year that Quesada returned to Spain, Loyola perfected the
Jesuit constitution. There was something sordid and savage
which gave Spain an air at once severe, fearful, and de-
fiant. Quesada fixed his hopes on Charles V, and Charles V
slipped from between his fingers. The emperor went off to
subdue the rebellion of Ghent, and the western world trembled under the impact of his horse's hoofs.

A short time before Quesada had left for America, King
Francis had fallen prisoner to Charles in the battle of Pavia.
Now Charles was crossing Francis's kingdom with his whole
armed force, and receiving from this same King Francis
a most splendid homage. Quesada stayed at court, litigating against Alonso de Lugo, while the emperor's figure
whirled on beyond the Pyrenees, enveloped in a cloud of
dust. Federmann, thinking himself cleverer, went after
Charles to claim the governorship for himself. The Welsers,
seeing him, laid hands on him. This German crook who
had asked so much money of them brought no sign of the
gold he had "ranched" in Venezuela. So the gentleman with
the red beard stayed caught in the toils of the bankers. Let
us drop him out of sight. He will die penniless in Spain a
little later.

           ❖     ❖     ❖

King Francis, stout and gallant, wily and unworried,
cheerfully patronized pleasant reunions in the castles of
France, where the nobility amused themselves without regard to convention; and at the same time he stirred up the
infidels against Charles V. The Spaniards who travelled in
Charles's train, like all those accustomed to amusing them-

selves in French cities, went singing the pleasures of wine and women as they were described in the most delightful outbursts of mirth by the most boisterous genius that ever made the sons of the Seine laugh. While Ignacio de Loyola was preparing his spiritual armies on the Spanish side of the Pyrenees, François Rabelais on the French side was bringing forth the life and deeds of Gargantua and Pantagruel. In Spain, men saw the world through the sufferings of the Inferno. In Italy, through the crude lessons of Machiavelli. In France, through the sensual life of the king of the drunkards. When one considers that Ignacio de Loyola, Machiavelli, and Rabelais all lived in the same period, and that men who were their contemporaries, like Quesada, had those three horizons to look toward, it explains many things. So, for example, it may explain why those who brought gold from America had little doubt as to whether they should waste it in Spain or enjoy it in France or Italy.

As Charles V was crossing France, reaching Brussels, entering Ghent, his ministers were getting documents in the mail from Spain which told of affairs of the Indies. What reached the emperor's ears was merely the sound of crumpled paper. Much more important than any tale of wild Indians was the maintaining of the European order which Charles V was going to establish when he had humiliated those freemen of Ghent. It was there in Brussels, with his mind fixed on other things, that the king decided the fate of Quesada and of Santa Marta by ordering that the governorship be handed over to Alonso de Lugo, and this in spite of all petitions to the contrary and without taking into account the fact that that great villain had already sold it.

❋     ❋     ❋

Charles V, entering the city of Ghent, was something to look at. It was not many weeks since, in plazas and taverns, markets and guild houses, the locksmiths, the weavers, the saddlers, the cabinet-makers, the bakers, and the butchers, boiling with democratic fervour, had raised their voices against the king's decrees and with clenched fists had threatened those who ruled them. Like the Spanish Comuneros twenty years earlier, or the German peasants fifteen years before, these burghers of Ghent asked liberty at the tops of their voices. Ghent was actually a small republic. The fifty-two guilds of manufacturers and the thirty-two tribes of weavers had their own government; the thousands who milled through the streets and stormed the city gates looked a turbulent mob which opposed the majesty of the emperor. But there was no lack of those who, in the depths of their hearts, preferred "the peace of despotism to the turbulence of liberty." And even more so now that Ghent had lost its equilibrium.

One day it was proposed to levy new taxes upon the citizens. The guilds met, and solemnly destroyed the famous "calfskin" in which Charles V announced that he would punish anyone who pretended to uphold city privileges which he did not concede. The mob poured through the narrow, twisting streets, with the banners of the guilds held high and shouts that shook the city's walled centre, singing their liberty and carrying bits of that parchment stuck in their caps like plumes.

But now that shout, a hymn to freedom only a few weeks earlier, was beginning to falter. Swiftly, but in silence, the artisans returned to their workshops. In the market no one talked of anything but wool, meat, or fish. For the emperor, with a great and thunderous retinue, was advancing across

France. Already the people of Brussels had acclaimed him. The populace gathered at the city gates, on the roof-tops, in house cornices, and gothic windows of stone buildings to look for the measured advance of the troops and the banners of the king waving between their gold rosettes. A witness says that entry was as if God had arrived in the city from Paradise. The emperor's train took more than six hours to pass a given point.

"Four thousand lancers, one thousand archers, five thousand halberdiers and musketeers composed his bodyguard, all armed to the teeth and ready for combat," John Lothrop Motley would say in his history. "The emperor rode in their midst, surrounded by cardinals, archbishops, bishops, and other great ecclesiastical dignitaries, so that the terrors of the Church were combined with the panoply of war to affright the souls of the turbulent burghers."

Never had such a thing been seen in Ghent. At parade pace this college dressed in velvet cloaks, ermine capes, golden collars, and cataracts of pearls went penetrating deep into the heart of the city. Seen from the roof-tops, the town looked a fantastic tapestry. The shining arms gave back the blue of the sky, light trembled and broke against the standards, the scarlet-clad heralds blasted the air with their long copper horns, the princes made silk creak under their silver-plated mountings, and precious stones sparkled in the nobles' hats. This mass of fine cloths, brocades, laces, was like a great machine which rolled over the voices of freemen, flattening them, reducing them to a miserable squeak.

A month after the emperor arrived they hanged nineteen rebels on the gallows as a warning to the city. Ghent, meanwhile, was emptying its warehouses in order to feed this army of foot-soldiers and horsemen, kings and warriors, which went scattering through the streets in search of amusement. A month after the executions were over, the decree which punished the city was announced. In order to repress all future violence they were to have a new constitution. The ancient democratic air must be transformed to a muffled living in humility.

And so that solemn approval of such capitulation might be expressed, there was to be a symbolic ceremony in which all would bow the head and bend the knee. On a designated day the chiefs of the weavers were to present themselves dressed in black, with uncovered heads, innocent of jewels or adornment, accompanied by fifty heads of the guilds and fifty workers, the latter in their shirts, and with halters about their necks, to implore the emperor's pardon. At the same time all the functionaries of the city were to fall on their knees "to say in a loud and intelligible voice, by the mouth of one of their clerks, that they were extremely sorry for the disloyalty, disobedience, infraction of laws, commotions, rebellion, and high treason of which they had been guilty, promise that they would never do the like again, and humbly implore him, for the sake of the Passion of Jesus Christ, to grant them mercy and forgiveness."

◆　　◆　　◆

Charles V was always like that. If he muffled the voice of victory in the shadows of the Cathedral, what would he not do with the loud shouts for freedom which the burghers had given? And Spain was like that. Even murderers and gipsies, Moors and Jews, crossed themselves in Spain, and said the "Ave María Purísima" with which one invariably knocked at the heavy Castilian doors or replied with the "conceived without sin" which was the invariable answer from the depths of the echoing entrances.

Those days of glory or of worry for Charles V were days of trial for the conquerors of America. Hernán Cortés was at court now, humbly begging that in return for the great achievements of his youth he be given rest for his old age. Quesada went intriguing like a petty lawyer; Pizarro talking loud and hard against the background of his riches; Belalcázar claiming the governorship of Popayán, which the emperor would have to give him if for no other reason than to lessen the power of the Pizarros; Alonso de Lugo asking for and getting Santa Marta, not so much because he was the son of Fernández de Lugo as because he had gold and was married to a lady of high degree.

All these personages went rubbing shoulders in the corridors, in the streets, in the taverns, in the house of the scribes. Those who, with their soldiers and their personal audacity, had doubled the world's landscapes and extended its horizons to infinity, now saw their vision shortened to the capital's narrow streets, the pallid faces of cautious ministers, and an emperor with a hard hand and a sober countenance.

Cortés wanted to prove his warrior's fortune in the Old World as he had in the New. In order to be near the emperor and reawaken an old affection he resolved to go with him on his expedition to Algiers. They went off one day in the same ship, cheered by the hope of conquering infidels again and beating the accursed soldiers of Barbarossa. After the white victory of Ghent it would not be a bad idea to add to Charles's record a red victory over the hosts of Algiers.

Twenty thousand men went with Charles in two hun-

dred and fifty vessels. Cortés felt hope spring again, and he
and Charles argued back and forth like two fighting men
who were old comrades. But this time fate was against
them. A storm rose during the night, and the troops nearing
Algiers were caught on a sand-bar. Cortés's ship foundered,
and fourteen of the galleys. Cortés and his son got ashore
by swimming. When dawn broke, the shipwrecked unfortunates stared at one another. The emperor stood shivering like a mongrel pup. Cortés then proposed an offensive,
but between the king's disillusionment and the army's hunger it fell to pieces.

From this day forward the old conqueror of Mexico
dropped from favour, and Charles thought of him only as
a person of bad augury who had gone with him on a disastrous journey.

Pizarro usually ran across Quesada in the gaming rooms.
In this absurd and contradictory court Quesada was losing
spirit, and he threw himself into the flowery path of pleasure, where women hung on his tales and his ducats, and
gamblers coveted his gold. One day he met with Pizarro,
Pedro Almírez, and another man at the gambling table.
Each card went down with an appropriate word of praise or
insult for their various conquests. A smiling maidservant approached the table. Pizarro, who had just won the hand,
gave her a crown. Pedro Almírez and the other man, cap-
tivated by the charm of the girl's big eyes and flashing
teeth, followed suit and gave her a crown apiece. Quesada,
taking a diabolical pride in his own defeat, Quesada who
was losing the game to Pizarro as he was losing favour at
court, looked the girl over from head to foot, and picking up
as many golden ducats as his hands would hold, tossed
them into the skirt she so willingly raised, saying, "I lost

the hand to these generous gentlemen, but I figure that in the number of ducats I give to you I win."

\* \* \*

While the lawyer Jiménez de Quesada was dividing his time between pleasure and petitions to the king and queen asking justice, a pile of papers was rising against him in the Audiencia. He had conquered a kingdom hardly smaller in size and wealth than Mexico or Peru; as someone said, he had set a beautiful emerald in the empire's crown; he had therefore a perfect right to expect not only that they would listen to him, but also that they would load him with honours. But it did not turn out that way; on the contrary, the pile of papers was threatening to engulf him. In Santa Marta, in Santa Fé, in the very court itself, the scribes spent day and night filling pages with accusations against him. The caravels that came from the New Kingdom to the peninsula carried fat packets accusing Quesada of fantastic crimes, or making his most necessary acts of discipline look ugly.

A Santa Marta soldier lodged criminal charges against him on the ground that he had once put the said soldier in jail, held him up to public shame, and given him a hundred lashes while the town crier proclaimed it, without giving him a chance to exercise the right of appeal. As a matter of fact, the soldier had been guilty of cowardice, leaving a cross-bow in the hands of an Indian. The denunciation was issued in Santa Marta, and Don Gonzalo was at court, but nevertheless the local judge ordered the constable "to seize the body of the lawyer Jiménez." The constable sought him, and came back, naturally, to say, "Sir, I have sought for the lawyer Jiménez and have not found him; they say he is not in this country." The judge insisted, and announced through the town crier that the lawyer must present himself in Santa Marta in nine days' time. As Quesada did not comply, he was declared to be a rebel.

Meanwhile the *residencia* charges (a form of impeachment) which Don Miguel Díez de Armendáriz was pressing against him in Santa Fé took form. There were also public demands that he appear before the Audiencia within twenty-seven days to answer charges. "On behalf of the king," announced the crier every morning in a solemn voice and to the beat of drums, "on behalf of the king do you, Gonzalo Jiménez de Quesada, answer before the royal justices." Don Gonzalo was wandering in and out of Spanish taverns. The call was repeated from corner to corner in the new-born streets of the capital of the New Kingdom. The twenty-seven days passed, and again Don Gonzalo was, by the mouth of justice, declared a rebel.

The list of charges preferred against the lawyer was a formidable one. That he took wicked measures against the Indians, committing many and cruel acts of force, robberies, and deaths, "ranching" and taking their farms and their fields, sending dogs against them and killing them, both through his own orders and those of his soldiers and captains. That he had burned many towns, and that through his cruelty those fertile and abundant lands were now depopulated. That having obtained from the Indians more than three hundred thousand gold pesos and many emeralds, he did not show them to His Majesty's officers at the time, but kept them guarded for a long while, and later took out what he wanted to keep. That when the booty was divided he took out a tenth part and the best jewels, saying they were for Don Pedro Fernández de Lugo, but keeping them for himself. That in addition to this, he took a ninth part of the booty on the ground that it belonged to him as lieutenant general. That in addition to the gold which he took from the chieftains, he carried to Castile fifty, a hundred, or a hundred and fifty pesos from each soldier, and no one ever knew what became of these. That of the gold obtained after the first division of the booty he gave none to the soldiers. That he took out three thousand pesos from the royal coffers as a loan to himself which he never repaid. That he tortured Sacresaxigua until he killed him, and took for himself the gold which that king had entrusted to him. That he sowed panic among the Indians until they fled from the Spaniards. That he gave secret instructions for the hunting of treasure, and gave nothing of what was taken in these raids to either the soldiers or the king. That he was cruel to his soldiers, and especially to Juan Gordo, whom he hanged, and to Lázaro Fonte, whom he exiled. And so forth and so on.

The judge of the *residencia* proceedings published the charges, and announced that the lawyer must answer within three days; as the lawyer did not reply, he was thereby declared to have confessed. Nor were these proceedings *in vacuo* to stay on the shelf in Santa Fé. All the hate and bitter envy which emanated from the accusations went to court, and at court men erected, with delighted attention for the most minute detail, a machine whose business it was to devour Jiménez de Quesada alive. One by one, the men who had lost went fleeing from the round table where conquistadors sat boasting of their deeds. And so Don Gonzalo fled. He fled to France, the happy, friendly, Rabelaisian France of Francis I. And while the conqueror was pounding on hard café tables demanding a glass of wine, the justices of Spain were seeking him throughout the court, for Queen Juana had ordered him to jail.

Those were days of bitterness and melancholy. Don Gonzalo, thinking he would find pleasures in France for the drowning of his sorrows, frequently found himself alone and badly treated, even though he still kept a fat purse. And as would happen more and more often from now on, he shut himself up in a tavern room and limbered his quill to write histories that no one was going to read.

❖   ❖   ❖

In France, the web of wars against Spain was being spun again. King Francis, having played the host magnificently to Charles V when the latter went to subdue the rebels of Ghent, now sharpened his sword that he might humble the Spaniard's pride. The history of these two kings is a tale of continuous watchfulness, veiled from time to time in courteous phrases. Now Francis supported the Turks, now the Italians, in attempts to ruin his powerful neighbour. With the defeat of Charles at Algiers still fresh, he now tried to undermine his power in Flanders. In the form of piracy, the war reached the coast of America. One day Robert Baal with four hundred Frenchmen appeared off Santa Marta. The city had no defence. Don Alonso de Lugo, who should have been in the plaza with his soldiers, had left for Santa Fé. The French sacked the town and burned it.

Quesada was bored in France. His very restlessness impelled him to wander from one country to another, as if he were trying to touch the interior life of Europe with his own hands. He watched the course of politics with a growing interest. In hours of boredom and annoyance he wrote. He had always had a love for letters. To deny the effectiveness of foreign metres which certain poets who loved novelty were bringing into vogue, he entered into long polemics with those who wrote verses. For Quesada, verse must be made according to the old Castilian metres,

*Those fitting and adapted to the language*
*Through being born the sons of its own womb.*

Quesada was now composing his first books. He polished and enlarged an account of his conquests, making notes, as he went along, on details of American life. Perhaps he edited his first essays on the wars in Europe and America.

For the rest, he went brilliantly dressed, but each day more solitary in spirit. He now shone not for the court, but among the people. Perhaps if men hunt some day through the archives of French jails they will find clearer traces of his life. The best way to reconstruct the lives of such men as Quesada is to lend an ear to what the prisons say. When curious men in later centuries tried to reconstruct Cervantes's life they found that the only strong threads were that scandalous affair of his daughter and the administrative duties in which the author of *Don Quixote* felt himself buried. If Shakespeare had been less honest, and involved in more legal proceedings, the men of the twentieth century would have found his life no such mystery as it is. The most definite thing about Quesada is the account of his bouts with justice. The rest—his books, his adventures— are light things that the wind picks up and forgetfulness carries away.

Well, then, not only was Jiménez de Quesada bored in France. Justice pursued him, and it became advisable for him to change his lodgings. He went to Italy.

❖     ❖     ❖

This Italy which Quesada now reached was receiving a daily horde of gay and licentious Spaniards who overflowed the streets, came to blows in the cafés, made certain changes in the life of Rome, Naples, Venice, and Genoa. They were chiefly women of the gay world who took part in the fiestas of the rich and crowded the churches. One day in Rome there was given in the house of Cardinal Arborence a performance of Juan del Encina's farce, *Plácida y Victoriano,* and the Duke of Mantua said that there were more Spanish wanderers than Italians in the salons. The courtesans spoke Spanish, and many words of Castilian origin began to make their way into popular speech. The glories of Charles V and the American conquests gave Spaniards the right to carry a certain air of superiority in the streets, and it was thanks to these mannered, flippant, and picaresque tourists that both fanfaronade and Don Juanism flourished throughout Italy. Those who found the life of Spain too oppressive, too full of convents and crusades, emigrated to the joyous cities of that other peninsula where the libertine spirit left by the Renaissance was reigning triumphant.

It was frequently the friars themselves who left Spain to amuse themselves in Italy, where they could doff their cassocks and surround themselves with complaisant women. These adventurers, who were crafty sneak thieves, robbers who cleaned out inns and stole from peasants, were held in horror. Croce, in his book on that period, shows how the word *"cappeare,"* which means to go about at night stealing the capes from poor peasants, got into common Italian speech. "The phrase 'to steal a cape at night as the Spaniards do' became proverbial." And not only the cape. "Is that a Spaniard coming toward you?" says the page to his master in the play, and the latter answers, "A Spaniard? Don't come so close! There—that's near enough." And in another passage, "God grant he is not deceiving us, and does not catch sight of this gold. Being a Spaniard and a friar, eh?"

So I say that a flood of Spaniards invaded Italy, and among them Gonzalo Jiménez de Quesada and the friar Domingo de las Casas. Domingo de las Casas came to spend the gold he had brought from America. He came to give free rein to those alms which he had, with such zeal and astuteness, inveigled from the soldiers of Castile in the New Kingdom on the plea that he would build for them that church near the Seville wharves. He became a layman with great grace, broke with the rules of his order, and was never to emerge out of the turmoil of these cities again. From this time on the chroniclers have nothing good to say of him. As a matter of fact, this was in accordance with the temper of the times. What happened with the Borjas and the Borgias was very like what happened in the Las Casas family, with Bartolomé becoming a passionate defender of the Indians in Spain and in America and Domingo a spendthrift and a pleasure-seeker.

❊       ❊       ❊

Quesada saw himself plunged into a whirlpool of passions. Yet American affairs were being listened to with growing interest. It must not be forgotten that the accounts of the voyage of Amerigo Vespucci were all published in Italian, and that they gave the world the first news of the progress of discovery—Book V of these accounts bears this dedication, *"Alberico Vesputio a Lorenzo Piero de Medici, salutem."* Books like the history of America by Hernández de Oviedo, the letters of Ferdinand Columbus, and the chronicle of the conquest of Peru by Agustín de Zárate were soon to be common throughout Italy.

Quesada gossiped in the taverns, made the girls laugh, and created more of an impression with his great moustaches and his florid beard which still carried the scent of American forests than he did with his velvet clothes. Italy could not resist the flood of gallantries which fell from Spanish lips when they set out to win the love of women, nor cry down the chivalrous ceremonies of those who adorned all this with the flowery speeches, the flattery, the "by your leave" of the peak of the Middle Ages, nor manage to laugh quite loudly enough at these swaggering soldiers and bullies who lived by flashing their swords but who were in sober reality the same men who had made the king of France their own at Pavia. Quesada had about him a bit of all of this, and it should not seem strange that Italy held him captive for several years and diverted his attention from his misadventures at court. Nor, by the same token, could he cease going over in his mind the scenes in which people lashed out against Spaniards, for whom there was very little love in all Europe. There were constant conflicts in Naples between the Neapolitans and the Spanish. At that very time "eighteen Spaniards were killed in the taverns of Chorrillo, torn to bits, and thrown from the windows into the streets; many Spanish women and old men were killed in the plaza of the Via Catalana and in the houses on that street."

Therein lies the explanation of a thick book which Quesada would be impelled to write in defence of his homeland, and which begins with gentle bitterness and a thread of melancholy in the title of the first chapter: "Whether the

ill will which many nations bear toward the Spaniard be a
matter of hatred or envy, and whether the causes they allege for it be just."

*     *     *

Thinking thus, and looking at the world through its history because he could not look it frankly in the face, Quesada grew bored with Italy. And one day he turned his
steps toward Portugal in search of other breezes. Again we
see him magnificently set up, seigniorial and elegant, pur-
suing life through the streets of Lisbon. For some days the
Andalusian in him was reborn, and flourished. He carried
the flavour of his province in his bearing as one wears a
brilliant cloak; it shone in his eyes, now hard from his military life, now luminous with the grace of his character. The
man knew how to stamp hard, and to tread softly. He was
in that maturity between forty and fifty, strong and virile
and hardly come to the middle of his life. Almost as many
years as he had spent wandering about the world still lay
in store for him. His long-suppressed pride was reborn amid
the ruins of his melancholy. He thought about America
again. This Europe, full of envy and misery, was a rotten
world. In America a man might be no worse or no better,
but at least there was still mystery there to be discovered.
The dream of El Dorado filled his mind again. There, come
what might, he could climb to the heights another time,
even though he did it as captain of mutineers, and could
live amid the savage struggle of virgin territories.

Thoughts like these raised his spirits, and his figure grew
taller in the Lisbon streets, so that merely in looking at
him the Lusitanians grew restless. He could not pass
through the city unnoted, even though he were the least

famous of caballeros, as he could not pass unnoted in Santa Marta when a company of soldiers devoured by hunger sought in him the man who should lead them to the top of the Andes.

> And they arrested him one day in Lisbon,
> Finding him with clothes that were embroidered
> (For there it seems that they are not permitted).
> And on the day they took him out of prison
> The jailer's wife requested that he give her
> A certain sum that was her jailer's fee,
> And he at once gave her a hundred ducats
> So she with such a generous fee in hand
> Swore nevermore to follow that profession
> Nor ever be another's jailer there.

❊   ❊   ❊

So Quesada went to Spain. And then a knight came into the world who was to be immortal—Don Alonso Quesada, the Quixote of La Mancha.

# IX. The Return

The Indies, shelter and refuge for Spain's despairing, shrine of the mutineer, asylum for the murderer, chips and a green cloth for the gambler, enticement for unattached women. . . .

—CERVANTES

Miguel de Cervantes Saavedra . . . humbly implores that Your Majesty will have the goodness to grant him a post in the Indies out of three or four which are at present vacant, one of these being the auditorship of the New Kingdom of Granada, or the governorship of the province of Soconusco in Guatemala, or the post of paymaster of the galleys at Cartagena, or of Corregidor of the city of La Paz . . . for his desire is to continue ever in the service of Your Majesty, and there to end his days as did his ancestors before him. . . .

—CERVANTES

# THE RETURN

QUESADA had eight or nine years of wandering through this wicked European world before the charges against him began to fade out and he was able to return to his own country. He entered Cordova like a man whose life has been pardoned. His uncle Jerónimo de Soria offered him an exceptional post as head of the House of St. Lazarus. Gonzalo's pockets were empty, but still it is more than a little sad that the man who had been the first to reach the heights of the Chibcha empire, and who had added so immense a territory to the empire of Charles V, should now have come to the point where he was candidate for the directorship of a lepers' hospital by virtue of the fact that his uncle was relinquishing it in his favour.

In order to understand Jiménez de Quesada's position in Spain after the conquest of the New Kingdom, and to measure the misery it inflicted on him, one must remember two things. When he arrived from America it was to meet the fury of the lawyers, the mounting pile of paper charges in the Council of the Indies, the cry of Cobos from the windows of the palace, "Throw that lunatic out of the plaza!" the jail sentence, the fines which the ministers imposed upon him—or, to sum it up in a few words, it was to meet this declaration which that same Cobos, the king's prosecutor, made against him: "I, Licentiate Francisco de los

Cobos, your prosecutor, state that Licentiate Gonzalo
Jiménez, Lieutenant Governor who was in the New Kingdom of Granada, and Hernán Pérez de Quesada, brother
of the aforesaid Counsellor Jiménez, during the time they
were in the said governorship, did and committed many
and grave crimes to the disservice of God and Your Majesty, and injuries to the natives of that territory, committing thefts, burnings, acts of force, death, and other injuries in order to rob them of their property. I ask and
implore that Your Majesty order the most severe penalties
imposed upon the said Counsellor Jiménez and Hernán
Pérez de Quesada, which by their aforesaid crimes they
have incurred; and that these be imposed upon each of
them, their goods and persons alike, that it may be an example to them and to others, and I swear to God in due
form that I neither state nor ask the aforesaid maliciously."
This was the first thing that greeted Quesada when he returned triumphant from America. The other was his uncle's offer of the post in the lepers' home, made when he
came back from exile.

But these were the hardships of his trade, and now at
least he would gain the king's ear, and for the first time in
nine years, for the doors of the court were to open to him
by way of the humble doors of a hospital. For the first time
he was going to tell the king about America, and to ask
him for a title. No longer would he waste time thinking
about a Europe that depressed him. Like those old men who
begin to remember their past lives with a precision of detail and a flood of incident, Quesada, who was now fifty,
painted for his king the life of America and pointed out
the principles which he thought necessary for good government there. I refer to an admirable work, full of op-

portune observations and Christian feeling, having none of the passionate polemic of a Bartolomé de las Casas, but done with the quiet skill and steady judgment of a man who can measure the worth of human deeds and who knows how to appraise the condition of the Indians. Life's eloquent lessons gave his words depth and dignity. The swaggerer who fell in and out of Lisbon jails, the conquistador of the round table who flung an apronful of ducats when Pizarro's tip was but a single castellano, had become an austere and simple man whose eyes sparkled with contained enthusiasm and suppressed joy at the hope of returning to the Indies. To the forest, the hunger, the gold, the adventure, the freedom of the New World.

  ✿   ✿   ✿

Of all that Quesada wrote, only two works were to reach posterity complete—his defence of Charles and his notes on the proper governing of New Granada. This last is the most nearly perfect that emerged from his pen. It is a compendium of all his experiences in governing, his political reflections, his circumspect study of reality. It is one of those sixteenth-century documents in which the reader will always find an even-tempered flow of Christian charity, a very rare thing in the flood of Catholic literature which burst from the depths of the conquest. No excessive demonstrations here, no show of dogmatic reasoning, but a simple explanation of life as it was lived in America and wise advice on behalf of the Crown's work as a civilizing influence. For writing these instructions for good government, Quesada had his own experience of conquest and voyages, the memory of his own cruelties, of the teeth of justice snapping at his heels, of the European panorama which he

had seen with his own eyes, of the history of Charles V and
of the courts of France and Italy which his investigating
eyes had surveyed. He had neither shut himself up within
the Spanish microcosm, nor let himself be deceived by life
in the rest of Europe, nor lost from sight the reality of life
in America. As of that time and place, his work has exceptional value. His counsels had two facets: on the one hand
he was, as will be said later, a statesman, that is, a man
who enters deep into complex matters of politics and eco-
nomics; on the other hand he was a good Christian. How
much do the counsels in this document remind one of those
which Don Quixote was later to give Sancho Panza for the
governing of his island!

His suggestions begin with an assumed humility—that
he was speaking primarily as one of the people and only
secondarily as chief captain and conquistador of the New
Kingdom. As one of the people, he had seen how likely
were injustices to be committed in America, how justice
was prone to be laughed at, the Indians to be exploited until they died and the land was left unpeopled.

In accordance with the usual order in these documents,
the first thing he asked in his suggestions for good government was that there should be a properly established
church in Santa Fé de Bogotá, that it be raised to a bishopric, and that the bishops should always reside in the New
Kingdom. That there be regular religious orders there, so
as to ensure the performance of apostolic labours with the
more zeal. For though there are priests in Santa Fé, there
are not enough for the conversion of the Indians, "the more
so in that they do not bother with this, nor care about it, as
though they had gone there to get rich and for no other

thing." As long as there are no better friars, the Indians "will be left unconverted to our Christian religion only because there are no men to instruct them with spirit and fervour."

Quesada then asked that the distribution of towns be confirmed, according to the boundaries he named. That grants of Indians be made fixed and permanent, as was done in Mexico and Guatemala, in order to fix what we might call the first property map of the New Kingdom. And that an exact tax-list be compiled showing how much tribute each chief was to pay, and taxing them with moderation. The Spaniards were levying tribute in bulk, without any order to it, and thus sowing terror and confusion among the Indians. It was necessary to take measures against this and against another custom of the Spaniards, which was to have no fixed day for collecting tribute, with the result that many Indians paid two or three times. Often they, "thinking that gold was going to be demanded of them again, rose up with their wives and children and went to the mountains and left the towns empty and lost."

Quesada maintained that the Indians knew more about working the emerald mines than the Spaniards did. If the traditional methods of hunting stones were abandoned, there would be an end of the mines; they would be left destroyed and forgotten, and men who had always lived by trafficking in these stones would abandon that region. The coming of new arrivals into this business had been slow and inept. In order to set aside the king's fifth, the royal officers took one stone out of every five, and many times that one was worth more than the other four put together. The lawyer proposed that the stones be put up at auction, and that the fifth be taken in the form of that due proportion of what the sale produced.

At the same time Quesada defended the Spanish entrepreneurs who were beginning to exploit gold mines or to take out cinnamon of the kinds his brother Hernán Pérez de Quesada had discovered. He thought that in principle the Crown ought not to claim a fifth of all products but a tenth, as was done in other parts. That the men who gathered cinnamon should not be required to come back through the ports of the New Kingdom, for the purpose of dividing it into fifths (or whatever proportion was agreed on as the king's share), for cinnamon came from a remote and deserted province which could more easily communicate with Spain through other ports, and it was absurd to regard as cheats or smugglers those who had to take the natural routes of the country in order to get their loads out.

But Quesada expressed himself with the most fullness and precision when he talked about the maltreatment accorded the Indians. Later he himself, with the Indians assigned to him, would give a living example of how they should be freed from excessive tributes and would become their defender in the New Kingdom. In the ten years since the founding of the colony, there had been terrible iniquities. He said it himself: "In the New Kingdom there was much mistreatment by the conquerors and other Spanish settlers, deaths, thefts, and cutting off of limbs, to such an extent that it is terrible to tell of it, and all for the purpose of forcing the Indians to give up gold and precious stones, and therefore many towns have been emptied of their inhabitants and a great number of Indians are dead." The governors and the justices did nothing to stop this wave of cruelty. They were afraid of the conquerors, and many times they were themselves responsible for deaths and robberies and many other kinds of crime.

*　　*　　*

Then he talked about the governors. When the governors knew that an inspector was coming or heard a rumour that one was coming, they hastened to name ordinary alcaldes who were their accomplices, and they anticipated justice by causing charges to be laid before the alcaldes and agreeing on a punishment. When the inspector arrived, the governor would go smiling to meet him, saying, "If anything happened here, it has already been taken care of."

Quesada not only condemned all this, but proposed a measure which, while strange, should not be thought unreasonable. He would forbid Spaniards to visit Indian towns which were not under their charge. The fact was that these Spaniards installed themselves in the towns on some pretext, such as going to the markets, and made the Indians feed them and serve them without limit. Quesada said, "If these Spaniards must go to the towns, let them go accompanied by a constable or a justice to watch them."

But the Spaniard had invented a whole system of multiplying his profits which extended into the subtlest details of life. He shortened the calendar so as to levy tribute three times in every year. He altered weights so as to get almost five pounds for every one the scales showed. Those who had land grants near the Magdalena hired Indians as beasts of burden to bring cargoes up through the mountain ridges of the Opón. For each of these bits of cunning Quesada pointed out the remedy he thought just, and he denounced still other things which shocked his Christian spirit, as, for instance, "The Spaniards never go to the New Kingdom without its costing a great number of Indians who die in the mountains of the Opón, for, as they come from a different region, in this other hot country they fall sick and die, especially when they are loaded down with cargo." The king ought to forbid this, even though the Indians say they do it of their own free will, "for Your Majesty knows what manner of free will the Indians have, and how the Spaniards make them say this by a thousand methods and inducements."

One of the things that most exercised Quesada was the problem of dogs. They were an important part of the conquest, and the verb *"aperrear"* (to loose the dogs) became a word in common speech, a word that sent cold chills up the back. The Spaniards loosed their packs against savage Indians and the dogs tore them to shreds. The dog was a terror to all the natives, but as the colony became settled, the Indians too began to keep dogs. There was already a pair on every ranch, and no town which did not number five hundred to a thousand of them. Quesada thought that a day would come when the Indians might rise up and use these animals as a living weapon against the Spaniards. So he proposed that the king order that no Indian have a dog, except the chief, and that "he might have one or two only, and only males and no females, so there should be no offspring."

In another paragraph Quesada set down certain arguments in favour of Spaniards' marrying, a paragraph which time would turn against him. He noted how the provisions of the king in favour of this basic way of populating the Indies were mocked at and defeated by a thousand subterfuges. In the New Kingdom, he says, "where there are in my belief three hundred land grants, there are not a dozen married men." It is therefore necessary that those who do not marry lose their grants, and that no excuses or extensions be allowed.

Then Quesada went into a thousand things in which the Spaniards contravened justice. In the tariffs, which they arranged as they chose. In the councilmen whom the governors named for the town halls, treating all this as though it were the greatest joke in the world. In the chancelleries, where they spent in litigation three times what the deal was worth. In the danger that the Royal Audiencia would interfere in things which were not within the scope of its competency. In the annoyance which resulted from dividing Indian towns when land grants were made. In the arbitrary acts which were committed because those who were at the head of public administration did not visit the towns.

And at the end the lawyer made two suggestions—that on naming ordinary alcaldes there should be no interference with their election on the part of "any of Your Majesty's officers or any titled or otherwise powerful person or anyone who holds any office of justice"; and, second, that the royal writs be kept in a safe with three keys, because anything could be lost or mislaid at the pleasure or convenience of interested parties.

*   *   *

Let us now put aside this political compendium and return to Santa Fé de Bogotá.

Santa Fé was beginning to take shape. The main plaza had its own type of straw house. Down the small streets leading off from the crossings the pigs, chickens, friars, Indians, and Spaniards moved lazily along. The backstairs gossip conveyed a certain human sense of the city, a feeling of social life. The carpenters began to build chests, wardrobes, beds—household furniture which would some day be receiving clean starched linen in peaceful homes. One walked across fresh grass, between white walls, under the eaves of grey roofs. Green, white, grey—all of them town colours, wrapped in the quiet atmosphere of the high plains. In the plaza, in front of the principal church which was made also of straw, lay the cemetery. Two limpid rivers wrapped the settlement in a crystal embrace.

In the afternoons, groups of the curious formed to listen to the fantastic accounts of a man at once gracious and reserved, suave and hard, and recently come from Europe. He was the post in human form, bringing news of old comrades; he told the tale of Naples and of Rome to those who once had made war in Italy. He talked of Charles V and of his extraordinary deeds, his entry into Ghent, his defeat in Africa. The Spaniards listened to him with respect. The Indians looked at him dully, hardly understanding what he said. He was Don Gonzalo Jiménez de Quesada, marshal of the New Kingdom, come to retrace his former steps and to see his friends.

Marshal Quesada! After so many years of lawsuits, of gay parties, of silent nights, of meditating on the grandeurs and miseries of power, he had won no great titles, no honour and recompense like those accorded Cortés or Pizarro, not even a governorship as had Belalcázar, but only the title of marshal.

> Since fish of greater weight he could not catch,
> He had to be content with what he marshalled. . . .

Others around him rose high, and with better fortune,

but fate was to leave them lean in their turn. Town life in
Santa Fé grew like the breath of rumour, and the marshal
followed it with eyes that were quiet and serene. His fifty
years, which no one celebrated, had given him a vigorous
body and put into his soul a certain grandeur which he had
learned to temper and to sun in the clear light of optimism.
Certainly he was one of the people. Perhaps one whom bad
luck had pushed to the edge of ridicule. The chroniclers
made jokes about his title, the marshal. They called him
knave and fool. But when the colony was confronted with
an uprising, all eyes turned naturally toward the "fool"
to ask his counsel and implore the aid of his strong right
arm. And if the "fool" should sound the trumpet for new
conquests, the soldiers would range behind him, bewitched
by the magic call of the conquistador. If you want an account of the way the chroniclers muttered about him, read
these verses by Father Castellanos:

> *Another also came on this occasion*
> *To that kingdom which he himself discovered*
> *And which with all his captains he had conquered:*
> *Don Gonzalo Jiménez de Quesada,*
> *More of whose fleece was cropped than left to grow,*
> *For what with games and quarrelling and women,*
> *Inventions, liveries, lies, and empty pomp*
> *And a licentious prodigality,*
> *He had run through the great sum of that money*
> *Which in those provinces he had acquired.*

\* \* \*

How different was this Santa Fé of 1550 from that which
Quesada had left when it had only the dozen huts of the

first settlers and when the only faces to be seen were those of the energetic and greedy captains of the conquest. Now men of letters were beginning to arrive, and the first stones to be laid where the building for the Royal Audiencia would rise. They were about to make the first clay tiles. Sheep and goats began to appear in the fields. But the most extraordinary sight was the Spanish women. They came with Lebrón, Alonso Luis de Lugo, and Doctor Miguel Díez de Armendáriz. In the list of those whom Díez de Armendáriz brought to the New Kingdom, we read "a barber, a surgeon, a blacksmith, two tailors, a hosier, tile-makers, scribes, two carpenters, six Negroes, three married men with their wives, and two widows to be married, each with daughters." He came "as heavily laden with men as with women," says Bishop Piedrahita, "though much discredit followed Miguel Díez on account of so many women, which continued until the end of his governorship. . . ."

Quesada's old friends had scattered. Almost all of them lived with Indian women on land grants. In those ten years, and perhaps because of the cold of those uplands, the hot energy of virile spirits had cooled and the men of the conquest had become a lazy colony. This was the colony where Eloísa Romero made wheat bread, where she prayed in the roadside chapel, and the first heads of grain began to yield.

Among those who had disappeared were Quesada's two brothers. Alonso de Lugo had clapped a judgment on both of them, more because he wished to have no rivals by his side than for any other reason. Of Hernán, Don Alonso said, "Not room for two cocks in a single henhouse." And therefore one day, well tied with judicial red tape, Lugo and the Quesadas went down the Magdalena. Díez de Armendáriz was just reaching Cartagena in his role as royal inspector. The Quesadas thought they might get justice from him. They set out for Cartagena in a small boat. They were all ready to weigh anchor when a storm arose. The Quesadas were on deck, playing cards with Captain Suárez and Bishop Calatayud. Suddenly a bolt of lightning struck. The Quesadas were both hit. Suárez had an arm crippled and the bishop a leg.

Of the death of Hernán Pérez, Ocariz says, "The bolt burned his hair and beard and all the hair on his body, for he was very shaggy; and it burned all his clothing and he was left naked, and part of his clothing was left in bits no bigger than grains of salt, all burned, and likewise his entire body, apparently without a blow, and black as a Negro's."

Thus in one fashion or another all the men of these conquests vanished from the stage, while Quesada, from a corner of the colony, watched the years go by without receiving any signal from death that it was time to bow his head. All the misery and the grandeur of the conquest had passed before his eyes; now all the grandeur and the misery of the colony were passing in front of him. Anyone who could succeed in penetrating the mind of the old conqueror would gain a most ample picture of the first half of the sixteenth century. The men who contended with him in Spain for glory became only a thin line of shadows. The hounds of justice followed them to the very tomb, not like peaceful old dogs moving in their masters' footsteps, but barking and furious, loosed against them as they once loosed hunting dogs against the Indians.

Sebastián de Belalcázar, accused of having unjustly killed Marshal Jorge Robledo, was condemned to death by the Audiencia. Belalcázar appealed to the court, was granted a rehearing, and left on his way to the peninsula just as Quesada arrived in Santa Fé. When he reached Cartagena he sickened and died. A friend of the conqueror, who was his executor, bought four yards of Rouen cloth for a peso and two reales, and had a shroud made for him. A woman charged a peso for cutting the shroud and preparing the body decently. Twenty pesos were paid to the church for the funeral. Thus for twenty-two pesos and two reales, and without further ceremony, they dispatched from this world one of those who had had his hands in Atahuallpa's treasure, the man who was Quesada's competitor in Santa Fé and who founded many cities which were to grow famous with the passing of the centuries.

Another was Don Alonso de Lugo, the robber son. He too went to the capital to answer the accusations that were raining on his head. There Quesada had seen him on the road to disgrace. And now it became known that he, virtually in exile, fighting with the king's troops in Mallorca, Milan, France, had died like any miserable soldier while Quesada was tightening his hold on this second chance which life had given him in the New Kingdom.

*    *    *

A colony's first days are never very peaceful. There is no lack of scandals, assassinations, thefts, excesses of all kinds. We are not exactly in a fool's paradise or a fool's court. But Santa Fé did not suffer from that wave of turbulence which, down in the lowlands and in Peru, stirred up serious trouble among the Spaniards themselves. La Gasca and the Pizarros fought in Peru, and Belalcázar hanged Jorge Robledo; down in Santa Marta French pirates seized the town; but the uplands had only individual

cases which justice handled as best it could. The new laws
of the Indies were proclaimed, and a great outcry followed.
No one was in favour of protecting the Indians. Díez de
Armendáriz told the king that this Terra Firma had caught
the contagion from Peru and that, seeing himself abandoned
by everyone in his desire to put the laws into effect, he had
decided to suspend them for two years. And that if the
king did not find this measure to his liking, he would have
no other recourse than to end his days of service to His
Majesty. . . . All of which did not prevent Díez from in-
forming the king that the laws were justified in that the
Indians of Hontibón, Guatavita, Bogotá, and Sogamoso had
been forced to work their eight months' stretch in the mines
or be put in prison, set upon by dogs, and punished in
other ways too ugly and immoral to be written down.

About the priests let us say nothing. They were the first
to rebel against the new laws. If, they said, you take from
us the means we have been employing for our support, we
will abandon the churches. Díez de Armendáriz, terrified,
left things as they were. But the priests went on asking for
more. Those who earned fifty thousand maravedis said that
if they were not given one hundred thousand, others must
be found to carry on their parishes. The rise in salaries was
approved, and the sacristans were then raised to fifty thousand maravedis. The worst of it was that religion did not
advance. One day they made the experiment of examining
a group of Indians to see if they knew the Ave Maria, and
not one could say it. Lawyer Góngora, who arrived during
those years, wrote the king saying that in suppressing Indian idols and sacrifices the churchmen did less than was
ordered. "Their prelates are occupied more with other
things than with doctrinal matters. The custodian of the

Franciscans was an old man and sick, and he resigned in favour of a restless priest who was deaf from birth. The Dominicans and Franciscans have ordered other priests to be brought; it would be better if they were men of forty years or more." Some time later, Doctor Venero de Leyva would be forced to insist on this same theme, telling His Majesty that he should put some order into the clergy, who come and go with a great deal of money, but without saving any of it, "for they spend it in raising dogs and fine horses."

At the bottom of all this disorder the malicious author of *El Carnero* always found some question of women. He took it upon himself to tell posterity all the tales of a city newly born. Why the judges fought among themselves, why the captains kept a jealous watch over their wives and daughters, why the friars lived in a state of perversion. It was remarkable that so few women could stir up such a scandal in the town. Jiménez de Quesada had reason for asking that all Spaniards come married. *El Carnero* has very curious notes on the trouble Antón de Olalla—Quesada's old friend who was with him through all the conquest campaign—had with the judges. There had been installed in Santa Fé a girl of the type that, as they say, can always start a war. A judge and a friar were in love with her. The two met in the woman's house one night. The wrath of the judge could hardly be contained, and on the following day he had the Audiencia exile the friar. The friar was an intimate friend of Antón de Olalla, and Olalla quarrelled with the Audiencia. When the judges left for Spain, Olalla went with them, but not in the same boat for fear they would kill him on the voyage. That was the tone colonial life was taking.

In a letter to the king, President Díez de Armendáriz

announced that for Lent he had taken much care to find
out about the married Spaniards and to make sure they
went to live with their wives. This moral gesture was new
in him. It had not been that way in Cartagena. For the rest,
this struggle for morality was to last three centuries, more
or less.

❖ ❖ ❖

The great conqueror who had dominated the almost
fabulous stage whereon the discovery of the New Kingdom
had developed was now reduced to being a mere spectator
of a simple and picaresque life. It was the greatest contrast
that could be obtained in a single lifetime. Díez de Armendáriz, formerly fierce and ardent, was now a royal inspector,
a gentleman playing the leading role in this comedy of man-
ners. This was the period of the Negress Juana García, the
first witch whom the bishop condemned one day to be
burned as an impostor and a procuress. Jiménez de Quesada
intervened, and the bishop contented himself with exhibit-
ing her on a platform at the hour of High Mass with a halter
around her neck and a lighted candle in her hand. The
Negress, who knew all that went on inside Santa Fé, did
nothing but moan and mutter, "We all did it, all of us, but
I alone pay."

Díez de Armendáriz bought an adobe house which was
being thatched with straw, so that he might live as be-
fitted the foremost authority of the nascent republic. He
was to be censured for this purchase later, and forced to
cancel the deal. The poor man began to be heaped with op-
probrium and complaints. Envious rivals sprang up about
him like weeds and the dirty waters with which they
drenched his good name did not fail to reach Spain through

the postal waterways. He wrote his uncle Luis to defend him before the court because he knew that Governor Heredia was accusing him of many ugly things unworthy of a Guinea Negro. Lugo, too, accused Díez de Armendáriz of having made away with seventy thousand castellanos. At this new affront, Díez wrote the king, kissing his feet, and asking that he send someone to come and impeach him for his so-called "wicked life," as though he were a highway robber.

Meanwhile as inspector he did only the good which occurred to him. The Indians of Hontibón, Guasca, and Sogamoso, who had risen up to protest against bad treatment, he brought under the king's easy yoke. When the chief came on a visit of peace, he dressed him in Spanish costume—shirt, shoes, and the rest—and even a coat of scarlet satin. While Díez was putting these gifts upon him, the Indian, uncomprehending, laughed. And Armendáriz laughed too in as kindly a fashion as if he were not the same man who, a short time before, in Mompóx perhaps, because Juan Rodríguez did not want to give him a horse had had him dragged from the temple and garrotted until he died. But here in Santa Fé, even wild beasts turn into domesticated animals, into barnyard fowls. It is, I repeat, the cold.

\*     \*     \*

If this were all there was to the Santa Fé colony, it might well go down to posterity as an agreeable gathering of gossips which the marshal would watch from his observatory with the same interest that the comedies of Lope de Vega or La Celestina might have aroused when he had the chance to see them in Italy. But no. That Don Miguel Díez, moreover, had another side. It was with much reason that Bishop Piedrahita said that coming with women did him much harm. Díez was one of those highly sensual gentlemen who had come to America to enjoy the pleasures of the flesh without restraint. Never in Cartagena did he bother himself with the king's instructions that married men be brought together. From the time he entered the kingdom, he behaved like the gallant in a musical comedy. He dressed in purple silk, with a short close-fitting jacket and a longer one over it, and he went through the streets of the port on horseback with great display. He raced across the flatlands amid the jingle of bells, said his enemies. And, they added, at night he went forth disguised, many times in a white blouse and wide breeches, with bare legs.

They said that the neighbours took their wives with them on their night watch, for they feared that if they left them alone in the house the lawyer would pay them a visit. They said he carried on love affairs with Doña Ana, the wife of Sebastián de Heredia, and with La Pimentela, and with Lucía de Alvarez, and with La Sotomayor de Alcocer, who belonged not only to Alcocer but also at times to Pedro de Orsúa. And he laid hands on Catalina López when she went to beg freedom for her husband, the carpenter Jerónimo. And the wife of Alonso de Olmos, a half-breed, had to let herself down by a rope from the window of Armendáriz's house, and fell to the street half dead. Once, says a certain illustrious historian, Juan Escalante did not want to go on watch; the lawyer had him seized and ordered him to walk guard through the whole town. He then took advantage of this opportunity to enter the house, where Escalante found him, and stuck a knife into his wife in punishment. The chronicler adds, "Out of respect for history I will not reproduce other details of the scandals created by Armendáriz."

But the wave of loose living did not end here. In the accusation against Armendáriz it was alleged that he robbed Christians as well as Indians, that he sold justice, that he trafficked in merchandise stolen from the ships. In an account by Restrepo Tirado, that erudite historian says, "The pen would blush to transcribe the scandals which occurred in Cartagena daily, and the list of those of high position in the clergy and in public posts who kept concubines."

Also the cruelties committed against the Indians increased. Baltazar de Párraga, the adelantado's lieutenant in Tolú, had forty of these unfortunates put into a hut, and "had their hands, arms, and noses cut off; and the Indians were knifed, and set upon by dogs, and the dogs ate them." This is the atmosphere of a colony in its early days. A suit against Gómez Carvajal accused him of having taken the free and Christian Indian woman Luisa to a rocky knoll and having lashed her to a tree and given her so many blows that her body was flayed and made all bloody, and had beaten her many other times at home because she did not pay him as she had promised for a machete, and had burned her belly with oil and fire. Of this same *en-comendero* it was said that he killed the Indian Juanillo with a single blow, that he lashed and beat another to death, that he loosed the dogs on many others, and burned them with oil. These folk were hard and cruel as the soul of the Middle Ages. So hard and so cruel that saying so is enough, and better not to insist on these dramas.

Bit by bit the cold of the high uplands, the frozen wind from the south that numbs the people of Santa Fé, and those dawns when the frost whitens the pastures and makes men shiver, tempered the Spanish spirit. At times Miguel Díez de Armendáriz seemed but a simple fool. His adventures were carried on in secret. A night lit by the frozen light of a round and simple moon does not invite one to go forth masked for adventure as do the warm airs of Cartagena. When Armendáriz left Santa Fé, everyone mourned his departure: that, they said, was indeed a good man.

&ast; &ast; &ast;

But the colony kept growing. The sound of hammer on anvil began ringing in Santa Fé at daybreak. For the first time the song of iron fell on the ears of the Andes. Clang, clang, clang . . . the iron's cry rang out from the blacksmith shop without let or respite.

The sparks fly up like musical stars to adorn a sky as blue and diaphanous as the banner of the Pure and Holy Virgin. The Indians stand in line, blowing the enormous flame. The bars, growing white hot, seem strips of taffy. The horses tied to the hitching posts stamp and whinny. Why so much work in the blacksmith shop? What new emprises make blacksmith and helpers sweat?

It was, alas, the affairs of justice. It was Counsellor Montaño who ordered fetters forged and prison bars. For weeks they did nothing but forge link after link of a great chain metres long which was to be the pride of the prison. Santa Fé must recognize that they had entered on a new phase of colonizing activity. Jiménez de Quesada watched, though always from a secondary plane, the movements of Montaño, who now was sending people to the gallows for trivial causes and having whipped at street corners men who had been discoverers and conquerors of the kingdom. When

Montaño crossed the plaza with his train of slaves, everyone fell silent, which exasperated him the more. In vain his wife made suggestions which were meant to be to his interest. No—Montaño desired that no one should disregard the tone of his rule.

Cruelty to the Indians increased. The Spaniards beat them, kicked them on any pretext, and robbed them when they brought their poor merchandise in to trade, "paying the miserable beings in the coin of blows, if they tried to charge any other," pretending that whatever was taken from them was for Montaño's house.

Everybody trembled. If the bishop managed to preach moral sermons at all, it was to empty air. Conflicts arose between the bishop and the Audiencia. One day a certain priest arrived from Peru whom the Audiencia at Lima claimed on the charge that a criminal judgment stood against him. The priest took refuge in his right to ecclesiastical asylum. The Audiencia set aside legal formula and seized the priest. The bishop was indignant, he protested, they did not listen to him, and he resolved to leave the diocese. There was a wave of terror in Santa Fé, for if the bishop went away, they would all be left without that symbol of protection. The Audiencia itself was disturbed, and the judges rode out several leagues to implore His Reverence to return. They kneeled to kiss his ring and ask his pardon. The bishop acceded to their request, but signified that, as penitence, they should return to Santa Fé on foot, and he went back to look after his flock.

But this did not mean that things would be much changed. The judges did not dare cross Montaño. Briceño, worst of all, trembled like a whipped pup whenever Montaño raised his voice, and humbly signed whatever he asked.

Men in the streets insulted Briceño and called him op-
probrious names; the name by which he would go down
in history was "Montaño's mistress."

There was only one person who dared defend those
whom Montaño in his madness attacked. That was Jiménez
de Quesada. Again the conquistador became the town's advocate. Again his quill was exercised in drawing up long
documents in defence of conquerors and Indians. In all the
town there was only this one strong voice to ask justice,
though without swerving from the plain path of law. Montaño watched him with growing jealousy, but there was in
that captain who had won these lands for the king a certain
grandeur which intimidated him. Defeated in the depths
of his soul, he tried to belittle the marshal's importance. As
a rule Quesada's defences went unheard by the Audiencia.
There was always some good Spaniard, some poor Indian
who moved slowly about the jail, making Montaño's chains,
Montaño's fetters, Montaño's bars ring. It was sad that the
voice of iron in Santa Fé should come only from the harsh
throat of the prison.

❈ ❈ ❈

From the depths of the hot country there reached Santa
Fé the shouts of certain mutinous captains, who were filling the kingdom with their sinister voices. As we already
know, the colony had, in addition to its other functions,
to serve as stage for the bandits whom Spain had thrown
out on the high tide of conquest. One day twenty-five Spaniards left Santa Fé bound on adventure. Two years later
they came back like savages, quite naked. Díez de Armendáriz wrote the king, "There are many vagrants whose sole
ambition is to have three or four Indian servants and go

from ranch to ranch stealing whatever they can find. I have told them to seek a job and an employer or I will throw them out of the country. Some have fled, and others have gone to the mountains to become highway robbers. I had one given three hundred lashes, but I did not have him hanged because he had taken nothing from Your Majesty's treasury, but only from private persons."

But now something more serious arose. It was announced that a Sevillian, Alvaro de Oyón, had headed an uprising on the banks of the Cauca, had knifed the alcaldes and others who had attempted resistance, and with sixty bandits was subduing towns. Even one of Quesada's nephews had died under the weapons of Don Alvaro. The Audiencia received this news with terror. Everybody enlisted to go in pursuit of the rebel. Montaño summoned to a council of war all the captains except one—Marshal Jiménez de Quesada. His exclusion was so absurd that even poor Judge Briceño ended by voting for Quesada and putting an army corps under his leadership. But Montaño had his way again: Briceño wavered, and it was arranged that Montaño should go at the head of the troops. The expedition left, though it was unimportant, for Don Alvaro had already been caught and hanged from the gallows which his treason against the king had prepared for him.

* * *

But it was clear that, if Santa Fé had one figure of moral value, even in the humiliating position to which he was relegated, it was Quesada. Montaño had put the former inspector Díez de Armendáriz in jail. He had made him come from Cartagena to answer charges that had piled up against him. After Armendáriz had been in prison several months,

Montaño decided to continue the case in Cartagena. The
day came when Armendáriz had to leave the Santa Fé jail
in order to go back to the prison in Cartagena. Although
Armendáriz had been accused of robbery and extortion,
he had not one centavo. The jailers charged him for the
food they had given him. He had nothing to pay them with
and said so. The clerk advanced and with plebeian hand
plucked from Armendáriz's shoulders the great-coat he
wore, leaving the former governor of the kingdom in his
shirtsleeves. Seeing this, Captain Lanchero felt indignation
rise within him. Lanchero was never a friend of Armendáriz's and had even suffered from his persecutions, but the
clerk's act and Montaño's unnecessary cruelty moved him.
And taking off his own coat of fine scarlet, he placed it over
Armendáriz's shoulders. The old governor turned to see
who had given him this unexpected gift, and Lanchero
asked, "But, sir, are there none of those favoured in former
times who would assist Your Grace now?" And Armendáriz, melancholy, answered, "No, Señor Lanchero, for during the time I was making friends I chose the worst."

Could Montaño continue to act that way as long as Marshal Jiménez de Quesada was there to watch him with wide
and tranquil eyes? In all his violence, his imperiousness,
his cowardice, something kept tormenting Montaño. It
was Jiménez de Quesada. A man, nothing more: one of the
townsmen, who sometimes sent a pen scratching across
paper and sometimes was silent. One day Montaño decided
to send him into exile. "Without any other crime," says the
chronicler, "than that of befriending the conquerors in the
lawsuits that dogged their every step." Quesada was ordered to leave Santa Fé and not show himself within a ra-
dius of six leagues. The marshal said nothing, and left. But

his absence was harder for Montaño than had been the marshal's presence. If he could kill him, if only he could wipe out that accursed shadow . . . But it was useless, for the more shadowy grew Quesada's silhouette, the deeper the shade it cast on Montaño; it pursued him the more insistently when it was not present.

The decree of exile did not stand. Quesada began to be stronger outside of Santa Fé than he had been inside. His friends made him come back. Montaño did not enforce his order. Santa Fé was already conspiring against him. A flood of petitions reached Briceño, asking that Montaño be jailed and that his impeachment follow. Briceño trembled like a frightened woman and tried to resist. He knew he could not withstand the tyrant's hard voice. At last they made such a fuss that he said he would act if he should receive a paper signed by the bishop, the prosecutor Maldonado, and Jiménez de Quesada. The conspirators turned at once to them.

The bishop and Maldonado agreed immediately. They said the patience of the kingdom had reached an end. If lack of jurisdiction should give the boldest subject pause, they added, it was also true that the extreme need for the remedy should of itself convert him into a legislator against the tyrant. The amount of law and theology which the lawyer and the bishop handled with such art and skill was designed to make legal the imprisonment which they so greatly desired. But the truth is that it would not have been legal. Quesada knew it, and thought that the tyrant would eventually be mired in the mud of his own misdeeds. Quesada knew the art of waiting; he was in no hurry, and he had more faith than the others. When they asked him for his opinion, he gave it with cutting frankness:

"I cannot accept this plan. We ought to let heads be sacrificed to the knife rather than raise a hand in resistance. Though Montaño cut off all the heads in the kingdom, and mine the first, and though in the course of such misfortune everything be lost, I will never assent to the seizure of a judge of the high court without express order from the king."

Speaking from the obscure point of view of one of the townspeople, as a soldier in the ranks, Quesada was showing himself to be as jealous of authority as he had been when he was captain of the conquest and held the soldiers in check with the hard law of his sword. There was a great difference between this self-contained marshal who saw the kingdom he had won being sullied by other hands and the Pizarro gang that knew no law other than their own greed, or the figure of Belalcázar who left Robledo dangling in the disgraceful noose.

# X. *Adventures of Don Quixote in America*

Then Don Quixote gave orders to gather moneys together, and by selling one thing and pawning another, and getting poor prices for all of them, a reasonable amount was secured. He himself adjusted a round buckler which he had begged a friend to lend him, and, mending his broken helmet as best he could, advised his squire Sancho of the day and hour he thought to set forth, so that he might make ready all he saw necessary for them; above all he charged him to carry saddle bags.

—CERVANTES

# ADVENTURES OF DON QUIXOTE
## IN AMERICA

THE Quesada family had always been like that. I have already told in the proper place how in times past the Princess Palomela had two blue doves on her shield as an emblem. But as time went on, the doves became ambitious, perhaps through dipping their beaks in Moorish blood. Or perhaps because the village of Quesada, which changed the family name, turned the heads of these ingenuous men and set them on the road to madness. Or, better still, because the accursed sixteenth century infected them with its spirit, made them dream of unknown lands, of fabulous governorships, of fantastic ladies. We have seen them embark in small uncertain boats, throw money about with both hands, fluctuate between arms and letters as though trying to put a sense of romance into steel and temper the alphabet with ideas of valour and chivalry.

Gonzalo, the lawyer with whom this history is concerned, held the middle place in the trio of sixteenth-century Quesadas. The first was Gaspar, who left Andalusia in Magellan's expedition when Gonzalo was about twenty. The last was Alonso, who was to go out from La Mancha, a man of fifty, when Gonzalo died an octogenarian in Mariquita. To a certain extent Gonzalo was disciple to Gaspar, and Alonso disciple to Gonzalo.

The history of Gaspar is not well known. It is known that he left Seville with Magellan in 1519, to go as the king's confidential man on the first trip around the world, and he commanded the *Concepción*, one of five ships allotted to the enterprise. Magellan was a hard man, and reserved. Even the captains did not know where they were going. They sailed for more than six months without the admiral's confiding his secrets to them.

Finally, desperate, they decided to rebel against that silence. After begging Magellan to hold a round-table conference with the men in command of the separate ships, and receiving his refusal, they resolved to carry out their plan. One day Magellan invited them to hear High Mass aboard the flagship and to take breakfast with him. The captains did not come. They stayed on their ships, and jeered at the admiral. Only one ship, the *San Antonio*, remained faithful to Magellan. At night, with a thick fog dimming the ship's silhouettes to mere blurs in the mist, Quesada and a few companions lowered themselves into a small boat and moved cautiously to the *San Antonio's* side. They climbed to the deck. The boatswain, Juan de Eloriaga, started up at the sound of their footsteps and advanced toward the conspirators, demanding an explanation. With six blows of his fist Gaspar de Quesada disposed of him. Then all was quiet. And when Magellan's sailors came over to the *San Antonio* the next morning, expecting to find her still loyal, the soldiers called down from the deck, "Admiral Magellan is not in command of the *San Antonio*, but Gaspar de Quesada, who is our captain."

But this Gaspar who was, like Gonzalo, a captain of mutineers was also, like Gonzalo and Alonso, a literate man. Also he was circumspect and discreet. He sent the admiral a letter couched in the humble form of a petition and raising the question of command. Neither he nor his companions wished to risk the ships further in an enterprise which seemed bound for no good end. If Magellan would grant this petition they would obey him faithfully. And if, up to that point, they had called him "Your Honour," from then on they would add "we who kiss your hands and feet."

Magellan, who was quick in decision, and silent, laid a trap for the captain of the *Victoria*, caught him, and knifed him. Soon he was again in a position where he could dominate the situation. The rebel captains fell into his hands, and he clamped fetters on them. Quesada he condemned to death. He also condemned Quesada's body servant, but told him, "If you carry out the sentence against Quesada, I will pardon you." The servant severed Quesada's head with a single blow. Stuck on a pole, which became the centre of a buzzards' merry-go-round, the head of Gaspar de Quesada marked in its day the point reached by certain Spaniards who had set out to go around the world.

In his youth our Gonzalo must thus have received teachings and inspiration in which sordid adventure was mixed with daring and with death. There, too, the lawyer must have learned how fate seemed always to veil or to cloud the family escutcheon. Gonzalo, who advanced along the ways that we have seen, also wanted to hold the world like a ball in his two hands, to make it spin with a philosophic air, or to drop it at his feet and gaze down at it with that careless melancholy which Albrecht Dürer was to depict, but for Gonzalo as well as for Gaspar the world slipped from between his fingers just as love slipped away from all the Quesadas. Love always kept its distance from their lives. Charity alternated with the clash of arms. A never-ending fantasy called him to adventure and thrust spurs into his horse's flanks. Ah, this is the family's fate, a fate which was to see itself raised to the verge of madness in the austere

figure and broad, dreaming forehead of Alonso. Alonso
Quesada came into the world as Gonzalo—his father?—left
on his second voyage to America. His life as a vagrant and
a trouble-seeker would be unknown to no one, for a famous
man of letters would write about it, a man who, if he
failed to embark for America, failed through no fault
of his own. This unfortunate writer was Don Miguel de
Cervantes Saavedra.

❈    ❈    ❈

The reader will forgive the fact that it is not possible for
me to seat Don Gonzalo in a broad leather armchair facing
a stone-arched plaza, where files of holy women pass slipping noisy beads through their bony fingers. Or that I do
not have him curling his long moustaches while the musical murmur of the bells echoes in the quiet air. This colony
is very poor and very new to have broad leather chairs, or
holy women with their rosaries, or stone arcades, or jan-
gling bells. The scenery is necessarily reduced to the adobe,
the straw, and the grass which we have already seen, the
poor women who light the flames of jealousy in conquerors'
breasts, two or three sullen friars, and the subject Indians
who tread out clay in the tile works or carry loads of potatoes.

Gonzalo Jiménez de Quesada will have to sit down many
times on a block of stone to talk with the townspeople,
while Montaño is combing his beard before the pigs and
chickens in the corral of his house. But the gentleman who
thus sits and talks will not be so much aware of the stone
that freezes his rear as he is of that Terra Firma on which
the stone rests. To be on Terra Firma, to have America under his feet, represents the first step in his journey, his first

adventure, the success of his first sally. His mind now wanders restlessly amid new plans for conquest. His long arm, the long arm of a knight and a gentleman, is stretched above the weak like a protecting wing. His dark and tranquil eye looks again toward El Dorado.

It is not in him that madness lies. It lies in his period, in that turbulent sixteenth century which turns all values upside down. And he is so much a part of that world that though we see him assailed by hunger, envy, misery, though we watch him cross rivers and mountains like a wraith escaped from an insane asylum, his words really give an impressive sensation of practical wisdom and common sense. Which is rather like what will happen to Alonso, called Don Quixote. Like the helmet made out of a barber's basin, these deluded men sometimes make one laugh and sometimes weep.

The king gave Gonzalo a coat of arms. First, there was on his escutcheon a mountain looming out of the waters of the sea, and many emeralds scattered on the waters "in memory of the mines which you discovered," and at the foot of the mountain, and crowning it, great trees on a field of gold, and a golden lion on a red field with a sword between his paws "in memory of the spirit and energy you showed in going up by river to discover and conquer the New Kingdom." Then a castle and a border of four gold and silver moons on a blue field, and for a seal a closed helmet, and for a device a black-winged lion with a naked sword between its paws, and cords and accessories with ornaments of blue and gold. . . .

There never was a more fantastic vision of the New World than this. Nor greater waste of enamel, nor more highly decorated poetry translated into the world of arms.

If only Alonso of La Mancha could have had one as fine.
. . . But Gonzalo was no less under the spell. This escutcheon was never to be carved in stone at the entrance to a
house, nor would its colours ever be seen except on a paper
which the marshal guarded in his strongbox and which
time would turn yellow while the letters turned brown
and the moths and mice and worms made it into dust and
powder.

*    *    *

One day the king's courier reached Santa Fé with a
dispatch which gave Quesada the right to use the title
"Don." (I suppose that Quixote would inherit it from here,
because where does Cervantes say that the king authorized
Alonso to use it? But let us not digress.) This was that
three-lettered decree of which the chroniclers speak and
which must have struck Montaño like a dart through the
heart. From now on Quesada would be Don Gonzalo in
the New Kingdom, as they would be saying Don Quixote
in La Mancha.

But while these honours brought a certain distinction,
they were out of keeping with the surroundings. Montaño,
finding himself powerless to demote this hidalgo whom
everyone loved, tried to get rid of him through another
form of exile—he named him governor of Cartagena. And
again Gonzalo, with a stream of honeyed words from Montaño sounding in his ears, seeing himself overwhelmed by a
flood of petitions, accepted this exile in silence and obedi-
ently.

When the news sped through the town there was no one
who failed to deplore it, no one who did not watch with
anxiety the marshal's departure, his flight, so to speak. The

bishop decided that Gonzalo should not be allowed to go while the synod was engaged in studying the conditions of ecclesiastical government and while reform was under way "in the irregularities in the Indians' catechisms, both ecclesiastical and secular, which pervert the very means by which faith should be implanted in them." In this struggle Don Gonzalo was the bishop's effective counsellor. It was with his help that the synod was called together. Here is the short account that Piedrahita would give of this affair:

"Bishop Barrios, seeing that eighteen years after the conquest of the kingdom the Spaniards were still divided into separate factions, that the priests, far from minimizing such internal jealousies, kept fanning their flames, and that scarcely any of the Indians had been instructed in the first rudiments of the faith, though all of them could have held professorships in the subtleties of Spanish greed, convoked a provincial synod for the reform of such abuses."

The synod brought to light many things which hurt Montaño. Don Gonzalo took the road to Cartagena; and, though the agreements which were reached fell to pieces in the bishop's hands because of the opposition of the judges, it is said that something was gained in restraining the unbridled greed of the *encomenderos* and in forcing the priests to recognize that the Church had punishments for the weakness with which they had administered their offices. And time continued its march. . . .

*       *       *

Though decorated with the title of governor, Don Gonzalo found his exile in Cartagena harder than the one which had decreed that he stay not less than six leagues away from Santa Fé. The hot Caribbean sun stifled him. A sickness which was eating at his skin seemed to gain new virulence at the seashore. For the first time the strong man, who had seemed unaffected by the sudden reverses native to America, felt himself weaken. Not even in La Tora, where he had gone out at the head of an army ravaged by fever, had he let misfortune sway him. Now, however, there may have been some connexion between his deep melancholy and the fevers that were devouring his flesh.

But his spirit still stood guard. One day he received certain documents from the court and, seizing on them as a pretext, decided he must take them personally to Santa Fé. He left the affairs of the governorship in the hands of a subordinate. It was the last time Quesada would ever look on salt water. That Terra Firma which had always drawn him, the heart of the Andes which claimed him, now took him back again. He looked at the bay once more, but without affection, then left it, and went up the Great River of the Magdalena, past the scenes of his great undertakings and great misfortunes.

* * *

Marshal Quesada was watching the life of Santa Fé unroll before his eyes. Once again Montaño must suffer the torment of his presence and this time hear the citizens name him captain general. There were new judges in the Audiencia, and a secret document, which Quesada had brought, for Montaño's impeachment. This document was in the hands of Tomás López, a shivering, cowardly lawyer who thought more about becoming a priest in the service of God than about taking part in the affairs of the Audiencia. Of him, Quesada said there was no minister better at drafting laws in favour of the Indians and no one worse when it came to executing them. Montaño became aware that there was plotting against him. Wishing to take the others by surprise, he invented a fantastic conspiracy which would, by making people believe his life was in danger, allow him to flee on pretext of fidelity to the king. Secret murmurs went about which put everyone on guard. No one dared to go out at night, and for greater strength the hidalgos to whom Montaño wished ill met in one another's houses. Finally Tomás López plucked up courage, paid Montaño a surprise visit, and notified him of his impeachment. Amid general satisfaction he went to wear the chains which he himself had forged for his enemies.

*    *    *

From the doorway of one of the big houses which were beginning to go up, leaning his still strong shoulders against the door-jamb, the marshal watched the evening light fade amid great golden clouds, while the twilight air wrapped trees, houses, mountains in a gilded violet mist. News had come from Spain about Montaño—he had been executed in the public square at Valladolid while a crier proclaimed his disgrace. A citizen arrived from Venezuela with a tale of how the tyrant Lope de Aguirre had flouted the authority of the king and was imposing his own will wherever he went. These events were passing through the marshal's mind as he watched the golden sunset, and he thought about sallying forth again. Many years had passed since he had come back to Santa Fé, and with a new access of youthful ardour he had begun to dream about new conquests. The dream took shape in the person of his brother Hernán Pérez, who, searching the eastern plains for El Dorado, had found cinnamon forests. There, beyond any doubt, lay the real source of gold which he had vainly hoped to find in the land of the Chibchas. It was there that the tyrant Aguirre was roaming. What more brilliant crowning of Quesada's long life than a discovery which should eclipse not only his first achievement but also those of the Pizarros and Cortés?

But the clash of Aguirre's arms came closer every day. Crossing the cordillera, the news from Venezuela took on fantastic colour and detail. No one in Santa Fé talked of anything else, and all began to arm. A military committee was formed. There was only one man who could head the troops. As when they had felt the threat of Alvaro de Oyón, so today there was no doubt that only Quesada could be captain. The business of war-making had been somewhat forgotten in Santa Fé. Setting up an army was a novelty which surprised everyone, pulled them up out of the round of daily gossip, set them to thinking suddenly, much to their own surprise, of the hazards which lay in adventure.

The veterans of the conquest, their eyes long drowsing over the petty struggles of small-town love affairs, took on new briskness. There was a polishing of steel, refurbishing of saddlery, racing of horses through the streets. Even the women enjoyed the novelty, for once again they saw in the men of Santa Fé those intrepid creatures whom they had known in the high pride of the old days. Everyone was eager to discuss what should be done. Should they go forth to meet Aguirre through Cerinza valley or through Cúcuta? This problem of major strategy soon split the soldiers, and two bands formed which kept arguing and gesticulating into the small hours of the night. Some said Cerinza valley was ideal for a battle. Others insisted that by going as far as Cúcuta they could trap and crush Aguirre.

The marshal sat through these debates with the air of a man only half there, his mind fixed on the actual encounter, his thoughts straying at times, perhaps, to another high emprise—the search for El Dorado. But the noise and the shouting reached a point where he had to intervene. The soldiers came to defend their own points of view with such passion that they began to challenge one another. Then the marshal published an edict that any return to that argument would be punishable with death. The responsibility for command of the troops was his, and the squabbling ended.

* * *

Quesada had been in Santa Fé for twenty years. He was nearing seventy. But his hard-muscled legs could still hold a young horse in check. "What you thought age, was resting." But to start out at seventy on an enterprise more risky and difficult than the discovery of the New Kingdom itself was madness. Yet there is something superior to the common run about this type of man whose mere presence draws other men to him.

He was eager to free himself from the press of stupid things. This life of petty gossip and small plots, of the witch Juana García and Armendáriz's love affairs, of the vagrancies of Inés de Hinojosa and the fights between the bishop and the priests—he wanted to fling it all out the window. It was time to put a final period to his own efforts to get them to give him, first, a sure income of three thousand ducats and then either an assignment of Indians or an adelantado's title. How many memorials he had had to send the king, reminding him of Cortés and Pizarro, who were never absent from his own mind! On one occasion he had asked the king to raise his pension from two to three thousand ducats, and to assure its continuance to his heirs; he offered this sad reminder, "On a certain occasion at court there was talk of giving me a reward for my services, and after some discussion it was agreed that I and my heirs should be given subsistence in perpetuity so that memory of my services might endure as did similar services of the Marqués del Valle [Cortés] and Pizarro, to each of whom were given twenty-one thousand vassals and fifty or sixty thousand ducats of pension, and very important titles, though they had discovered and settled provinces no better and no richer than those I have brought. . . ."

Santa Fé had grown. And other towns had grown. When Quesada obtained permission to go forth to discover El Dorado he issued a call for good soldiers and horsemen. A throng of Spaniards offered themselves to follow this formidable old man who raised money, got horses ready, gathered weapons and supplies, and recruited Indians with a diligence and an energy that had not been known of him in Santa Marta when he had had no more than half the years that now weighed on his shoulders.

The capitulation which Quesada signed in order to go forth to El Dorado could scarcely have been conceived in the mind of a youth of thirty. Now he was contracting for the future. He went ahead as though he were a millionaire. Before his eyes a fabulous vision beckoned.

Listen well—this is the inheritance he will leave his son, the stipulation says. Ah, it is a phantom son who must be going about Spain now, but who will some day sally forth in search of that El Dorado which his father is never to find.

He is to equip the army at his own expense. The troops will go under his command. He guarantees to the Audiencia that he will raise four or five hundred men, completely equipped with arms; eight priests; supplies for everyone; horses, mares, cows, pigs, and hens; he will not load himself down with untrained Indians; "of all my conquests will I take possession in the name of the king. And when I found towns, which will be within four years' time, I will put into them no less than another five hundred Spaniards, and I will take married men, and officers and workers, and five hundred cows and three hundred mares, four hundred horses, a thousand pigs, three thousand sheep and goats, five hundred Negro slaves, both male and female. . . ."

All this is hardly credible. But the Audiencia accepted it, the Spaniards believed it, the Indians came to offer their services. Quesada authorized Rodrigo Suárez, captain of cavalry, to have banners displayed and drums beaten in Tunja, so that everyone might get ready for the conquest of El Dorado. According to the terms of the agreement, if Quesada succeeded he would be given the title of marqués for himself and for his son. In short, the fact is that in the month of February 1569, very early of a morning when cold pierced to the bones, all Santa Fé got up to bid the marshal farewell. When the Host was elevated in a Mass sufficiently solemn for the occasion, the silence and the piety were deeper than usual, and there were those who remembered when a fever-ridden General Quesada had set out from La Tora to the discovery of the New Kingdom.

Three hundred Spanish soldiers were already mounted. Fifteen hundred Indians, both men and women, followed carrying hammocks and supplies, driving pigs and other livestock. There were eleven hundred horses and other pack-animals, and six hundred head of cattle, and eight hundred pigs. There was a multitude of Negro slaves, both men and women. How much greater all this seemed than the Santa Marta expedition, when Quesada was merely a lieutenant for Fernández de Lugo! This was the rebirth of conquest within the colony itself and, like all renaissance, more optimistic and ebullient. It knew from experience that in the end victory crowns all the marches.

*      *      *

The enormous train of men and animals, white, black, and copper-coloured, moved slowly, first along easy upland roads which wound like a serpentine river, then across the rocky spurs of the cordillera and through the dense growth of underbrush. Drums and banners set the pace. At dawn the bugle woke the warm mass of men and women, who stretched themselves and made ready to go forward again. For the first few days there was whistling and singing as when boys out of school go forth on vacation. Later the hardships of the march muffled voices, and hunger and lowland heat tempered pleasure. They had forgotten what it cost to go forth on discovery in America. Adelantado Jiménez de Quesada remembered his marches of thirty years before, but also he was remembering that at the end of those thirty years he had won the title—adelantado— which had now put him at the head of his own troops.

Their first contact with the Llanos, those plains which were to be the beginning of this conquest, was full of adventure. One day fire spread through the wild grass surrounding the camp. The spark that caught fire and fled crackling under the rapid hand of the wind got as far as the very canvas that covered the adelantado's supplies. There followed a terrifying blast which made the voice of conquest heard through all the flatlands—a barrel of powder in Quesada's stores had exploded.

Then came acquaintance with another new world—the boas ("*culebras bobas,*" silly snakes), which swallow a deer whole and turn it into delicious juices as it travels the long dark channels of their bodies (the first of them measured twenty-seven feet long); the Indians who burned their huts before the Spaniards got there; the marches in which hunger kept pace as they walked, and the soldiers were forced to chew palm shoots in order to keep going. After many days of nothing to eat, they found a town with good fields around it; they named it Matahambre (Hunger-Killer). It was all as it had been twenty years before.

One night three soldiers fled with three pack-horses. It was absurd, they thought, to embark on conquest when Santa Fé was back there, safe and peaceful, waiting for them. This example soon infected the others. One night six or seven more tried to flee, but the guards were warned and stopped them. The adelantado decided to hang Juan Gil in order to maintain discipline and so that those who were meditating desertion might know the risk they ran. Notwithstanding that, the suffering was so intense that forty more tried to escape in a single night. They were surprised, and ten of them taken prisoner. But morale went on weakening, among the captains as well as among the soldiers. Captain Gonzalo Macías tried to flee, in company with several Negro men and women. Caught, he killed himself.

The march went on, not any longer to the beat of drums, but at the pace set by hunger and by death. At times they gnawed even the leather on their shields. There were no pigs left, and it was hard to protect the horses. An unknown fever began to undermine the lives of men and animals alike. The thick underlip of a horse would start trembling, and the soldiers came to recognize it as a sure sign of death. When they struck camp, arms, clothing, jewellery would be left behind because no one bothered to pick them up. How many weary months had these soldiers been wandering behind that mad old adelantado!

Months? No, years. Two years had passed since they left Santa Fé, and they had got nowhere. The enthusiasm they had once had for the adelantado was weakening. Stubborn, imperturbable, unconquerable, he alone went armed in search of mystery. But the troop could do no more. Those who had pressed kisses on his stirrups in Santa Fé, who were so happy that a song about his banners bubbled on their lips, now marched with dry mouths, their wounds festering, their vitals gnawed by the fangs of hunger. And in many a tormented mind there was only one solution— knife the adelantado. Kill Quesada in order to get back, if that was still possible, to land that belonged to Christians. They were weary of slaying Indians for no good end, of reaching towns and finding them in ashes, of watching those slow-moving prairie rivers which flow on into infinity and which must be crossed with water to the waist and wild animals lying in ambush. There was no remedy but to kill the adelantado.

The conspirators met at the ranch of a certain Don Gabriel. The decision worried some of them, but the saving of their own lives was more important than the faithful following of a madman. They argued as to whether it would be better to stick him with a dagger or to behead him with a sword. Someone remembered the terrific powder explosion at the start of the expedition, and they decided to do something similar—"to burn him alive with powder." It was a hard decision for soldiers who all knew what point Quesada had reached in his struggles; how, in his maturity, he had softened the harsh life of the colony, and how ardent and able had been the good right arm of this gentleman in defence of the humble. Perhaps the very difficulty of carrying out a plan which gave them such sorrow made for a certain vacillation in its execution. The fact is that the plot was discovered, and justice done to Francisco Gómez and Juan de Hermosilla, and a Portuguese, Gaspar, not to mention fetters for Don Gabriel, at whose ranch they had met.

But Quesada recognized that it was absurd to insist on keeping tied to him only those who followed through terror. He had to play a last card, and free the troop so that they might follow him of their own will or go back to Santa Fé. He knew only too well that there would be few who would follow. It was all so uncertain, and so mad, that there was no room for doubt as to the future of the undertaking. There was a certain Juan Maldonado who did nothing but argue night and morning with Quesada about going back. In order to save his sanity, Quesada said to him one day, "Señor Camp Master, if Your Grace wishes to return to Santa Fé, there is no one to stop you." And the camp master, who was only waiting for this, took the road to Santa Fé in company with Father Guisado and Friar Murueña, who were also bored by this adventure. The adelantado decided to get some advantage from those who deserted him, and so he took over six women whose husbands had fled.

* * *

In the face of the old conquistador's stubbornness, no argument was of any use. He explored here and there, as though seeking acquaintance with every hand's-breadth of his future kingdom. He met none but miserable Indian tribes, but this did not matter. The same thing had happened when he conquered the New Kingdom. He must reach the authentic El Dorado. There was only a handful of loyal men left. Those who had fled would be sorry some day. And torn by brambles, their eyes red with hunger and fever, the leaders sought new trails, sometimes cutting through heavy forest lianas, sometimes swimming the current of broad rivers. The horses were all scabbed and mangy; the soldiers, full of parasites which caused their death.

Suddenly they heard the sound of drums. The scouts announced that a great army of Indians was coming. The approach of battle gave Don Gonzalo new strength. With nine other horsemen he lined up to conquer a thousand Indians who came on in good formation, with a display of arrows and shields to defend them. They sought better ground for combat. The soldiers made ready for battle. Behind them a confused tangle of sick men, women, animals allowed no passage, and their cries of "God give you luck!" were lost amid the clash of arms. The adelantado, armoured in quilted cotton, his bearded face showing stains of white, lifted his lance on high and invoked St. James, as knights were wont to do.

And St. James was with the men from Spain. The horses broke across a gay little brook on whose opposite bank the Indian army was gathered. They were lively and treacherous Indians, whom wrath had made boisterous. Quesada advanced first. But the battle was reduced, as in a tale of

enchantment, to a loud noise and a cloud of smoke. Rodríguez Pérez de las Islas shot an arquebus against the Indian leader, and his death sent the others fleeing to the
mountains, without leaving even the murmur of leaves to
mark their going.

✣　✣　✣

That was the last heroic stand on the march. The troop
continued to be ill, and weakened more by undernourish-
ment than by fever. On hard nights they had stewed the
very coverings of their shields in order to sup on the softened leather. Almost never did they stumble on cultivated
fields which would nourish them. When they dropped from
the cordillera to the plains they saw an endless prairie covered with sunburned grass where the afternoon sun rolled
down like a great blood-red wheel. At night it was so still
they could almost hear the rising moon brush her silken
skirts across the meadows, or the snakes slip imperceptibly
amidst the grass. How far away from all this was the white
bell tower of Santa Fé! Some of them even became homesick for the music of the chains which Montaño's idea of
justice had had forged. The adelantado resolved that no one
should feel himself kept prisoner by his wishes, and now he
opened wide the doors to returning. He himself was going
forward, but anyone who wanted to go back had only to
come to his tent and say so.

> *Let enter here who will; this is the door,*
> *For my part it stays wide for evermore.*

And ten, twenty, fifty came in. Don Gonzalo never weakened. He went on giving all of them leave. He had sworn
to give it to them, and no one was to suffer lack of confi-

dence. Don Gonzalo was first and foremost a knight and a gentleman. Those who were to go back were now grouped together. As there were many of them, it would be best for them to have a captain and a priest. Don Gonzalo appointed these, and gave them military orders. Those companions of so many days of bad fortune took their leave with much emotion.

And the marches went on. The Indians killed the horses, and one day seven more Spaniards asked leave to return. Quesada gave it. Of these, only one reached Santa Fé alive. There were only twenty-five men left now. You remember how many went out with him from Santa Fé? You remember that splendid train that milled about his harsh, commanding voice? Out of all that only a handful of people were left, and they now besought Quesada to turn back in his tracks. If he wished, they would go on with him to the end of their days, even to the end of the world. But it was absurd that he, torn by the evils that beset them, should force himself to go further, in order to die tomorrow. He needed to regain his health in a good climate. He owed it to his country and his friends. They had had three years of this journeying, and there was not a pig left, or a dozen horses. Twenty-five of such friends as Quesada never would see again gathered about him to implore him. There was nothing more that a knight could do. And so he went back to Santa Fé.

The final upshot of the journey could not have been sadder. Of three hundred Spaniards, only sixty-four remained alive, and almost all of them died on the way back to Santa Fé. Of fifteen hundred Indians, only four were saved. Of eleven hundred horses, eighteen survived. But the adelantado was the adelantado.

*Arrived, then, at the kingdom, Don Gonzalo*
*With lack of health and money both, alas,*
*There rose a war with natives, the Gualíes,*
*Headstrong and rebel Indians of the place*
*Near to that city known as Mariquita,*
*And the king's mandate gave him total charge*
*Of bringing peace to that unruly land*
*And he, although he ached and felt age-weary,*
*Would not refuse to meet the king's command*
*And so made preparations for the battle.*

# XI. *Sunset and Evening Star*

Letters say that arms could not stand without them, for war also has its laws and is subject to them, and laws fall under letters and the men of letters. To this, arms reply that laws could not stand without them, for it is by means of arms that republics are defended, kingdoms held, cities guarded, roads made safe, the sea freed from pirates, and finally, that, if it were not for them, these same republics, kingdoms, monarchies, cities, and highways on both land and sea would be subject to the terror and confusion which war brings with it during the time it lasts and is allowed to make use of its privileges and its forces.

—CERVANTES

# SUNSET AND EVENING STAR

ALMOST always after Mass, or as prayer rose in the afternoon, and the main plaza, which was also the only one, filled with pious old women, judges and *encomenderos*, Indians and slaves, a stout old hidalgo set out, of whom years, labours, illness, and fatigue were beginning to take their toll. Seldom did he follow the king's highway. Rounding the corner of the church he took a higher street, then zigzagged toward the north and went on climbing until he reached a poor house cared for by Indians and a housekeeper who regarded the adelantado's white hair with respect. A few steps beyond, the street lost itself among the mountain underbrush. One or two lean horses moved lazily in the paddock, and a dog or two in the archway flicked at flies with his long tail. The hidalgo was sparing of words. Asthma overcame him, and he fell heavily into a leather chair. He might spend half an hour covering a few blocks, dragging his feet and leaning heavily on a stout stick. Whole weeks would go by without his being able to move from the house.

The hidalgo passed hours, long days, in a wide room which held a single table heaped with books bound in parchment, one or two armchairs, the image of Our Lady the Virgin with a candle almost always burning before it, a lance and a sword in the corner, a coat of mail hanging from an ornamental hook; the indispensable stag's head which was lost beneath the brim of a broad hat and a cape with many folds that almost touched the floor. Air and light entered through a not very large window, air from the mountain, cold and fragrant, light that was milky blue. There were no panes of glass yet known in Santa Fé, and the doors were made of hide with the hair left on.

The city was increasing in size. Two leagues roundabout it the Indian towns were forming, ruled by the corregidors, but having a certain city shape, with streets well laid out and church bells hung at some high point. The houses had well-cultivated gardens and fountains of pure water. Wheat grew in many places, and herds multiplied in the pastures. Groups of friars kept arriving to found monasteries. Under their straw roofs, new churches guarded images brought from Spain, lighted with small lamps burning vegetable oil or with candles made of tallow. Manzanilla and yerbabuena perfumed the patios.

Before setting out for El Dorado, and when the ingenious gentleman of this story was writing short memorials to the king, he filled in the long closing phrases of the letters with a rapid "etcetera" and signed them proudly "The Marshal." Now, when he wrote long supplicating communications to the king, he did it in these terms, "The humble servant and vassal of Your Royal and Catholic Majesty, who kisses your royal feet and hands, the Adelantado Don Gonzalo Jiménez de Quesada." Nevertheless, he kept a certain suppressed pride which came out now and then between the lines. After all, he had conquered a kingdom, and would conquer it twice more if need be, for the day it was necessary to give battle again he would shake off his sickness and become again a knight mounted on his battle charger. Therefore, when he sent his last service report, after calling himself captain of the hazardous adventure which was the conquest, he said, "After conquering and settling the New

Kingdom I returned to Spain to beg Your Majesty for the recognition of such a service, and this will be my hope until I draw my last breath."

*    *    *

People watched with respect and sorrow the solitary old man who shut himself up in his house to scratch at reams of paper with a badly sharpened quill. Now he was in a fever to write books. He had written some before he set out for El Dorado. First came the *Ratos de Suesca* (*Suesca Moments*), with notes about the natural history of the New Kingdom, the customs of the Indians, the rare and curious things which he had been observing since he first touched American soil. Something like the letters of Cortés, and the first descriptions of America. Then *La Refutación a Paulo Jovio* (*Refutation of Paulus Jovius*). In this refutation he reaffirmed his Spanish pride. He recalled how badly Spaniards in Europe were regarded, and tried to set forth a defence of his country. His feverish imagination dreamed in terms of literary and historical polemic, and he cleaned his arms and unsheathed his sword as though making ready for single combat. The mere plan of the work shows its broad scope, and in the first chapter, as I have said elsewhere, is a breadth of bitterness which gives the polemic shape and form.

That first chapter is the one which treats of "Whether the ill will which many nations bear toward the Spaniards be a matter of hatred or envy, and whether the causes they allege for it be just." Then Quesada sets out to review Jovius's entire history. He was a bishop of Nocera, and fond of reviling Spaniards. Quesada sets before him the real achievements of Charles V and his kingdoms. He refutes

the Italian in what he says about the Comuneros of Castile,
tells in what state Charles V received the crown of Spain,
talks at length about the visits which the kings of France
and England made in the first half of the century, shows
what Spain's conduct was toward Luther's heresy, recalls
the taking of Geneva and the election of Clement VII, relates how the battle of Pavia and the capture of the king of
France took place, how Suleiman's wars in Hungary went,
and the capture of Tunis by Charles V. All this he knows
through the quantity of reading he did in Europe and
America, and through what he gathered in the camaraderie
of the New Kingdom from the lips of soldiers who themselves were in those campaigns. That is to say, this is a compendium of European history, done with the critical sense
of a Spanish patriot and the forcefulness of a fighting hidalgo.

This book against Bishop Jovius the adelantado dedicated to Luis Méndez de Quixada, and Don Gonzalo wrote
"Quixada" because, as Cervantes will note later, no one ever
knew when the Quixanos were Quesadas or the Quesadas
spelled Quijadas. But the initial tone of the work deserves
to be remembered, for it gives a good picture of the adelantado. "There remained," he said at the end of the prologue,
"the need for pardoning the faults of this book on account
of the short time in which I wrote it, which was a little more
than five months, and the barbarity and crudeness of the
people with whom I had talked for so many years. . . .
The honest indignation which I feel on seeing the Spanish
nation so unjustly accused was the reason I hastened to
get this book out, even though it be not as polished and
finished as is required in this period when all arts and letters
are almost at their peak."

Now Quesada was composing his historical works at the same time as others which were touched with frank mysticism. This Christian spirit became tempered in him with the years. If as a general he had found it not inconvenient to have his orders obeyed under pain of death, as a man he had a certain background of pity. The last years of his life were full of contradictions—at one moment we see him moving about, scarcely able to drag one foot after the other, at another he is setting out at the head of his own troops; one day he has Indian towns burned, the next he is begging that the Indians be treated with benevolent tenderness. He is like lamplight about to go out: the flame goes up and down, now burns with disproportionate brilliance, now folds its wings into black butterflies of shadow.

Quesada wanted to leave a complete history of all his conquests, and started on the great work of his *Historical Compendium*. He devoted the first book to the period of his discovery, his entry into the country of the Chibchas; the second to his return to the colony, to the synod which was meeting in Santa Fé before he left for Cartagena, to the disastrous conquest of El Dorado. As his work went on, history became confused with the actuality of his latter days. More than with anything else was he preoccupied with the ordering of his accounts with God. He criticized the greed of the enterprises which he himself had commanded. Telling, for example, about the sack of the palace of the king of Tunja, he said, "Certainly it was something to see Christians carrying loads of gold on their shoulders, they who also professed to carry on those same shoulders the cross of Christianity."

Quesada also wrote a collection of sermons which were to be preached at the feasts of Our Lady. On all Saturdays in Lent, even after his death, he wanted a Mass sung with music, a sermon, and responses for all the conquistadors, living and dead. And for many years Santa Fé would listen to those mystical discourses by the founder of the kingdom from the lips of priests who garbled and distorted them. . . .

So Quesada went back over his own footsteps, retraced his history, examined his conscience, and, in a manner of speaking, prepared to leave this world. He was already old and tired, as the chroniclers keep saying, and yet he still thought about returning to El Dorado. He had promised the soldiers that he would come back to Santa Fé to regain his health, but—so help us Heaven!—on his honour he would not fail to return to the Llanos.

All looked at him with respect, respecting even his madness, except the president of the Audiencia. This was Don Andrés Díez Venero de Leyva, who had taken a dislike to him and of whom Quesada was to write words in which bitterness was mixed with resignation:

"It was a heavy blow to me, though not all that my sins warranted, that he should come forth from his study to wage cruel war, under the title and colour of justice, on one who before he was born (or at least before his beard appeared) had gained white hairs in the service of Your Majesty."

❈   ❈   ❈

Before leaving on the El Dorado campaign Quesada kept saying that he had not strength to climb a stair or to go ten steps on foot except with great effort. He declared then that to oblige him to marry in order to acquire the right to an *encomienda* was to open to him the tomb. What can be

said of the old man now, impoverished and infirm as he was!
As someone said, he went bent double, leaning against the
wall and loaded down with debts.

But alarming news kept coming from the hot country.
There was an uprising among the Gualíes Indians. A chieftain stole a half-breed woman who had turned his head
and who belonged to the *encomendero* Francisco Jiménez.
To make a long story short, the chieftain killed Jiménez
and his two nephews and took the woman off to sleep in
his own hammock. The rape of the half-breed, the killing of
the three Spaniards, the terror of the whites, had given the
Gualíes extraordinary courage. These Indians who lived
near Mariquita, in an ardent and stimulating climate, not
far from lands rich in gold, were not docile and tractable
like those of the uplands. On the contrary, they carried
treachery to the point where, not content with doing
shameful things to the Spaniards on the banks of the Magdalena, they climbed to the tableland of Santa Fé and committed all sorts of daring deeds. A group of chiefs federated
themselves with their towns, and again the vision of war
rose before Spanish eyes. But who could serve as captain
for the men from Spain? Don Gonzalo Jiménez de Quesada.

Farewell books, farewell all care for one's health. *Encomenderos* and soldiers gathered at the call "To arms!" The
adelantado, though he had to be carried in a litter, was in
command. The hot lands would be good for his worn frame,
and it could be said almost that he was filled with the energy of other days. Amid the jingling of horses and the clatter of arms the sons of St. James entered the rebellious
towns. They killed without pity, they burned whole settlements, they took gold as in the good old times. Quesada's
spirits rose to such a point that he founded a town just as

in his good days—Santa Agueda, which should be a sort of fortress for the Spaniards' defence while they were "skimming" the mines they had discovered.

Quesada went to the land of the Gualíes merely to "put down thievery," as the foremost authority of the kingdom wished. The army reached the town where lived the chieftain who was responsible for the uprising, and resolved to surprise him by night. When the Indians woke, the town was already on fire. The chieftain, leaving the half-breed woman in his bed, leaped to his weapons. The fight became a matter of single combat, and the chief perished. Broken and leaderless, the Indians fled. The Spaniards followed, "ranching" a town one day, following the fugitives through the mountains on another. They found agreeable climates and a land of gold in which the conquerors established themselves. As these conquests went on, not an Indian was left alive. It is the hard way natural to war.

Quesada summed up his whole campaign in a report which gives a perfect picture of his character: "Wishing to strengthen myself, though completely out of health, so as to go ahead with my plans for El Dorado, it happened that Briceño, your president, to whom be honour, found this kingdom much wrought up on account of the uprising in the sierras, where the natives had rebelled against Your Highness' service, and the matter was of such nature that the rebels left the lowlands in order to rob, and in such manner that it was no longer possible to work the gold mines in this province, nor to do anything here (especially in the hot country) which demanded peace and quiet; and then your president and judges, seeing this, and the urgent need for remedying it, turning me aside from the work I had in hand, commanded me to undertake this other, and, because I had discovered this kingdom, ordered me to restore it and to gain it back again, for it might almost be said that that was what was meant by pacifying the said sierras and quieting this province. And I, like another Hercules (I say this without boasting, well knowing that I do not deserve this name, nor do I by any means assert that I was born for the labours of the Indies or for being to this New World another such as he whom I have named was for that other ancient world, although all that be invention rather than a world, but let us call them thus), then took charge and raised a force and went to the said sierras carried on the shoulders of other men (for I could not go on foot on account of my indispositions) and in this way I began the said pacification, and completed it, though the savages killed many of my men in the process, among them my nephew Jerónimo Hurtado de Mendoza y de Quesada, the one on whom my hopes in this kingdom were centred. . . ."

*     *     *

Through the burning lands of Mariquita and Tocaima ranged the old conqueror, circling around his death. "He is poor and needy," said Marshal Hernán Venegas, "and has no possessions, nor house of his own in which to live in this city of Santa Fé, nor in the town of Tunja." Captain Tafur said, "He is poor, and much encumbered with debts." Gonzalo de Martos declared, "I do not know of any goods or chattels which belong to the adelantado, nor even a house to live in, save for the tribute which he has from Indians in this kingdom as is well known, and this is pledged on account of the heavy expenses of the recent expedition. . . ."

Apart from the conquest, the adelantado was a man who

looked upon the Indians with sympathy, and who would not dare to stain his estate with Indian blood. How many times he begged Montaño and the priests for the welfare of the aborigines, how often he insisted, in the Santa Fé synod, on a little Christian pity, how many bitter words he directs in his history now against the *encomenderos,* now against the priests. But this was not mere literary exercise or a desire to quarrel; it was because his conscience, the conscience of a good man, moved him voluntarily to proceed thus, even against his own interests. When he was given the *encomienda* of Chita, and went to collect the work tribute due him, he found, and so told the king, that the tax levied against the Indians was excessive. "They are," he said, "too heavily burdened because, being fewer than five hundred Indians, they are taxed fifteen hundred mantas, and so far as that is concerned they should be relieved of this, and until this is done I shall cease to charge them the work tribute, even though this be to my own detriment."

Quesada's petitions were growing fewer. Scarcely did he beg that they would not oblige him to marry. That they make life a little more agreeable for him. His life was slipping into an atmosphere of resignation. His skin was cracking, and his legs could scarcely carry him, with the weight of his eighty years heavy on his shoulders, through Mariquita's two or three streets under the vertical fire of the tropics as far as the straw church. There in the light which shone beneath the Virgin's image his dreaming eyes, already dimming, watched the last golden ray which would take him to that El Dorado in which none could fail to believe, the El Dorado which no one would snatch away from him, the El Dorado of the Christian God which he sought no longer with the fury of his lance but only with tearful love.

More than a conqueror, Quesada had been a discoverer. First among valiant captains though he was, he had known how to be silent, how to still the clatter of his steel, to incline his head, to listen to the voices of the Indians and discover the secrets of their hearts. How different his attitude from that of the purely sensual soldiers who squeezed the heart of America until their hands dripped blood. About him had risen men fortunate and men disgraced, whom the push of ambition had placed on the crest of the wave and the envy of imitators had cast into the trough of misery. Every day new gentlemen of dubious habits appeared in Santa Fé, and with their lewdness dragged life and honour into the dust. "At least," thought the adelantado, "may this light which gleams beneath the Virgin's image envelop them in its divine clarity some day."

The realities of American life reduced the discoverers to beds of misery and rendered the conquerors proud and blind. In that long twilight when the wild deer stands clear against the horizon and the sun of America drops between his spreading horns, Quesada advanced toward the shades of night with the same melancholy certainty which had moved Columbus's lips to prayer. How alike were those two lives as they faltered in the porticoes of death.

When Columbus was old and ill we see his son Diego negotiating at court that his father may be allowed to go from Seville to Toro and from Toro to Segovia on muleback. The roads of Spain were bad, but from the time of King Alfonso XI on the use of a mule was forbidden except to a certain small portion of the population. Ferdinand the Catholic forbade its use to laymen, and decided that only children, women, and clergy could make use of this mode of transportation. Columbus wished, therefore, to be given the same consideration as a child, a priest, or a woman in order that he might travel on a saddled and bitted mule, and the time Don Diego had to spend and the trips he had to make in order to acquire this dispensation were not a little humiliating. Thus the man who had discovered the endless routes of the sea, who had put them under the banner of the Catholic monarchs, who had mounted the frenzied back of the mad Atlantic in order to tame it and put it at Spain's service, had, now that he was old and ill, to beg the king's permission to be allowed to mount a mule. . . .

And Quesada, who had conquered a New Kingdom, who had found the emeralds of Muzo and put them into the king's hands, who had spent a hundred and fifty thousand ducats in the conquest of the Llanos, suffering in a thousand ways, "I and my people such labours, such misfortunes, and such strange and extraordinary happenings that it terrifies the mind to bring back such unhappy memories, for even though they have been told it seems impossible that they should all be believed. . . ." Quesada, I say, was forced to get down on his knees and beg that his creditors should be appeased and that he be allowed to die in peace. It was exactly the same as Columbus, of whom Humboldt would write on ending the history of his life, "The man who had given Spain a new world asked only a corner of earth in order that he might die in it peacefully."

*    *    *

When Quesada turned his attention to the matter of an estate which he might will to his heirs, he found himself poor and without any fortune. What Bishop Las Casas wrote of Columbus might be said of him—"He passed from this life in a state of deep anxiety, bitterness, and poverty, and without a roof in this world under which he might crawl to rest or to shield himself from the damp." Quesada had merely a few vague rights which would not bring in enough to pay his debts. And his books. His library which became a recreation for his mind when his body would no longer work for him. The parchments which piled up on his work table, mixed up with the papers which his own genius had created. The conqueror who had presented himself at court with gold and emeralds for the king, had on his second voyage returned to America with chests of books. Now, at the end of his life, he went over those volumes for the last time, and willed them to a monastery in Santo Domingo. Let the priest, and if so it be, the barber, do with them what they pleased.

What else had he to will? His titles constituted a treasure that was strictly personal. He had always regarded them with affection, first because they carried the signature of his king, second because they marked long notches in the measuring rod of his life, and third, perhaps, because among those who had certified those titles appeared one of His Majesty's ministers whose name was indissolubly linked with the name of the most illustrious lawgiver of Spain, the finest of the poet kings, and the most scholarly prince that the peninsula had ever known. That king was Don Alfonso the Wise, and the minister, Gregorio López, copyist of the *Siete Partidas* and their most authoritative commentator.

So the monarchs had given nothing to Quesada but a few titles. How different the treatment Cortés and Pizarro had received! At the end of his life Quesada might well have written something similar to this, which Columbus left in his will, "To our lords the King and Queen I gave, when I handed them the Indies, something which was as though mine own, and I might well call it so, for I besought it of them when the Indies were unknown and the way to them hidden; and when they were located and discovered Their Majesties spent, aside from the gift of my information and of my person, nothing nor wished to spend anything, except a sum of maravedis, and I had to spend all the rest."

Quesada, too, gave the monarchs a kingdom without their having staked on the hazard anything more than a banner. And now, with the kingdom in their hands, they had no eyes for the discoverer, who was left without even the shade of his own roof.

But there is the flame burning before the Virgin to mark the way. God grant that his debts may be paid with the income from the *encomienda*, that just as his creditors will forgive him, if they do, so will God save him from his debts. He has no one on earth to pardon, but he must ask forgiveness for his own lacks. His words are veiled in tenderness. He thinks—of what does he think? His son? But does he know anything of his son? There is no reason for naming him—may God guide him from on high. On the other hand he thinks, as Quixote will think, of his niece.

There is an extraordinary likeness between Quixote's will and that of Quesada. Both declare that their madness has passed, and that they are in the full possession of their faculties. Quesada begins by talking of the kingdom he has conquered, thus, "I, Don Gonzalo Jiménez de Quesada, adelantado of this New Kingdom of Granada, which I as captain discovered, conquered, and settled in these Western Indies along with many soldiers and gentlemen of the said armada who came with me . . . believe in the Most Holy Trinity, the Father, Son, and Holy Ghost. . . ."

Of Don Quixote, Cervantes says that after having written out the heading of his will and ordered his soul with all those Christian sentiments which were required, he referred to the kingdom he had conquered, and, turning his eyes toward Sancho, exclaimed, "If, as in my distracted state I procured him the government of an island, I could, now that I am in my senses, procure him that of a kingdom, I would readily do it."

The same return to reality occurred with Quesada as with Don Quixote. Says Quesada, "At present I find myself very ill of body, though sane of mind to dispose of whatever is fitting."

And Don Quixote, "Sirs, let us go softly, for there are not this year's birds in last year's nests. I was mad, and am now sane; I was Don Quixote de la Mancha, and I am now, as I said, Alonso Quijano the Good."

Quesada turned his eyes toward his niece and said, "As Your Majesty has done me the kindness of allowing me to name a successor to the grants of lands and Indians which I hold in trust in this kingdom, I hereby name as my successor, in accord with the said decree, Doña María de Oruña, daughter of the late Colonel Hernando de Oruña and Doña Andrea Jiménez, his wife and my sister, both deceased, and I hereby direct that all my debts be paid, those which I seem to owe in the Indies as well as in Spain and other places, and if my estate is not sufficient for this, I order that my successor pay them out of the bond-servants and the work tributes and the proceeds of Indian women and the grants that I leave."

Don Quixote says in his will, "I bequeath to Antonia Quixano, my niece, here present, all my estate, real and personal, after the payment of all my debts and legacies, and the first to be discharged shall be the wages due my housekeeper for the time she has been in my service, and twenty ducats besides for a suit of mourning."

Says Quesada, "I name as my witnesses and executors in this kingdom the most excellent archbishop of the said kingdom, and the most illustrious gentleman who is or was president of the Audiencia."

Don Quixote says, "I appoint for my executors Señor the Priest and Señor Bachelor Sansón Carrasco, here present."

And, as Cervantes says of Don Quixote, "The will was then closed, and, being seized with a fainting fit, he stretched himself out at length on the bed, at which all were alarmed, and hastened to his assistance; yet he survived three days; often fainting during that time in the same manner, which caused much confusion in the house. Nevertheless, the niece ate, the housekeeper drank, and Sancho Panza consoled himself, for legacies tend much to moderate grief that nature claims for the deceased. At last, after receiving the sacrament, and making all such pious preparations, as well as expressing in strong and pathetic terms his abhorrence of the books of chivalry, Don Quixote's last moment arrived. The notary was present and protested that he had never read in any book of chivalry of a knight-errant dying in his bed in so composed and Christian a manner as Don Quixote, who amid the plaints and tears of all present gave up his spirit—I mean to say, he died."

# XII. Quesada and Mankind

In his last years he was afflicted with leprosy, which made it necessary for him to stay in a desert place near the city of Tocaima which they call the hill of Limba, where there is a stream of water whose unpleasant odour comes from passing over sulphur deposits, and he rested amid its fumes. He left a sum of money with which to keep a jar of fresh water on that hill for wayfarers, for there was none near and the site was hot; and at last, without having married, and being poor, and owing more than six hundred thousand ducats, he died in the city of Mariquita. . . .

—FLÓREZ DE OCARIZ

# XII  Canada and Education

# QUESADA AND MANKIND

Four hundred years had passed since the day on which Gonzalo Jiménez de Quesada founded Santa Fé de Bogotá. The city put on its finest clothes to celebrate that event. It was agreed that the remains of the founder, which were reposing in an old cemetery, should be taken to the Cathedral.

God forgive me, but homage of this sort brings to mind a ridiculous situation which Pirandello recounts in one of his stories. Two men died in a small town near Rome on the same day. The first was one of those great personages to whom fame is accustomed to render posthumous tribute. The other, a poor devil, some town barber of the sort to whom earth bids farewell with four spadefuls of dirt. The two bodies were taken to the town undertaker to be made ready for burial, and while their relatives were preparing the last honours word reached Rome that the great man had died. There were obituaries in the press, meetings in the academies, flurries in the ministries. The dead man had belonged to all the illustrious societies, and he had filled, in his own manner, three or four pages of Italian history. Obviously the undertaker would soon receive instructions for sending the corpse to the Romans, while the corpse of the little man would remain in the funeral parlour with his arms crossed, awaiting the judgment of God.

In a special railroad car hung with crape the famous corpse left for Rome. The poor corpse, followed by two or three weeping relatives on foot, took the road to the town cemetery, feet foremost, and was put into his small stone house.

In one of the outlying stations of Rome the ministers and the academicians climbed into the mortuary car and then, unbuttoning their overcoats and lighting their cigars with all the ceremony proper on such occasions, they approached the coffin and looked at the dead man's face. Horrors! The undertaker had erred, and it was the little dead man, the village fool, who was sleeping on the silken cushions. How he would like to have seen himself, even after death, travelling first class with the gentlemen, and received as a member, even though a dead one, of the best academies! The sages and statesmen anxiously exchanged ideas. In a few moments they would arrive in the city of the Cæsars, where the Prime Minister, the newspaper men, and Parliament in a body awaited them. At a time like that they, who were accompanying the dead man, were to play as important a role as the corpse itself, if not a more important one. In their tortured imaginations they saw the whole crowd of photographers and newsreel men waiting at the station entrance. The matter was clear. It was not possible to slip the poor little corpse out and away from ceremonies like that. What the devil! There was nothing to do but to take it to the Basilica, pour out all the speeches over it, hang the laurel wreaths on it, and lay it away for ever in a marble chapel. . . .

\* \* \*

When the procession of notables, and the town of Santa Fé *en masse*, took charge of the remains of Don Gonzalo Jiménez de Quesada, or, if you prefer, of the Adelantado

Licentiate Gonzalo Ximénez Quijada, I asked myself anxiously, "Whose remains are these? Whose are the dust and ashes travelling thus amid clouds of incense, leaving the Catholic cemetery, which belongs to everybody, in order to enter the Cathedral, which is the pantheon of the very few elect?" For it is well to know, in spite of all I have written here, that we have very little information about the death of Don Gonzalo Jiménez—remember that four hundred years have passed since then—and are scarcely even certain that he died in Mariquita. Once the curious editors of the *Illustrated Journal* asked their readers, "Is it possible to see the remains of Gonzalo Jiménez de Quesada? Is it certain that they lie in the presbytery of the Cathedral, on the Epistles side?" And from then on that question has been a puzzle to all honest historians, for the identification of a corpse is a more delicate problem than are the legendary tales of great deeds.

The founder of Santa Fé wished, and so declared in his will, that the stone which covered his bones should not contain his name, nor any sign of his identity, but only this Latin legend, "*Expecto resurrectionem mortuorum.*" He wanted to be the anonymous dead who arises on Resurrection Day with his Quixotesque soul seeking bones with which to reconstruct his lean and discoloured figure. Without pretending to be skilled in these matters, I think that this is the way the dogma of the resurrection explains it. For my part, I believe that when the resurrection comes, and in case those bones are still enjoying their temporary repose in the Cathedral, Don Gonzalo will do well if he gets a thumb-bone or a poor lost vertebra out of them. His tormented shade will go wandering from Mariquita to Veracruz, from Veracruz to a dark corner of the Cathedral, from the Cathedral to the cemetery, and in the cemetery he will go reeling like a drunkard, snatching up a skull here, a femur there, a set of ribs out of a common grave, until, exhausted by fatigue and disconcerted at noting an incomplete hand or a cheekbone missing, he will put an index finger to the cranium that held his memory and making a recount will go back to the Cathedral, set aside a certain rare marble statue which they say is his likeness, and moving aside the slab which says, "*Expecto resurrectionem mortuorum,*" will find—and what a great feat!—his lost thumb, the poor forgotten vertebra, the cheekbone which his admirers had juggled.

Returning, then, to the tale in the *Illustrated Journal*, let me say that its editors were accustomed to formulate curious and intriguing questions which supposedly stimulated the mental activity of their readers. "Which is the elephant that carries towers on his enormous shoulders?" "Is it possible to see the remains of Gonzalo Jiménez de Quesada? Is it certain that they lie in the presbytery of the Cathedral, on the Epistles side?" I do not know whether the reply to the last question may seem amusing or tragic to my readers, but here it is:

Quesada died in Mariquita on a Monday in February, or perhaps in the month of June, of the year 1579. For ten or fifteen years his remains stayed in the cemetery which the Franciscan friars had in their church there. Don Juan de Castellanos recalls the matter thus:

*And now, having forsaken confidence*
*In the deceitful strength of being human,*
*He left behind the struggles of this life*

*With pious offices of all good Christians,*
*A man respectable and understanding.*

And he adds:

*But his will was badly carried out.*

The heat in Mariquita was terrific. Dead bodies began to
decompose within a few hours. The process of becoming
dust and ashes, or food for worms, was a matter not of years
but of days. When the precentor of the Santa Fé Cathedral,
one Dean Clavijo, took the matter up in Mariquita and the
tardy hands of the Spaniards went to pick up Quesada's
bones, there were no bones. But that did not matter. And
in truth, what did it matter? A few bones more or less are
mere trifles in the hands of death. So they brought that dust
to Santa Fé, and put it into a hollow in the church of Veracruz.

Five years later the city notables said, "Why not take the
remains to the Cathedral?" No sooner said than done, and
they laid the dust on the Epistles side.

Two hundred and eight years later the Cathedral was on
the point of going to pieces. There was suspension of services for years, rebuilding, etc. On excavating the presbytery
twenty years later "they found," said the archbishop, "on
the Epistles side, *certain* remains of Marshal Quesada." To
add to the confusion, certain relatives of Quesada had,
through privilege, been interred in that same crypt. But
even though they were dust, though they had been moved
about, mingled with others, there should have been some
remains of the founder there. Then the editor-in-chief of
the *Illustrated Journal,* fulfilling the mission proper to us

journalists, resolved to plumb the puzzle, and he himself went to see the crypt which ought to contain something which, to our way of thinking, would be what was left of the remains.

At half-past ten on the morning of a day in the 1880's after having lifted a heavy slab, Señor Urdañeta, editor of the *Illustrated Journal,* Don Lázaro María Girón, Don Manuel María Narváez, the Cathedral sacristan, and certain of the curious, went down an improvised stairway into the crypt and began to search. Here is the result, as it appeared in a March 1883 number of the *Illustrated Journal:*

"After the natural confusion produced by the sudden change from light to shade, we were able to distinguish at the bottom a vault six metres long, three metres wide, and two metres high, and in the bottom of it a coffin whose remains were dressed in velvet and purple silk, showing it to be of archbishop's dignity and belonging, we understand, to the most Illustrious Señor Doctor Fernando Caicedo y Flórez, Archbishop; in the corner were two smaller coffins with remains of the same clothing, and many bones belonging to at least two skeletons, all mixed, and without the least sign of military dress. We also descended to the crypt on the opposite side. There, in good condition were found the remains of Doctor Margallo in the centre of a vault like the former, and in the corners two small boxes and another of a child of ten or twelve. They seem never to have been touched. We will publish our carefully studied opinion on this matter in the following number."

In the following number nothing was said. Nor in the one after, nor in any one of those published for two years. Perhaps it was thought, as in Pirandello's tale, that the best thing was to bury the corpse, without identifying it, but to bury it.

I have carefully read the notes in the *Illustrated Journal* which followed the announcement that the conundrum posed at the beginning of these paragraphs was to be solved. They contain the information that Paris newspapers describe a concert in which our compatriot "*Mlle. Teresa Tanco a joué avec autant de talent que de sentiment.*" That "our friend the estimable gentleman Señor Don Ricardo Becerra, his charming wife and gracious family have been back in Bogotá since the beginning of the month." And finally, "Giving thanks in advance to the charming señoras and señoritas, we propose a new enigma by the famous poet Schiller: Who is it that takes us thousands of leagues away, and yet remains where he is? Having no wings to spread, he draws us rapidly through the air. It is the swiftest boat that has ever borne any voyager, and carries one across the width of the seas with the speed of thought. All this in the opening and shutting of an eye."

*       *       *

I judge that the lines transcribed above will be most informative for the reader concerning the adelantado's remains, and I do not think it necessary to continue a history which would have three new chapters—the moving of the remains from the Cathedral to a small park in front of the Catholic cemetery, another trip from there to the interior of the cemetery, and, finally, the splendid, the magnificent demonstration of affection for the founder, the quadricentenary, with a new transfer from the cemetery to the Cathedral. . . .

For a man who for eighty years ranged through Europe

and Terra Firma to have moved in three centuries and a half through such small adventures does not seem much. I have some doubt as to whether it was really he who made these posthumous voyages, or a minor friar of Mariquita, or some one of the Berríos who, because they were relatives, crept, after they were cold, to lie beside what was left of Quesada's remains. At any rate, the end of the discoverers was always the same. What survives is not so much the consequence of their audacity; it is the memory of those great achievements which their spirits, dogged by the envy of contemporaries, rendered fruitful. I think that Quesada, at least while he was opening a way through the tangled brush of the Opón, took more care to go ahead with the soldiers than to keep his beard combed. Yet for a painter, the adelantado's beard is more important than his deeds. It is a matter of taste and opinion.

But as I said before, four hundred years had passed, and everything is confused. I see nothing sure and certain in the details about Quesada which come to light today. I do not know whether his portrait is truly his, or whether his remains are really his remains, or whether his beard was full or thin. The most erudite and reasoned work which was written about the founder of Bogotá for his quadricentenary was a book by Don Enrique Otero D'Costa, an incomparable expert in minute investigations. That book proves that everything about Quesada and his whole history is uncertain. From a practical point of view, it establishes the triumph of the novel over history as such. Which is a very good thing. It is far more discreet to take refuge in the novel, the romance, the fabliau when you are painting the lives of gentlemen who undertook such fabulous enterprises as discovering a land of butterflies (Muzo was the first step in Quesada's explorations) at the cost of scores of unfortunate lives, or putting a whole army underground on the search for the mythical land of El Dorado. It is only that the romance of Quesada is a sad and melancholy one; this matter of not knowing who is who, this uncertainty which veils his whole history, is merely the mirror which reflects the final passion of his own life.

I do not know what anyone who was eager to put his likeness into marble or bronze could possibly do. There would always be hesitation as between the energetic lineaments of the soldier and the wistful smile of the disenchanted, between the cruel leader who had the rebel soldier hanged and the soul that carried on imaginary dialogues with the Virgin in Suesca or busied his pen writing sermons for the priests to recite at churchly festivals. When Quesada reached eighty his life struck a balance between the years of high adventure and the years of melancholy, without counting those he had passed in Europe among books and amorous adventures. Thus his figure is completely human and complex, and eludes the simplified versions which historians writing in an heroic vein make ornate and cloying.

Going back to the book and the writings of Don Enrique Otero D'Costa, we find that Quesada's departure from Santa Marta—when, as Fray Pedro Simón, Flórez de Ocariz, and Rodríguez Fresle, the fathers of our history, affirm, he set out to discover the New Kingdom in 1537—really took place in 1536. That the 162 soldiers with which he emerged from his great adventure were, according to one conqueror, 162, according to another 165, according to three conquerors 166, according to two conquerors 167, and according to four conquerors 170. That the Lazarus fever which ate at Quesada and has surrounded his memory with a tormented legend that he was a leper was not Lazarus fever at all, but a simple skin irritation very frequent in those days of filth and licence, which was commonly called, and as the quick way out of further argument, leprosy. That the charming ballad by Father Lescámez, that group of admirable verses in which he relates how Quesada

> . . . *had to leave Granada*
> *For some miscreant deed* . . .

was not written by Lescámez in the sixteenth century, but in the twentieth century by one Franco Quijano, and that the portrait of Jiménez de Quesada . . . Well, in this matter of the portrait it is better to go a little slowly. . . .

❖  ❖  ❖

In this ineffable homeland of mine there is no one who does not carry in his mind the image of the founder of the New Kingdom. It is a noble portrait of "a mature man, with black and luxuriant beard, dreaming eyes, an aquiline nose, and dressed in a gold-braided doublet." It does surprise one, of course, that a person so vigorous and hard-working should give such an appearance of freshness and fashion. Nevertheless, we all see him with these identical features in the first pages of our country's history. This is the way the hero of the conquest looked. Very well, that portrait happens to be of one of the kings of France—Francis I.

The matter could not be simpler. This fate befell not only Quesada, but all the other personages who came to America in the sixteenth century. Not very long ago there was erected in Cali a most noble piece of sculpture commemorating Don Sebastián de Belalcázar, founder of that city. It was the work of the Spanish artist Victorio Macho. It represents the conqueror as a figure of elegance, chest high, military garb resting well on his masculine shoulders, and facing the wind, the face of . . . the famous scientist and Nobel prize winner Don Santiago Ramón y Cajal. Everyone knows that the great Macho made one of the most beautiful monuments in the world, dedicated to the wise Cajal, and standing in the Park of the Retiro in Madrid. Macho, a man who knows how to see, fell in love with the head of the sage and, finding nothing better to serve as model for a conqueror's head, reproduced it.

Quesada's fate was similar. Don Constancio Franco, admiring the patriotic ardour of the editor of the *Illustrated Journal*, who was keen to glorify the fathers of our nation, once gave him an oil portrait of the adelantado, and from then on this portrait, and the wood engraving which Urdañeta had made from it, became the basis of Quesada's whole iconography.

Don Constancio Franco was a celebrated historian, to whom Colombian letters owe great finds. He was, moreover, in charge of the National Museum. He was most of all preoccupied with the fact that there was one lack in the museum which it did not seem possible to supply. There was no viceroy, judge, or president of whom future generations would have a true picture. With this praiseworthy ambition in mind, he contracted for the services of a painter and began to form the gallery. The artist in his service— and the service of the nation—finished a likeness of Viceroy Sebastián de Eslava. When he reached the museum with it, the director looked at it with infinite approval. How much humanity there was in that face with its fine rosy colour, and in that wig of whitest cotton! For some moments the director examined it with delight, and then he ordered,

"The portrait is magnificent. Unfortunately, we already have Eslava. Let's have this for Amar y Borbón, who is missing, and put his name on it and his titles."

In the case of Quesada's portrait, the trick happened to be discovered a great many years after he died, but, as in the case of the dead man himself, what was there to do if the documents in the history of the matter had already been set in print?

* * *

The reader already knows what there is left to tell about Quesada. His books were all lost. Mixed in with histories by Hernández (or Fernández) de Oviedo, by Piedrahita, or by Plaza are bits which may or may not be part of those works of his which, going from the Indies to the peninsula, from the frozen hands of the king's ministers to the parchment-like hands of old book merchants, ended by falling to pieces in the white hands of forgetfulness. Out of them all there are only phrases now and then, uncertain words floating in mid-air, which historical research tries in vain to make exact. Quesada himself had a certain genial divination of all these things, and with that penetration which at times illumines the judgment of men nearing the grave he penned that solemn epitaph which contains an infinite disdain for what men do. An epitaph which is the mortal leap of one who rises above all human falsity to enter the blessed meadows of eternity: *Expecto resurrectionem mortuorum*. . . . All pride and vanity are ended there, and his stubborn hope is shattered as he sees the fickleness of the world through the clear light of faith.

It is necessary to go back over Quesada's last experiences in order to see what depths his life reached when the greedy

profiteers of the colony had deprived him of all privileges
and had stolen from him the power for whose holding he
had little ambition. There was a substantial difference between the sensual appetite of a Pizarro, an Almagro, an
Alvarado, and the careless, unworried life of a man who,
returning from conquest to Spain with the rents in his
clothes mended, and cloaked in velvet, went gaily through
France and Portugal, amused himself in Italy, and, like the
quiet sun of Santa Fé, scattered gold dust over life and
over women. And who then sought in solitary places the
silence and the peace which are the need of candid or for-
getful souls, in order that he might carry on dialogues with
the Most Holy Virgin Mary, She who is without original
sin.

❈          ❈          ❈

Let us now return to something which was implied some
pages back. In Quesada's last days there was an intimate
and internal tragedy which gives a clue to much that would
be otherwise hidden in his life. In tardy acknowledgment
of his merits, the Crown conceded him a coat of arms, the
status of marshal, and honorary titles which obliged him
to live with decorum, but which put no lining into his velvet purse. Then began the interminable struggle to have
himself allotted a grant of Indians who should be subject
to his orders. His memorials, in which humility is mingled
with pride and hope with desperation, went from the New
Kingdom to Castile while he was enduring anguished hours
of great poverty, and not knowing how he, a marshal of
Spain, could appear in ragged clothing. But then fortune
imposed an even greater humiliation. And in a way Quesada was to be the victim of his own invention, for in his

instructions for good government he had continually counselled the king that Spaniards who asked for land grants
should be made to marry "so that the land may be populated and held in perpetuity." He marry! Quesada, now
that he was nearing seventy and when all the passions and
powers of youth had left his body!

In his instructions for good government, Quesada had
said, "Let Your Majesty be pleased to order that within the
said kingdom all those who have grants of lands and Indians shall marry within a period Your Majesty shall name,
and that when that is past, their grants shall be lost, or given
to others who are married, or put under Your Majesty's
charge; to the end that they shall clearly understand they
are to marry within the said period and that this period be
adequately long for them to comply, without Your Majesty
here or the judges there having to accept delays or excuses."

So then, how humble was the allegation with which the
adelantado, old now, prostrated himself at the feet of Archbishop Juan de los Barrios, begging that he would open
the ecclesiastical court to the hearing of testimony which
should prove that he, the adelantado, was in no condition to
marry! "I am the *encomendero*," he said, "of the grant of
lands and Indians at Chita, and of an age which makes it
impossible for me to marry. To take up married life with a
woman now would be, as is well known, to open to me the
door of the tomb." The original text of the allegation says
it all with a realism that makes one weep. And after the allegation came the proofs, the testimony, the slow labour of
that sturdy soul who had once climbed the ridges of the
wild Andes and who now, trembling and withered, laid
himself bare to the gaze of his companions and the city he

had founded, and did it with a desperate prolixity. Here are some of his words:

"I am not of an age to be able to marry, nor have I the necessary health for it, for I have for more than twenty years been ill of asthma, a disease which is notoriously incompatible with the married state. . . . And though my age and this impediment are both well known, for my appearance is that of a man of sixty more or less, and my illness quite as obvious, so that I am not able to ascend a staircase, or to walk ten steps without great effort, yet am I ready to give a greater abundance of information concerning all the aforesaid."

But there was something else. In Spain there was the son he could not acknowledge. The son who scarcely existed as more than a shadow in a single line of the contract concerning El Dorado. The son whom no one then named.*

\* \* \*

---

\* The author's implied identificaton of this unacknowledged son with Alonso Quixada, known to the world as Don Quixote, is an interesting example of literary intuition. What is known is that Cervantes, ransomed from a Moorish prison and returning to Spain about the time that the heirs of Jiménez de Quesada were trying to get to America to claim their inheritance, met and married a relative of theirs, Catalina Salazar. When he came to write his most famous novel, he named his hero Alonso and said, "Some . . . have concluded that his name was certainly Quixada, and not Quesada as others would have it." The assumption, supported by evidence which is at least provocative, is that the original possessor of that name was a gentleman of uncertain status named Alonso Quesada, "tall, lean, romantic, slightly mad like all the Quesadas," and a great talker, whom Cervantes met in the home of his wife's family; that this "cousin or uncle" was the son of Jiménez de Quesada, born of one of those love affairs of which he never spoke; that Cervantes was amused by his character and fascinated by his tales of the family great man. So, says Señor Arciniegas, Cervantes, who tried to get to America, would have liked to write about Don Gonzalo and lay his novel in Terra Firma, but failing that, and with Spain as his locale, "let Don Alonso become the prototype of Don Quixote, a character half child of the imagi-

Quesada reached the heights of eighty years and, turning his eyes toward the past, watched his various enterprises move past him as on some infernal moving-picture film. He remembered the labour and the hunger suffered in the ascent of the Opón. He thought of those days when the troops, their insides gnawed by hunger, ate, as one of his comrades said, "lizards and rats and bats and many other reptiles, and for very hunger chewed on our leather shields, and ate straps, and dogs, and other dead animals." And more recently, when his steps were coming close to the portals of death, there was that adventure of El Dorado, and the sufferings in the Llanos, where the soldiers, worn with misery and suffering, tried to flee and even thought of doing away with the adelantado, if his death would free them from the spell which had carried them forth on the road to an imaginary paradise. And he thought of the burning plains, and the fiery forests of the green inferno.

But soon his fever-driven imagination, his memory which was retracing its steps, as they say of souls in the other world, stopped to remember a hill browned by the sun. Up there was nothing but the dry rock, the hard tropical heat, and no shade from the trees, trees that had no compassion on men, that spilled no single green drop of freshness out of the inverted bowls of their foliage. The old wanderer who had disciplined the souls of those greedy men maddened by thirst, who had put all their pleas to the test, felt his throat grow dry and his tongue thick as he remembered the hill of Limba, which was in the land of Tocaima, and he felt that it was there that his shadow, from the limits of the other world, should provide relief for wayfarers. That

nation, half mirror of that passionately human life of the great dreamer, Don Gonzalo Jiménez de Quesada."—TRANSLATOR.

he who had led the men of Spain and the Indians of the New
Kingdom across such miserable crags, through such inhos-
pitable flatland, such wild uplands, should redeem his soul
from the sin of such mad undertakings by some such act
as extending the hollow of his hand forth from eternity to
give a draught of water to the thirsty. And out of this desire
came his will, touching the depths of melancholy and reflecting his life much better than the haughty escutcheon
with which the Spanish monarch had decorated him, which
orders in a slow clause that on Limba hill, in the land of
Tocaima, there be always kept a large earthen jar full of
water in which travellers might quench their thirst.

It is clear that the will was lost. Not one of Quesada's papers was to pass intact to posterity. Loose, without a bind-
ing, the will wandered through the archives of Spain. And
concerning the attention which was given it, Castellanos's
phrase would come down in history, "But his will was badly
carried out." Nor was the earthen jar even once filled with
water on Limba hill. His heirs, much less enthusiastic than
Quesada, would content themselves with construing the
direction to mean setting up a little fountain on a Santa Fé
street. This is the old Calle de los Plateros, which apparently takes the place of Limba hill.

If the things of this world turn to dust, smoke, and ashes
in any one person it is in Don Gonzalo Jiménez de Quesada.
Out of the great volume of his life there remain only neg-
lected leaves which turn yellow in the autumn of history,
while the little breath of irony takes them as a toy to play
with and scatters them gaily throughout the world. In the
lawyer's case, as in that of Christopher Columbus, there
is ever the double play of truth and falsehood. The shades
of the two heroes flee through its labyrinths and all the

rich human accents that filled their lives are lost there.
The Spaniards have always known how to fix the level-
ling power of death in mighty phrases. Philip II was very
right when he said that he issued the decree for reform-
ing burial abuses "so that what had been spent in vain
demonstrations and appearances should be spent and dis-
tributed in what was for the service of God, and the in-
crease of the divine cult, and the welfare of the souls of the
deceased." In the *Dance of Death,* written by an anonymous poet of the fourteenth century, Death calls the two
maidens:

> *They came unwillingly and with bad grace*
> *To hear my songs, for they are mournful ones.*
> *But flowers and roses will not save them now,*
> *Nor all the gewgaws they were wont to use.*
> *If they could, they would avoid me ever,*
> *But that cannot be; they are my brides.*
> *For their acquired graces, these and all*
> *Shall in another life have ugliness*
> *And I will trade them nudity for clothes—*
> *For evermore a very sore vexation.*
> *And for their palaces I'll give just measure*
> *In darkened tombs that foully smell inside,*
> *And for their tastiest viands, gnawing worms,*
> *Which from within shall eat their rotted flesh.*

Like that of the two damsels became the flesh of Quesada
and of Columbus. Little Gonzalo, the lawyer, well knew
that his armour was falling from him, that his head was
seeking the warm hollow of the pillow earth provides. That
the conquests of this world were slipping—and this time
for ever—from between his fingers. And that men would

not carry out his last wishes as set forth in his will, nor give his bones repose. And with a bitter disdain, mingled with vows of charity, placing no faith in men, he took leave of them until a later day—*Expecto resurrectionem mortuorum.* . . .

# Bibliography

# BIBLIOGRAPHY

Aguado, Pedro de: *Historia de Santa Marta y Nuevo Reino de Granada*

Alcedo, Antonio de: *Diccionario geográfico-histórico de las Indias Occidentales ó America*

Amunátegui y Solar, Domingo: *Historia social de Chile*

\* Belalcázar, Sebastián de: *Probanzas de Servicio*

*Boletín de Historia y Antigüedades*, Bogotá (Also see *Documentos del Archivo General de Indias*, Seville, published in this *Boletín*)

Bonilla y San Martín, Adolfo: *Luis Vives y la Filosofía española del Renacimiento*

Carrión, Benjamín: *Atahuallpa*

Casas, Bartolomé de las: *Historia de las Indias*

Castellanos, Juan de: *Elegías de Varones ilustres de Indias*

Cervantes Saavedra, Miguel de: *El ingenioso Hidalgo Don Quijote de la Mancha*

Cieza de León, Pedro de: *Crónica del Perú*

Croce, Benedetto: *Scritti di storia letteraria e politica* (V. 8: *La Spagna nella vita italiana durante la Rinascenza*)

Díaz del Castillo, Bernal: *Historia verdadera de la Conquista de la Nueva España*

Federmann, Nikolaus: *Belle et agréable narration du premier voyage de Nicolas Federmann le jeune d'Ulm aux Indes de la Mer océane et de tout ce qui lui est arrivé dans ce pays jusqu'à son retour en Espagne* (Original first published in German, then translated into French and into Spanish.—TRANSLATOR)

Fernández de Oviedo y Valdés, Gonzalo: *Historia natural y general de las Indias*

Fernández de Piedrahita, Lucas: *Historia general de las Conquistas del Nuevo Reino de Granada*

\* These titles are listed in the Spanish edition, but are not to be found in the catalogue of the New York Public Library or the Library of Congress.—TRANSLATOR.

Fitzmaurice-Kelly, James: *Miguel de Cervantes Saavedra*

* Flórez de Ocariz, Juan: *Genealogías del Nuevo Reino de Granada*

Franco Quijano, J. F.: *Fantasmas* (See note on *Romance de Ximénez de Quesada* in 2º *tranco, Los Molinos de Viento*)

Gómez Restrepo, Antonio: *Historia de la Literatura Colombiana*

Herrera y Tordesillas, Antonio: *Historia general de los Hechos de los Castellanos en las islas i tierra firme del mar oceano. En 8 decadas*

Humboldt, Alexander von: *Examen Critique*

Ibáñez, Pedro María: *Crónicas de Bogotá*

Jijón y Caamaño, Jacinto: *Sebastián de Belalcázar*

* Jiménez de Quesada, Gonzalo: *Instrucciones para el buen Gobierno (Boletín de la Academia Nacional de Historia, Bogotá)*

Leonard, Irving Albert: *Romances of Chivalry in the Spanish Indies*

Lewis, Dominic Bevan Wyndham: *Charles of Europe*

López de Gómara, Francisco de: *Historia general de las Indias*

Motley, John Lothrop: *The Rise of the Dutch Republic*

Navarro y Ledesma, Francisco: *El ingenioso Hidalgo Miguel de Cervantes Saavedra: Sucesos de su Vida*

* Notaría 2ª: *Documento sobre la Conquista del Dorado* (courtesy of Don Guillermo Hernández de Alba)

Otero D'Costa, Enrique: *Gonzalo Jiménez de Quesada*

* *Papel Periódico Ilustrado*

Prescott, William Hickling: *History of the Conquest of Peru*
*History of the Conquest of Mexico*
*History of the Reign of Ferdinand and Isabella*

Restrepo, Vicente: *Los Chibchas antes de la Conquista española*

Restrepo Tirado, Ernesto: *Historia de la Provincia de Santa Marta*
*Descubrimiento y Conquista de Colombia*
*De Gonzalo Ximénez de Quesada a Don Pablo Morillo: documentos inéditos sobre la historia de la Nueva Granada* (Documents from the Archivo General de Indias, Seville)

Rivas, Raimundo: *Los Fundadores de Bogotá*

Rodríguez Fresle, Juan: *El Carnero*

Simón, Pedro: *Noticias historiales de las Conquistas de Tierra Firme en las Indias Occidentales*

* Torre y del Cerro, José de la: *Gonzalo Jiménez de Quesada*
    (*Boletín de la Academia Nacional de Historia*, Bogotá)
Triana, Miguel: *La Civilización Chibcha*
Velasco, Juan de: *Historia del Reino de Quito*
Vergara y Vergara, José María: *Historia de la Literatura en
    Nueva Granada*
Zavala, Silvio Arturo: *El Derecho de Indias en la Conquista de
    América*
Zweig, Stefan: *Conqueror of the Seas: the Story of Magellan*